It Starts with an Idea

How a little software company competed against
the big software gorillas by turning an idea into
practical software

Jan McCleery

DEDICATION

To my wonderful husband Michael, who put up with my long hours at work and learned to cook so we could both survive.

To my two beautiful daughters, Julie and Kristin, who loved me even though I was not a stay-at-home mom, and who have become strong professional women in their own right.

To my big sister, Kathy, who has always been there to help me learn and grow, love me unconditionally, and cheer me on.

In memory of my loving mother, Clarice, who became a working woman in the '50s in Utah when working women were frowned upon. She read the dictionary cover-to-cover many times to prepare for a Secretary's job and ended up being indispensable to her company. She showed me that a woman can have a career.

CONTENTS

ACKNOWLEDGEMENTS

I would like to thank my business partners, John Miller and Stephen Gold. Without their imagination and willingness to take a risk, the adventure would never have been started. My appreciation also goes to our Board of Directors, who gave us their wisdom, support, and encouragement throughout the journey.

I would like to thank the extremely talented and hardworking Intelic software engineers, who created one of the highest quality, best performing, and unique software products on the market. Without their expertise and commitment, the experience would not have been as successful or nearly as much fun. In particular, I would like to thank Freeman Michaels for his talent in designing the product and his ability to make every day fun and enjoyable, Arun Bhat for his brilliance and support, Ketan Soni for his continued commitment to making product advancements, Kevin Hoang, QA, for his endless commitment to the company and unfailing support for me, and Chaiya (now Dr. Chaiya Laoteppitaks, M.D.) for his willingness to take on all tasks, his always positive attitude (now great bedside manner), and his never ending ability to think up new pranks.

From the management side, I greatly appreciated the expertise of prior Ford Aerospace managers Anita Wotiz and Gary Brink who, like me, took the plunge from a big aerospace company to a tiny start-up. Together we applied the right software methodology and process to insure high quality, on schedule, and low cost - our practical software methodology.

Thanks also goes to Julie Flaig for her intelligence and knowledge, her willingness to be a woman of all trades, and for being an unwavering champion of the company.

I would like to recognize Rich Stephens, who came aboard to provide customer service and has shown for years what that really means.

Posthumously, I would like to thank Ed Ducey, our pricing expert, who drove the pricing model and gave credence to our initial product due to his stellar reputation in the semiconductor industry. And Michael Bailey, our exceptional training manager, for his ability to turn complex concepts into understandable units of knowledge and for bringing his warmth and wisdom into the company – and Easter jelly beans.

INTRODUCTION

Intelic was a software start-up in the late 1990s.

The company was led by three co-founders: Stephen, a man with marketing flair and a true entrepreneurial spirit; John, a salesman and a visionary; and Jan, a technologist and an experienced software engineering manager. They were followed by an energetic, creative group of employees who together created a new kind of software company, where the software is geared towards what their customers want, need, and hope for. Intelic's focus was truly on their customers.

Their software was high quality, robust, scalable, and loved by the users. In an era where software full of bugs had become the accepted norm, where jokes about "the blue screen of death" were common, and where companies were willing to pay millions to giant Enterprise Resource Planning (ERP) companies for each implementation and millions again when they upgraded to the next release, Intelic was different. This new renegade company was a quick success, rapidly becoming the sales automation, quoting, and pricing software leader for semiconductor companies.

As the company grew and became more prominent, Intelic became a target for the software giants – known as "gorillas" in the software industry. The gorillas were increasing their grip on the software industry each year as they grew larger and larger on the road to becoming unstoppable behemoths. Information Technology (IT) managers were coerced into thinking that the large gorilla software was the only safe, smart choice. In turn, the gorillas' hard-to-implement, hard-to-upgrade software brought the gorillas billions in services contracts. Once installed at a company, the gorilla's position was sustained by their proprietary technology and the high costs a company would incur if they tried to change to another vendor's software.

After 9/11, as semiconductor companies faced a downturn in their businesses and put a hold on buying IT software, the little software company struggled to stay afloat. Yet the employees continued to fight to keep the gorillas from gaining any traction in their marketplace.

This book is a fun romp through the adventure of a start-up in Silicon Valley. During those years, Stephen and Jan would often say to each other "We should write a book. No one would ever believe this!"

"It Starts with an Idea" reveals how Intelic created a dedicated and enthusiastic team - a team that worked hard and had fun - and a great product.

In addition, it paints a vision of software that every company should demand from their software vendors. The book gives software engineers, managers, and CEOs insight into how to build software that is high performance, scalable, reliable, and robust - software that is on-schedule at low cost - using Intelic's "Practical Software" development methodology, a methodology that is more agile than "Agile." That's practical software!

THE CRISIS (2004)

"Warriors, warriors we call ourselves. We fight for splendid virtue, for high endeavor, for sublime wisdom, therefore we call ourselves warriors." - Aunguttara Nikaya (Way of the Peaceful Warrior)

It was raining, but it was June. It's not supposed to rain in June in California. Evening fog regularly rolled over the Santa Cruz Mountains and under the Golden Gate Bridge, creating grey morning skies in Silicon Valley. But the fog would always burn off by noon for the typical clear, brilliant California day. But not rain. Today the sky was grey with real storm clouds, not fog. The drizzle had caused Jan's windshield wipers to automatically begin a rhythmic swish, swish. The grey misty skies matched her mood. She was headed into work but wasn't sure what she'd find there.

She imagined the worst case scenario: Arriving at work to find the early-rise employees milling around the parking lot (or sitting in their cars to avoid the drizzle) and a Sheriff's padlock on the front door.

Yesterday, a group of developers had returned from lunch to find a Sheriff's Notice of Eviction on the door to the main entrance. Stephen, the CEO, had tried to explain it in a way to ease employee concerns. "It was just a miscommunication with the landlord, a mistake," he'd told them. Hence there had been no panic. Even though they were all aware that the last few months' sales had been flat, everyone had complete confidence in Stephen being able to lead the company through any lulls.

3

The executive team knew there was a real possibility that the unreasonable landlord would shut the little company out, padlock the doors, just out of spite. They had quietly loaded Jan's SUV yesterday with all the older and excess computers - desktops, laptops and servers - plus the recent backup tapes. Whatever they were able to sneak out the back door without the employees noticing, they took in order to be able to quickly set up a command post in an alternative location. John was already arranging high speed internet lines into a large warehouse on his property, just in case – to enable them to set up operations and stay connected to their customers and the rest of the outside world no matter what happened.

It wouldn't look good for the small company to suddenly go "off-the-air." That could be the death blow. For small software companies, appearances were key. Competing against the "software gorillas," the big billion dollar software companies that ruled the enterprise application market, had always meant appearing larger than you were.

Their customers, large semi-conductor manufacturing companies guided by the Information Technology (IT) professionals that managed their computer centers, believed that they needed big software from big vendors to sustain their mission-critical business processes. That was the message the big gorilla software vendors had touted for years.

It wasn't true. Their little software company had proven for years the ability to handle big manufacturer's needs. They had built reliable, high-performance, high-quality enterprise software and provided excellent service to their customers. They provided it much quicker and more cost effectively than the mega-software companies.

However, it was hard to compete against the gorilla marketing approach. The gorillas had huge marketing budgets. They wined and dined IT managers, offering the managers the opportunity to meet other professionals at huge user meetings where they awarded and recognized key IT managers. Being recognized by a software gorilla was reported on the cover of IT magazines and greatly improved the IT manager's professional standing. IT managers evaluating vendors were quickly convinced that the safest job decision was to go with a big vendor. In the '90s, the IT saying was, "No one ever lost their job for choosing Big Blue," (referring to IBM hardware). When choosing Enterprise Resource Planning (ERP) software, the belief was similar regarding the big gorillas like Oracle and SAP. IT managers felt secure with their choice when going to one of the leaders in the ERP space.

The gorillas had been buying up the smaller software companies as fast as they could, growing larger and larger. Some would buy the smaller company, take their customers, and throw the old product away, forcing those customers to convert to their solution. Others ended up either with huge, fragmented software offerings or spent years trying (usually unsuccessfully) to convert it all into a reasonable single solution.

The little company had stayed under the radar as long as it could. The gorillas had woken up and taken notice. The gorillas were not happy that this little company had been able to provide significant functionality to a large market share of companies in one vertical, the semiconductor industry, while they themselves had not been able to make any inroads into the same companies for automating key, mission-critical functions: sales quoting and pricing.

The gorillas knew how to spread rumors, innuendo, and enough flack to worry large, conservative semiconductor manufacturers who were considering taking a chance on a small company. While the gorillas had been unable to steal any of the little company's current customers or divert any new sales, they had been successful at slowing down sales. The manufacturers were taking a "wait and see" attitude after 9/11, while the economy was down. The little software company's sales had come to a standstill.

Jan wasn't about to panic. She was sure Stephen had a plan. She just needed to get to work and find out what the next steps would be. The battle wasn't over.

IT STARTS WITH AN IDEA (1997)

"If your actions inspire others to dream more, learn more, do more and become more, you are a leader." - John Quincy Adams

Jan hadn't expected to be jumping into a new start-up in her late 40's. When she discovered that John and Stephen were getting ready to start their own venture, she'd thought it would be an exciting opportunity. She respected both of them, and John had an interesting product idea.

John had years of experience in the semiconductor industry and believed he knew just the software tool that sales managers were yearning for. Stephen was outstanding at marketing, communications, and market analysis and had come from a company working with semiconductors. Both had done start-ups before.

She had asked John for a breakfast meeting and pitched the idea of them adding her to their team as their software development lead.

John had surprised her by saying, "We were hoping you'd ask. Planning on it. What do you want from the job?"

She launched into expounding about how it was her desire to build great software and deliver products customers want.

He said, "But I meant what do you want as your compensation package? Because I think we should be three equal partners."

She hadn't expected an equal share and was stunned. "That certainly works for me!"

Her background had primarily been software engineering in big companies – initially working as a software engineer for Ford

Aerospace, a government aerospace and defense company, rising through the ranks until she was a senior software manager. She'd then left the aerospace world for a mid-sized commercial software company. Later she discovered that she enjoyed working for even smaller companies. She was eager for the opportunity to be involved at the beginning of a start-up.

She liked John's product idea. As Vice President of Sales for one of the largest semiconductor company in the world, John and his friend and associate, Ed, had grown tired of the way sales people needed to manually determine pricing which resulted in inconsistent quotes. John felt that pricing should be more globally consistent. Ed built a software tool on the Microsoft Access database for John and his sales team to use. Ed was a pricing expert, someone the semiconductor industry looked to for advice and consulting about price setting and price management strategies. The tool was a big success at his company. From there, John was co-founder and managing director at a semiconductor start-up. There, again, he and Ed built their Access-based quoting and pricing tool. John was convinced there was no such tool on the market and that there was a strong need in the semiconductor industry.

John had started pursuing his own company a few years prior but instead had encountered James, CEO and Founder of eMarket.com, a dot.com start-up and one of the first web-based trading systems. James' trading system provided purchasers of semiconductor components the opportunity to review part prices and availability with a number of distributors and purchase parts online. The software was sold to distributors of semiconductor parts. There were distributor systems installed at various distribution companies and a central server that customers could access via the internet to search for part availability at the various distributor warehouses. The concept was similar enough to John's dream that John accepted the VP of Sales position there instead of starting his own company.

John wanted to bring Stephen in as VP of Marketing. He had worked with Stephen, who did marketing at a distributor company in Florida. Stephen wasn't very interested but John, the consummate salesman, knew the right approach to take.

John had suggested to Stephen that maybe he "just wasn't ready" for a start-up. Maybe he didn't "have what it takes" to take command of an entire company's marketing direction and strategy. Stephen was rankled and told John he would take the job. John's reverse psychology worked every time.

Jan joined the dot.com as VP of Engineering.

Ultimately James decided he needed his Sales VP to have software sales background instead of John's semiconductor background. Both Stephen and Jan spent time with James arguing how important it had been in sales meetings that John knew exactly what the customers were wanting. However, James and John parted ways, which gave John the opportunity to return to his dream of starting his own company.

Although John had the initial vision and was the driver for the new company, he asked Stephen to be the CEO/President. John considered himself more the product evangelist. Stephen, John said, was a better front man to talk to the press and analysts. Stephen, although not yet 40, had started, managed, and sold a successful computer company by recognizing and leveraging the infant, but quickly-growing, PC clone market during the days of the IBM look-alikes such as Eagle Computers and others. He had been voted Pittsburg's Entrepreneur of the Year at age 29. He was energetic, charismatic, and well educated with outstanding communication skills.

The three new co-founders started working on the product and company basics. Since both Stephen and Jan were still working at the dot.com, their time was limited to after hours, but that didn't stop them from putting in 8 hours/day on the new company. They just got little sleep. John was able to focus full-time on selling his product idea and getting feedback from his peers.

John and Stephen decided on the company name "G2 Technologies" to combine sly intelligence and high tech. They named the product "ProChannel" for professional channel software.

Stephen had been busy creating a business plan: researching

competitors, market potential, and staffing needs over the next five years versus revenue potential.

He categorized their new product as Customer Resource Management software. CRM was a growing market space which included sales force automation tools. Their goal was to build a vertical CRM solution aimed at the large semiconductor market.

They researched the current CRM vendors. The vendor that was closest in product offering to what G2 would provide, and hence their primary competitor, would be Siebel Systems, a company founded by Thomas Siebel in 1993. Tom Siebel had previously been an executive at Oracle. By the late 1990s, Siebel Systems was the dominant CRM vendor for sales quoting and pricing software.

The G2 business plan was, like everything Stephen produced, a marketing feat: charts and graphs with convincing marketing detail and a thorough, detailed cost, budget, and revenue analysis all packaged in a neat spiral binding with a snazzy color cover. He produced multiple copies which he and John distributed to potential angel investors and leaders in the semiconductor industry.

In parallel, all three worked to develop a product demo. John had the vision. It was Jan's job was to convert it into a demo. To avoid any issues with software propriety, Jan worked hard to ensure there would be no conflict of interest with their current employer. She bought a personal laptop and began developing an HTML demo for their new product starting from scratch. (HTML is the markup language used to create web pages.) She was meticulous about not using anything from their prior company's product - not even the little red dot used in the eMarket.com product, which she was sure was just a standard icon. Instead she recreated her own red dot using the Paint software program. Stephen and Jan both made sure they were still putting in sufficient energy and focus at their current jobs.

John would talk about his vision, but since he was more salesman than product designer, his vision didn't always make sense to Jan who had little experience in the semiconductor industry or with semiconductor sales organizations. Her first 20 years were spent at Ford Aerospace. In aerospace, the Sales & Marketing "organization" was often one guy in Washington working with the Army to find out about upcoming programs. It was much different than the big semiconductor companies' sales organizations whose reps had the need for real-time quoting and pricing support and whose sales managers needed help with managing rep firms, commissions, and distribution. She knew a little about software sales, but the software business was much different than the semiconductor business. Often she was at a loss when John talked about ship and debits and the sales organizational structure.

Fortunately, Stephen was able to bridge the gap between John's vision and Jan's need to build a demo. Stephen knew the industry's sales users' needs, plus had an appreciation of graphical layouts and a keen understanding of usability.

Stephen would translate John's vision verbally into use case scenarios that Jan could work from to build demo screens and flows. Stephen also provided feedback on the look and feel, pushing Jan to be more creative graphically.

Jan worked to make the demo screens, which were simple HTML/JavaScript forms, look active and real. HTML screen mockups were quick to create. There wasn't time to develop a real Java product underneath, but adding JavaScript functions made the screens look like they had a real product behind them including active buttons, pop-ups, and meaningful data. For example, all date fields auto-calculated back from today's date so the demo data never looked stale or out-of-date.

Since the demo actually had no real functioning program underneath, she had carefully reviewed with John what the sales demo navigational flow was (which buttons to hit) and what to type into each input box on the screen so that the data coming up on the next screen would make sense.

"Always type 'ab' in the customer search field," she instructed John, "because once you hit the 'Next' button, only customer names starting with the letters 'ab' will be on the search results screen. If you want it to look real, you'll need to follow the script," she admonished.

John and Stephen went out making the rounds, showing the

demo to their expansive network of friends and associates in target Silicon Valley semiconductor companies and returning with suggestions and changes to fine-tune the ever-evolving demo. Jan worked on the demo updates in the evenings, often until 3 a.m. in the morning.

Their business contacts viewed ProChannel as an exciting, new, and important strategic sales tool. They loved the new concept and it was clear there was no other vendor using the same approach.

Early in the spring, Jan was invited to join John and Stephen to meet with a prospective customer, Vantus, a spin-off company from Advanced Micro Devices (AMD). AMD was a large semiconductor company that volume-produced Intel microprocessors plus its own Intel clone for the then booming PC and PC clone market.

Jan arrived early to meet John and was introduced to Julie, who was new to the team and had been working with John on Sales, pro bono. John knew Julie from the industry. Julie was previously with AMD. Julie wore a summery outfit with her strawberry blond hair in cute pig tales which made her look even younger than she was. Jan loved Julie's energy. Julie was excited about the prospect of getting in early at a start-up. She had introduced John to Lars, Vantus' VP of Sales, and had orchestrated the meeting.

John had arranged to use a conference room at a local hotel. The Vantus team arrived and they all sat down and exchanged business cards. John had produced business cards, so their sales efforts had a professional look. Lars had brought two women with him to the meeting. One represented the IT organization and the other the pricing team. Then the door flew open and Stephen strode in with his tie over his shoulder and an eager windblown look. He had a charismatic presence that immediately drew attention and he joked in an easy but professional fashion. He quickly set up his laptop and started the demo. Shortly after the meeting, Vantus wanted the software. Since they were the first customer to show interest, John wanted to offer Vantus the ability to start using ProChannel without requiring any up-front cash, as a show of good will and to expedite the process. John was sure as soon as they started using it, they would love it and gladly pay the software costs.

Besides the sales meetings and demos, Stephen had found a lawyer in a prestigious law firm willing to represent the new start-up with stock as his only compensation. Jan and Stephen met with their new lawyer and prepared the initial paperwork. The business was valued at an initial $10 million; John, Stephen, and Jan were each awarded 3.33 million shares of founder stock.

There were no paychecks yet, no official company. Yet by mid-summer John had commitments from many of his friends and business associates to be angel investors. After their prior negative experiences with Venture Capitalists (VCs), neither John nor Stephen wanted anything to do with VC money. John called VCs "bottom feeders." John and Stephen had obtained commitments adding up to an initial $1 million nest egg. They also had two very interested customers, Vantus and QuickLogic.

That called for a celebration. In July, John invited Jan, Stephen, and Ed, the Pricing expert, and their spouses plus Julie to his condo in Santa Cruz, sitting on the bluff above the Santa Cruz wharf. John was hoping to convince Ed to join the team.

John was successful and the small team of five were ready for business.

GETTING READY TO LAUNCH

"It's the little details that are vital. Little things make big things happen." - John Wooden

They leased a small office area in San Jose between Highway 101 and the 880 on-ramp. It was a brand new row of small office areas, more amenable to a mechanic shop than a software company.

On the first floor was a small entrance area with a reception desk and three cubicles, next a wide hall with a kitchen area on the right and two bathrooms on the left. The hallway lead to a two-story main room, which was a big empty space but was large enough to convert into six cubicles for developers. Stephen had arranged previously for carpeting to be laid, since the main room only came with concrete floors.

There was a small upstairs loft over the entrance/kitchen area which could be converted to contain three small co-founder cubicles. The loft had a small window that looked down on the larger room below where the developers would be working. Stephen thought that was an advantage to stay "on top" of the developers. Jan thought Stephen's desire to always know everything that was going on was humorous.

Behind the developer room at the back of the office space was a large two-story warehouse, which Stephen also had carpeted in order to use the area as a conference room. A large two-story roll-up garage door at the back opened almost directly onto the on-ramp connecting Highway 101 and 880. Rolling the door up in the summer would cool down the un-insulated warehouse room, but bring traffic noise right into the building.

Jan had been working on recruiting the engineering talent they would need, but without as much success as she'd hoped. Java was a fairly new programming language and all of her key engineering contacts from companies prior to eMarket.com used C or Fortran, and had no web-based experience. Java was the software language of the internet that they planned to use for their new product. Jan didn't want to recruit the Java-experienced eMarket.com engineers since it would already be a big hit to James when two of his exec team, Stephen and Jan, left eMarket.com.

She had been able to hire Martin, a software manager Jan had worked with before she worked at eMarket.com. Although she wasn't able to offer him a management job and wouldn't be able to for some time, Martin was willing to do coding and eager to be an early employee in a start-up. Martin was bright and energetic, and although he didn't have any hands-on experience with Java, he believed he could ramp up quickly and was willing to roll-up his sleeves and do hands-on coding to build his Java skills. Jan felt that as the company grew, Martin's management skills and prior real-time, mission critical software experience would make him effective at leading the day-to-day development tasks plus help to produce a reliable, high performance system. Since Martin was willing to do coding, Jan was glad to add him to the team as one of the developers. Besides, she felt that it was important for managers to really understand the product they were building. She didn't think it was effective to hire engineering managers who knew nothing more than how to manage. That seemed to be a waste and wouldn't earn the respect of the developers they led. Having Martin spend a year or more with his sleeves rolled up doing coding would earn him that respect.

And then there was Freeman.

Jan had originally hired Freeman in 1996 when she was working as an IT manager at Varian, a Silicon Valley manufacturer. She had been recruited to join Varian by Don, a prior associate of hers from

Ford Aerospace. Don had become the CIO in charge of Varian's Corporate IT organization. Although Jan had never worked in an IT organization (only software development and engineering) the position was to manage the company's SAP Technology department, which was interesting to Jan.

A few years earlier, after leaving Ford Aerospace, Jan had worked for ASK Computer Company which built MANMAN. MANMAN was an ERP program that helped manufacturing companies plan materials purchases, production schedules, and other administrative functions. At ASK she managed the MANMAN/DEC product line of 100 employees including developers, product marketing, and customer support teams on the East and West coasts. With that span of duties, she had not had the chance for much hands-on involvement with the MANMAN product, which she felt made her less effective as a manager. She thought that working in Varian's IT organization, supporting the SAP ERP software, would be a good opportunity to increase her ERP knowledge and make her more effective as a software manager for a company similar to ASK. Also appealing was that as part of her SAP ramp-up, she would be able to attend the intensive, 5-week SAP UNIX developer training.

Varian had an IT organization staffed with employees that had all been with the company for many years. Don hoped to rejuvenate his organization by infusing it with new talent. Jan was brought on to replace a prior manager who used the "old school" management style. Don knew the type of manager Jan was, from working together at Ford Aerospace, and thought she would be a fresh addition to Varian. In addition, Don had received approval to hire a dozen college grads to infuse life into the stagnant IT organization.

Freeman was one of the candidate college grads. He hadn't made the initial cut of new-hires. He was from UC Davis, like many of the other candidates, but had an Economics degree – not a typical IT background. The others had resumes that were a perfect fit for the SAP projects. However, there was something about Freeman that stood out, and Jan was disappointed he wasn't a fit for their openings. Freeman's father, who had a Master's in Physics, had sent Freeman off to college with computer parts in a box telling him that when he figured out how to assemble it, he would have his school computer. Which Freeman did. Jan thought Freeman would be a perfect fit to be part of her systems and networking team. Jan convinced Don to add one more hire - Freeman.

Jan was proven right. Freeman came into the team and a few weeks later, the senior network engineer admitted Freeman was running circles around him and the rest of the network engineers. They were all amazed at how bright Freeman was and how quickly he picked up the technology.

At one point, Don asked Jan to create a web-based survey about email systems. Varian had many diverse email systems at different divisions and locations. Don wanted a corporate standard so people could communicate more effectively. Jan expected to assign the project to the IT Webmaster, Meryl, but quickly found out that Meryl didn't have web development experience. Meryl's role was solely from the network side, to monitor Varian's Internet site to be sure it was up and running.

So Jan put Freeman on the job and she and Freeman both taught themselves HTML, JavaScript, and Perl - the programming languages of the internet.

They completed the survey project successfully and learned a lot in the process. That expertise was going to come in very handy in the future. Having caught the internet development bug, Jan took a Java development course at Santa Clara University. Waiting in line to enter the classroom, she saw Freeman and his friend, also attending the course.

A couple of years later, Jan joined the dot.com as their VP of Engineering. The dot.com's software was web-based and so she quickly solicited Freeman to join her as an HTML designer. That was no surprise to Don. He'd figured that both were destined for more challenges than he could offer within his IT organization. Besides, Freeman had come to Don a short while after he was hired and asked, "Is there any growth opportunity at Varian?"

"Sure there is," said Don. "Why do you ask?"

"Well, Meryl has been at Varian 30 years and is still in the same job."

Don told Jan after they left, "I figured if he hadn't gone with you, I wouldn't have been able to keep him anyway."

To her surprise, Freeman wasn't sure he should make the move. He'd discussed it with his father, who Freeman had great respect for, and was counseled against job hopping, especially so early in his career. Jan could certainly appreciate that advice, having chosen to spend almost twenty years at her first company. However, her choice to stay was because Ford Aerospace offered a wide variety of job opportunities and growth. Jan didn't see the same opportunities for Freeman at Varian.

Freeman agreed to work as a contractor in the evenings at the dot.com while remaining at Varian during the day. He was quickly sold on the start-up software endeavor. It was fast paced, technically challenging, and he loved it. He joined Jan as a full-time employee at the dot.com.

When Jan joined eMarket.com, their product was based on a proprietary software language owned by their partner, Tibco. Tibco was a leader in stock and financial network exchanges. The partnership with Tibco was outstanding in getting eMarket.com credence for being able to host a secure web-based marketplace. However, Tibco's proprietary language, a complex Lisp-like language favored for artificial intelligence system development, made it difficult to expand the business with new engineers, since few developers were trained in the language. Worse, the network protocol software Tibco provided, Rendezvous, although a state-of-the-art protocol, was a version specific to eMarket.com. As Tibco maintained and improved their mainstream Rendezvous product, eMarket.com would not be able to take advantage of those improvements because of their customized version. These were big technology issues.

Jan talked the CEO into upgrading to Java, the emerging "preferred choice" of web-based applications. Nine months later, the eMarket.com development team was close to completing the new Java-based object-oriented system and Freeman was quickly picking up the language.

At that time, Jan began working with Stephen and John on their new venture. To make it easier for eMarket.com when she left, Jan hired a Director of Architecture and a Director of Applications, who were senior enough to report directly to the CEO/President after she left. She had no plans to solicit any of their key engineering personnel.

But, she reasoned, Freeman was another story. Since she had hired Freeman from college and brought him to eMarket.com, and he was a junior developer, she didn't feel that she was exactly "robbing" eMarket.com of a key employee. Although Freeman was a bright engineer, he only had a little real Java experience. She thought his energy and drive would be a good addition to her new company so she asked him to join them in their new venture.

Again, Freeman wasn't convinced he should make the move.

John arranged for a company outing. He purchased a box at an upcoming A's game in Oakland and invited the team (Jan, Stephen, Ed, Martin, and Julie) and their spouses. He also invited Freeman and his girlfriend. John and Stephen had decided to help work on Freeman, since Jan thought he would be a valuable addition.

The area was stocked with appetizers, beer, wine, etc. The group had a lot of fun sometimes watching the game on the monitor, other times going out to see it "live" from the high seats right outside the box. Jan, Stephen, John, and Julie each took some time to talk to Freeman and show him what a fun time they were going to have in this new start-up.

Even though Freeman was still a junior developer, the partners all felt that it was vital to get him on-board because of his amazing attitude and energy.

But it took another lunch outing with Jan, Stephen, and John to close the deal. One of the issues had been with Freeman's father. His father was upset the first time when Freeman had quit Varian after such a short time to go to a start-up, and now here he was, as his father put it, "Job hopping again." His father was again concerned that wouldn't look good on his resume.

"But Dad, I've always worked for the same manager," Freeman retorted.

Freeman gave his two-weeks notice the next day to eMarket.com, but wouldn't be able to start until early October.

With Martin and Freeman signed up, there were still four more developer slots she needed to fill.

The partners had found the office space and signed the lease, but Stephen originally wasn't completely happy with the new facility.

"This linoleum looks cheap," he said a week before the first official day of work. He was staring down at the flooring in the kitchen/hallway going between the reception area and the main room. "We need tile."

Stephen and Jan drove to the nearest tile shop and bought nice gray tile, gray grout, and signed up for a rental tile cutter. They arrived back at the office. Ed had dropped by to hang out and was relaxing in his cubicle in the front office/reception area looking at the stock market reports.

Stephen and Jan got right to work. Both had done some tile work in the past so made quick progress. They'd made quite a mess in the main room cutting tile and Stephen called to Ed, "Ed – vacuum this room."

Ed grumbled as he reclined with his feet on his desk, "Not my job description. Besides, we haven't started work officially yet."

Stephen scowled. Ed relented and got up to vacuum up the mess.

After setting the tile in the quickset, Stephen mixed up the first batch of grout. Stephen and Jan were about halfway through the grouting when John came in the front door. Stephen jumped up to greet him and John looked over and said, "Just what I like, a working woman." Jan scowled and they laughed.

John said to Stephen "Do you have clean clothes here?"

Stephen said, "Yep – I'll go jump into them," as he washed his hands off in the sink. He dashed upstairs and returned looking ready for business.

Stephen said to Jan, "Sorry – sales call. Finish up, OK? You know how to mix the grout. See ya later." Off they went.

Jan wasn't happy but by the time they returned, the grout was finished.

"Looks perfect," Stephen said, pleased with the upgrade.

They were almost ready for their first official day of business, but they still needed to complete their Board of Directors.

THE BOARD

"Life is 10% what happens to you and 90% how you react to it." - Charles Swindoll

At the beginning of the endeavor, John and Stephen had targeted two businessmen for the board of Directors. Both were from the semiconductor industry with rich experience and a substantial rolodex that would come in useful. Both men had proven business expertise as demonstrated by their personal wealth. Bob had been CEO/President of a large semiconductor distribution company. Keith had in the past been John's boss at National Semiconductor, then had been the VP of Asian Sales Operations. Both Bob and Keith, like John, were avid retired race car drivers and car collectors.

John and the initial two board members also agreed that Stephen would hold the lead position of Chairman of the Board.

Years before, Jan had met a start-up founder she was impressed with and thought they should consider as a board member – both because of his success and his accessibility.

She'd been at an SAP User Group meeting, going through a cafeteria-type lunch line. She had chatted amiably with the person in the line behind her. When they got to the end, he said, "It looks like there are a few seats over there."

They sat down to eat and continued chatting. He was CEO and Founder of a very successful start-up in Silicon Valley. It was an interesting connection because he had started his company by commercializing software originating from a different aerospace company. The CEO told Jan that there had been three aerospace companies developing similar artificial intelligence workstations at the time. One was Ford Aerospace, where Jan managed the far-thinking Research & Development projects including the development of a smart workstation that could consume a wide variety of data coming from various systems, condense it, and identify when issues, like army water crossing or tanks on the airstrip, should be alerted to the analysts. He and Jan had similar backgrounds and he had asked her about joining his company, but she had just hired on at her current company and didn't feel the time was right to make a quick jump, even though the job and company would have been very interesting.

The one thing he said that impressed him as he was starting his own company, was the number of CEOs that were willing to sit down with him and give him their time and insight into how to start a business.

Now, as John, Stephen, and she were thinking about board members, Jan thought of that CEO and wondered if he would be as willing to help her in a new start-up, as his mentors had helped him. She had run his name by Stephen as a potential board member and prepared a board packet to send to him. Then Stephen called from his cubicle next door "Wait! Don't send that packet!" She went into Stephen's cube. "Look who his board members are," and he motioned to his monitor. There was the list on the internet – names that meant nothing to Jan. But Stephen said, "Compare that list to Seibel's Board of Directors." Seibel was going to be their biggest competitor. And sure enough, the same list of people were on both boards, including Tom Seibel himself.

"Never mind," Stephen chagrined. "Those are people we don't want to give a heads-up to about our new product. Sorry, he's out."

John had invited Jan and Keith, one of the prospective board members, out to lunch to meet each other. Keith respected John highly and was ready to be on the board.

Over lunch he asked Jan questions about product development and her role. Then said "What will your title be?"

She hadn't actually thought much about titles. "How about just Jan?" she grinned.

They decided on "VP of Engineering."

John, Stephen, and Jan decided on a five-person board. Besides Stephen as Chairperson, Keith, and Bob, the two other positions would be filled with an academic and a technical member. Stephen had met Al, a Santa Clara University Business Department professor, on a recent trip and recommended him as the academic member. The fifth member was still being sought.

The two sat in the filtered light in the two-story warehouse which would serve as the conference room for the fledgling start-up. It was a hot August day, and the overhead lights were off to help reduce the heat already starting to build in the large, un-insulated area behind the air conditioned office space. There was a little light coming from the overhead windows above the large roll-up garage-type doors at the back of the room. The constant din from outside came from the cars and trucks taking the Highway 101/880 connector ramp just a few feet behind the office complex.

The two had been meeting for about an hour. For Jan, it was her chance to get to know the man Stephen was recommending as the technology representative for their Board of Directors. She already knew Scott's history. He had participated in start-up software companies multiple times. Each time, he had grown the business and then successfully sold it for a substantial profit. At the first company, he was the VP of Engineering. At the next few, he was CEO. Now he was currently sitting on boards for various start-up ventures. He definitely knew software technology and had a proven track record of success.

His background was just what Stephen wanted as the final seat on the Board of Directors. The three partners all agreed that with the current business trends, a likely exit strategy would be an acquisition, rather than an Initial Public Offering (IPO). They needed at least one board member with a proven history of selling software companies successfully. Since she represented the technology side of the management trio, she would be the one this board member would be scrutinizing the most carefully, and he would be the one she would look to for advice regarding technology direction. Even though the three partners would manage the company day-to-day, they would be reporting to the Board of Directors who would be representing their investors' interests.

Although Jan's assignment was to convince Scott to join the board, it was also her chance to make sure he would be a good asset for the management team. She was hoping to understand his style, his reactions, and his way of thinking.

For him, it was his chance to measure up the partner who would be the small company's Vice President of Engineering. This was his final step in deciding whether to commit to be on their board. The board would be a financial commitment, a time commitment, a legal commitment, and moreover, could affect his reputation on other boards if the management team performed poorly. He had been quizzing her on technology thoughts, management plans, and software process concepts.

They were getting to the end of their discussion. She had made her decision about him, determined he would be an excellent asset to the board when he asked, "What keeps you up at night? What about this venture scares you the most?"

She quickly reflected to see if there was anything that was particularly worrisome or concerning and answered. "Nothing," she said. "I've been in large companies and small, grown successful teams from scratch. I just can't wait to get going."

He had not expected that answer but no answer would have made him feel more satisfied. He smiled slightly as he had also made his decision. They had their final board member.

WEEK ONE (SEPTEMBER 1998)

"The only way to do great work is to love the work you do." - Steve Jobs

Jan woke up energized. It was a beautiful California day with none of the early morning cloudy haze typical during the summer months. September had brought with it clear, blue skies and the day was already starting to get warm. As she drove, she went through a mental checklist of what had to be done to get a development team formed and product development underway. It was September 15, 1998 - the first official day of work for the newly formed company.

Stephen and John were standing near the entrance when she arrived.

"Glad you finally showed up," John teased as she came through the front door. "Engineering hours," added Stephen smugly. It was only 8:30 a.m. but Stephen and John, who liked to get started around 7:00 were eager to kick off the first day. Julie the new Sales Rep was also in the office already. She had been spending time with John and Stephen on sales calls the past three months, eager to be part of the new start-up. The past three months had been pro bono, so she was also eager to start getting a real paycheck.

As soon as Ed, the pricing expert arrived, Stephen, their CEO and President, called their small team of five together for their first staff meeting.

It was clear this wouldn't be the same as other staff meetings she'd been used to in the large corporations she'd worked for before. She'd never been part of the initial stages of a start-up before and had never had to think through the basic operations of a company.

First item on the agenda: purchasing office necessities such as paper towels and toilet paper. Stephen gave that assignment to Julie but she immediately objected. "Just because I'm female doesn't mean I need to be the one to buy the toilet paper."

John's interjection didn't help the situation as he teased, "Well, who *would* you expect would do the shopping?"

Stephen quickly tried to smooth the situation saying, "It's not that, Julie. You're the only one with an SUV. We need lots of paper towels and other bulky items. Don't worry. There are plenty of chores to go around." To which Julie acquiesced and agreed.

Both Julie and Jan put their foot down though when Stephen suggested that the women take on the bathroom cleanup task. "No way," said Julie. "You men are going to take care of the Men's room, we'll take care of the Ladies' room. We're not cleaning up after you. Ilk!"

Stephen acquiesced.

Stephen continued down the list. "I'll get a postal meter and lease a copier. Jan, do you have a FAX machine you'd like to contribute to a worthy cause? Anyone have a spare coffee pot?"

The agenda certainly contained items Jan wasn't used to seeing on a company meeting agenda.

The next day Stephen called Julie, John, and Jan into the warehouse. He had his laptop set up and asked them to stand behind him. During the prior months, John had encountered another start-up named G2 Technology so they had finalized instead on the company name of Intelic Software Solutions, Inc. Intelic stood for <u>Intel</u>ligent <u>I</u>nternet <u>C</u>ommerce.

Stephen assigned himself to design the logo. The marketing pitch said the software was "ProChannel" since it would help turn every one of the semiconductor company's sales reps into "pros" in increasing their sales "channel" margins and revenue.

They started out picking the logo color. John wanted red. "It has more of a punch," he explained.

Stephen felt that since their prior company's logo was red and black, he wanted to go with something completely different.

Julie liked the eggplant color from a recent event she'd been to. They narrowed it down to a variation of blue or purple.

"OK," Stephen said. "Which one do you like best. This? Or this?" He brought up two color panels, each a shade of bluish/purple: one eggplant, one bluer. They each pointed to their favorite.

"OK – now which one?"

It was like taking an eye test where you look with one eye and then the other. The color they thought was too blue ended up too purple in comparison with the next example. On and on Stephen went – a perfectionist in color and perspective.

Finally, they had narrowed down the color choice, and Stephen was off to design the logo. "Intelic," he pondered. "How to best represent it?"

Stephen decided on a Times New Roman font, small italic "i" - a white letter against the blue/purple background.

Stephen designed the logo, ordered letterhead stock, and coffee cups from a company that was very economical. Unfortunately, the coffee cup company was limited in their color choices and delivered cups slightly more blue than Stephen's color choice. No one else noticed but Stephen wasn't happy. He was the perfectionist in the group.

The next day, Jan heard a lot of noise as Stephen started up a table saw in the central kitchenette/hallway with board ready to cut in half. She yelled over the din, "Stephen! Shut that off!"

"Huh?" he said as he turned the saw off and turned around to see what the problem was.

"What are you doing?" she complained. "Don't you realize what a mess you'll make of the entire office if you start sawing in here? Out! Out!" and she spirited him and his table saw to the alley outside behind the warehouse. "Here," she pointed. "This is the sawing place!"

"You sound like my wife!"

"I guess it takes two to keep someone like you out of trouble."

Stephen grumbled but set up the table saw in the parking lot out back. He donned his tool belt and went about making shelves for the large supply closet under the stairs to turn it into a "computer room." One of the angel investors had provided 26 desktop computers as his investment and they were all in boxes waiting to be set up.

While Stephen was carrying the shelving into the office, Martin, the new software manager, arrived for his first day of work.

Jan introduced them. Holding the shelf with one arm, Stephen shook hands with Martin and motioned to the rows of computers in the hallway outside the development offices and said, "A developer. Good. See those computers? Get them set up."

"Aye, aye, sir," replied Martin with a snappy salute and smile.

Some of the computers would be used as central servers and went into the new "computer room" closet. The rest were for employee workstations, and integration and QA systems. Over the next few days, the shelves were built, painted, and the centralized computers assembled, loaded with software, and moved to their new shelves. All those computers in a small space generated too much heat, so Stephen sent Martin to the hardware store for fans. It wasn't impressive enough for Stephen to have all those computers in "just" a closet so he measured the opening, removed the door, and went to Tap Plastics to buy smoke-colored plastic to cover the door space. Then he set each computer's screen saver to 3D text so that "Intelic" rotated on each screen. As visitors walked by, it would look like a fancy control center filled with computers ready to compute.

A sign company came to install "Intelic" above the door.

A few days later, John had a paint brush in hand and was touching up the paint on the walls in the main room.

Then Jan saw Stephen standing in the open 2-story main room looking up at the ceiling and then he left the building. He returned an hour later with bright plastic triangle flags – red, yellow, and blue – like you'd see at a race course. Next he was on the tall ladder near the

20 foot high ceiling hanging the banners. He couldn't quite hang them as far out from the wall as far as he wanted and stretched precariously with one foot on the ladder and the other in empty space while everyone watched and held their breath. Jan thought they'd better take out extra insurance on Stephen. Up and down the ladder a dozen times, moving the ladder from position to position.

Then he stood in the doorway with a pleased look on his face, crossed arms, looking up at the colorful banners overhead, and said, "There, that's better."

THE FIRST CUSTOMER VISIT

"Less isn't more; just enough is more." - *Milton Glaser*

Stephen had scheduled a site visit at Intelic by their first potential paying customer. QuickLogic's CFO wanted to "kick the tires," so to speak. Although QuickLogic was a start-up company itself, they were going to IPO soon. Winning QuickLogic as a customer would start the fledgling Intelic off in the right direction.

Stephen and John had spent the last few months talking to QuickLogic and demoing the new product. Now QuickLogic wanted to take the next step. While Stephen had been up-front with them that Intelic was just getting started, both he and John had been aggressive in their assumptions about how quickly they would be able to pull the initial funding together and get started. QuickLogic's CFO had been pushing to move forward.

Stephen finally had agreed to a visit no later than the next week. With only a handful of employees on-board, the company certainly wouldn't look very substantial. The team had a lot to do in the first week.

Hiring was already a top priority. Frank, a senior developer from eMarket.com had approached them about a position. He had exactly the senior Java experience they needed. They were hesitant to take any more people from their prior company. A junior developer was one thing but this was a senior, experienced developer who had been with the prior company from the beginning. However, Frank convinced them that he would ensure their prior company's CEO knew he had come to Intelic, not vice versa, and was planning to leave eMarket.com regardless. They needed a strong engineer so they relented and were glad to have another slot filled. The only problem was that he wouldn't be available until the end of October.

That still left three more developer openings. Jan had been reviewing developer resumes for months, from job fairs and recruiter friends who would help her out for free. She also reached out to engineers she'd worked with before but most were C developers or, if from Ford Aerospace, Fortran or Ada developers. None had any web experience. John and Stephen were regularly asking her for a hiring update but the fledgling company had no budget to pay for any recruitment services.

The valley was on an upswing and the job market was so hot that good developers had job offers the day they posted their resumes. More promising experienced developers were securing VP or CTO slots in other emerging start-ups. The few candidates she was able to bring in quickly for interviews either weren't up to her standards or wanted more money than the company's start-up budget could afford. She'd been able to attract Martin and Frank with good stock packages instead of high pay, but not all developers were willing to make that trade-off.

Since recruiting was slow, Jan sought a contract company to fill Intelic's developer gap. Jan had worked with the owner of one contract company previously. Although he himself was not available for Intelic, he was a very intelligent, skilled engineer and Jan hoped he represented the talent his company could offer. His company offered H-1 Visa engineers from India on-contract. In addition, he was willing to provide engineers at a much better rate if Intelic was willing to give his company stock options. Stephen always preferred offering stock instead of cash to limit the cash outflow during the early years.

One part of the contract bothered Jan and she had asked the owner if he would consider removing the clause for Intelic. His contract included a "non-conversion" clause where Intelic would not be able to hire any of the engineers who came to contract for them.

The owner was adamant on the point, though. He said he didn't want to spend all of his time traveling to India to recruit engineering talent, cover the cost of processing H-1 Visas, and relocate them to the U.S. just to have the companies he contracted with recruit them to become their own direct employees. Jan worried about retention because his company paid the engineers they hired fairly low wages, taking quite a bit off-the-top for themselves, and didn't offer the engineers any stock options. The main incentive the engineers had for staying with the contract company was that the contract company held their H-1 Visas.

The negotiations with the contract company and associated legal paperwork had moved slowly. The contractors wouldn't be on-board in time for the QuickLogic visit.

Other than Martin, the developer cubicles were still empty.

The day before the QuickLogic meeting, Stephen called the team together. Because they already had the prototypes, a design, and would soon have Freeman and the contractors on-board, the team knew they could deliver the product QuickLogic wanted. The offices were empty and Stephen wasn't sure how to convince the QuickLogic CFO that Intelic was a good bet.

John already had a plan. "We just need to make the place look occupied and sound lively. I'll ask Keith (one of the board members) to come over to meet the CFO. My daughter, Jenn, can be at the Reception desk. We'll add radios for some background noise."

"I'll set up the offices," he continued. "But we need to get some developers in here."

Jan had an idea. She arranged for one of the developers she had a résumé for and was interested in to come by for an interview at 4 p.m. the next day. She then called Freeman and asked if could juggle his work hours and come over, around 4 p.m. to help interview a potential Java developer. Since Freeman was an early starter and typically arrived at work by 7 a.m., she hoped he could leave his job early enough.

"Sure," he said.

"Great," said Jan. "Actually, can you get here a little before 4 p.m.?" "Use the office by the Conference Room. Say 'Java' a lot. Draw on the white board. Use technical jargon."

"Huh?" Freeman was puzzled. Then, "Sure – whatever you want."

John and Martin spent the day setting up the developer computers. They put a desktop computer in each developer cubicle. Jan set up an office for herself downstairs in the first developer cube after entering the room. Just before the QuickLogic CFO was about to arrive, Martin turned on the computers in each cubicle, each to different pages with the screen saver off. John was busy adding the personal touches in each empty developer cube – open magazines and books in general disarray, open briefcases, coffee cups, and family pictures (all pictures of his family). He gave each office a "lived in" look. A radio in the front office and one in the back, plus coffee percolating, made the office feel homey and busy. John felt confident with the approach. He knew in two weeks this is how the offices would look and everything they would tell the CFO about the software and delivery plans was completely true.

At 4 p.m. when QuickLogic's CFO arrived, John and Keith were talking business in the reception area and stopped for introductions. John's daughter Jennifer welcomed him and telephoned upstairs to Stephen. Ed was visible in his office cubicle just off the reception area. Julie was in the kitchen making coffee. The office was humming. Stephen then escorted the QuickLogic CFO through the developer office area. Jan and Martin were on their computers, Freeman and the developer candidate were drawing on the board and discussing Java, and signs of life were everywhere else. Stephen, John, and the CFO headed into the "conference room" warehouse and shut the door whereupon Stephen turned on the projector and proceeded to dazzle the CFO with the Intelic marketing briefing. Stephen colorfully and succinctly painted a vision of the upcoming product and provided industry perspective. After an hour, the door opened and they exited through the building to the front door where the CFO shook hands with Stephen.

"Very impressive. I look forward to working with your company."

The deal was as good as sealed. The first paid customer was on-board. The team danced around the office giddily. Even Keith, the board member, was caught up in the excitement of the first deal and Freeman was hooked. He, like the rest of them, had bought into the dream.

THREE MONTHS TO DELIVER THE BABY

"Nine women can't make a baby in one month." - Fred Brooks in "The Mythical Man-Month" and Ray Zachary, Ford Aerospace.

The next day, John, Stephen, and Jan sat down to discuss schedules. Stephen said, "OK. QuickLogic is hooked and wants the product. They want to install it in January."

"What?" Jan asked. "January of what year?"

"This coming January, of course."

When John, Stephen, and Jan were writing their business plan and formulating the first year's strategy, Jan estimated that they could produce a basic product in nine months. John felt strongly it must be available sooner. So Jan gave a revised estimate of an initial release with only the primary modules (quoting, pricing, orders, debits, and samples plus basic administration modules including catalog, account management, and user management) which she estimated would take six months using six developers.

The original plan had been to start the company in June. But the reality was that all of the logistics - finding the funding, the building, hiring, etc. - meant they didn't open the doors until September.

"I'd said six months at a minimum. It's now September. That means no earlier than April."

"But," John complained, "you said in June we could have it in six months. I told QuickLogic we'd have it for them by January!"

"We've only hired a couple of people: Martin, and Freeman who will be starting in a couple of weeks. The contractors will be on-board next week but Frank won't be able to start until the end of October. I'd planned six developers on-board for six months to get the product out."

They both looked at her like disappointed children.

Jan raised her eyebrows, looked over at them, and took in a slow breath to stay calm. "Well… Let's re-group," she said slowly. "When we talked about schedules last June, I said the minimum time possible for pulling a first release, minimum time for a minimal product, would be at least six months and you both said that would work."

"Right" Stephen said enthusiastically. "We told QuickLogic that. Since that was last June, they've since been thinking they could have a product in January. We did such a great job yesterday convincing them we had a company up and running. We don't want to discourage them at the start."

"The prototype we've been showing customers has 14 modules plus a framework. Even with the reduced plan of quoting and pricing – we can't possibly deliver that in 3 months."

"We have a commitment for more money now – how about if we get some more contractors from the company you signed – how about that?" Stephen proposed like an excited kid.

"The contracting company is already not able to deliver enough resources," said Jan. "Regardless, if it takes 9 months to deliver the baby, adding more moms isn't going to speed up the process. There's a code size-to-team size ratio that is like a law of physics. Er, of software. This baby's going to take 6 months minimum."

The look of dismay on Stephen's face was obvious.

"OK, let's think about this," Jan loved a challenge. At Ford Aerospace, one of the trainers who came from Ford Motor Company was from Tennessee and taught about the "Fuzzy Peas." He was referring to the 3 Ps that drive a software project: People, Plan, and Product. "People" are the number of developers you can put on the project. And while you can't gather nine women and produce a baby in a month, there are some impacts that can be made if the right resources are allocated to the right schedules. "Plan" is the schedule –

moving the schedule in or out is an obvious choice and one of the ways a manager can affect the end result. That wasn't an option here. "Product" refers to how much product (how many enhancements) is built. Remove some features, save some time.

"The 6-month plan was for a subset of modules, not all fourteen. Can we reduce it even more? What's the minimum feature-set QuickLogic needs to start with?"

Stephen paused only a minute. He saw the twinkle in Jan's eyes and knew there was hope after all. He appreciated her warrior side and had seen her rise to the challenge many times in the past. His wheels were turning. "QuickLogic's crisis, and why they need the product quickly, is that they want to be ready to IPO, but don't have any predictability for their revenues. That's because they don't know what the sales force is telling the customers since it's all done over the phone and not tracked anywhere. In addition, they have several rep firms that do direct sales for them, but QuickLogic doesn't have good visibility to their deals. Those guys are giving credits to their distribution partners and QuickLogic has no visibility into that either. They can't go public with no revenue predictability."

"So," said Jan. "If we could automate their sales quote activity initially, that would allow them to demonstrate the controls needed to IPO?"

"Probably. Except they also need to be able to give their sales reps direction about what prices are valid – they really need our pricing engine also. We can put off design tracking, asset management, and other modules."

"What would they need to be able to do online quoting and pricing?" she mused. "We'd need the full-up browser-based quote screens and the pricing engine."

"Right."

"Can we just load their user names and passwords in the database for sign-on and not give them any GUI initially for user management?" Jan asked.

"I think they could buy into that for a few months," Stephen agreed.

"Would they need to be able to search for parts?" Jan continued. "Would they need that part attribute search screen we'd prototyped?"

'Yes, afraid so. Plus they need to be able to add new customers on-the-fly and convert their quotes to debits or orders."

That was a brick wall. Jan lamented "We can't try to automate linkage to the ERPs for order management in 3 months," as any hope at a plan fell quickly apart.

"Not a real interface up-front," Stephen quickly interjected to keep Jan in her previous "can do" attitude. "We'd make them — 'rip and read.' Their sales users can capture the order and debit info but they will need to have their admins print out the forms and re-enter the data manually into their ERP. No worse off than they are today."

That got Jan back to seeing a glimmer of possibility.

To try to solicit a 3-month plan from Jan, Stephen added: "Make it a prototype — anything to get it to them quickly."

"No, no, no — that's not the right approach. We're too little to be building throw-away code. We need to architect it the right way from the start. We'd end up never being able to get rid of the prototype code and the architecture would get convoluted. Let me see what we can do. The contractors start next week and we can brainstorm."

The next few weeks were a flurry of activity. Freeman arrived and two of the three developer contractors from the contracting company, Vimal and Sanjiv, were available to start.

Julie was working on sales in addition to helping Stephen with any other company start-up activities required. However, when Stephen ran by and asked her to pick up his dry cleaning, he noticed the "Excuse me?" look on her face and quickly added "Pleeease? Look at me. I spilled ketchup on my shirt, have a phone call with a CEO right now and need to be at a meeting at Linear in a half an hour. I know you're not my secretary or my wife." The little-boy pleading look on his face made Julie laugh and she said, "I'll get right on it boss. Plus I've got an SUV."

The initial demo screens had been developed, but underlying pricing algorithms needed to be designed. Stephen had designed pricing software before, and Ed was a hands-on pricing expert.

Ed gave whiteboard training to Jan and Julie on pricing methodologies and practices: how price curves should be optimized, what business parameters need to be considered, where the distributor book cost value should fall on the price curve based on what variables, and why. Ed was often called on by pricing managers in various companies to provide consulting and feedback on their pricing methods and strategies. He was well known in Silicon Valley. Having him on the team was a definite plus. The initial pricing engine delivered to QuickLogic would not include all of the advanced functionality Ed was explaining, but having the right data structure was important for the longer-range product plans.

While Jan was writing down specifications for the developers with the graphical user interface (GUI) based on the HTML demo screens and adding the underlying algorithms and database design layers, Freeman was performing investigations of third party tools for supporting the database and Java application.

CHOOSING THE RIGHT ARCHITECTURE

"Simplicity is the ultimate sophistication." - Leonardo da Vinci

Some software companies start out going down the path of building a quick prototype, with the idea that the code will be scrapped later and product re-done. However, that wasn't Jan's first choice. In her experience, there is never time to go back to the beginning and rebuild totally from scratch. Especially in a fast-paced environment. Instead, the teams get stuck with the half thought-out code and discarded modules. Jan hated putting resources into what later would be wasted code. A quick mockup HTML demo screen was one thing. A complete product delivered to a customer then later thrown away is another. She felt it was best to make the right architecture decisions up-front. Build the code in a way that it was high quality and solid and, if due to lessons learned, some features and functions needed to be revised, they could be evolved. But the entire product wouldn't need to be rebuilt.

Even though Jan preferred Sun/UNIX as a platform, John had been adamant from the start that the initial releases had to be on Windows. Most Sales VPs, the buyers of Intelic's software, would normally have discretion over their own budget for desktop hardware and software purchases. On the other hand, UNIX systems - like Sun Microsystem computers which needed to be maintained in a company's air conditioned computer room - required getting the customer's IT bureaucracy involved. That could mean extra months to close the deal. John was convinced that he would have an easier time closing the deal for a product that would run on a simple Windows desktop computer and not require IT support.

The strategy worked well for QuickLogic. As a start-up, QuickLogic had minimal IT resources and wanted a turnkey system.

The Intelic system would be a modern web-based application with a central server contacted via the internet by users using their own desktop or laptop computers (typically for business, Windows PCs).

There were three "layers" to the architecture. The bottom layer was the database. The middle layer was the application itself. The database and application would reside on separate servers in the customer's building. The top layer was called the client software and was what would be on the users' desktops or laptops for their browsers to use. The "client" was the web-based screens and forms users would interact with.

Although the early years of Java were not without their difficulties, Jan believed Java was the right language for a web-based application. She was convinced that a standards-based technology was key. Since Java was a very portable language, writing the software in Java would make it easier to expand support to Sun/UNIX and other hardware vendors later.

For the software that would run on the user's desktop or laptop when accessed from the web, the "client" software, Jan wanted to stay with the lightweight HTML and JavaScript, similar to what she built the demo with. The other option was "client-side Java," which was an entirely different compiler than the application's "server-side Java." Client-side Java, if used, would actually be downloaded on the users desktop or laptop and executed there, similar to how cookies are downloaded and used.

When at eMarket.com, one of the engineers, a very opinionated Russian engineer from Sun Microsystems, was adamant that client-side Java should be used for eMarket.com's product. Jan wasn't as convinced. Client-side Java created a heavy footprint (a large amount of data that needed to be downloaded to the user's PC, also called a "thick client"). This was known to cause performance issues. In addition, downloading client-side Java required the user to go to the Sun website and download the latest version of Java to his or her private desktop or laptop system. It wasn't as automated back then as it is today. This added a burden that many sales users would not have accepted.

During Jan's SAP experience at Varian, she observed the problems IT organizations encounter when upgrading to a new version of "thick client" software. It required the new software to be loaded on each desktop computer. Even worse, when the software had a thick client, periodically every user in the company needed to upgrade their PC operating system to remain compatible with the SAP software residing on their desktop computer. When there are thousands of PCs in the company, a full company upgrade to a new version of Microsoft's Operating System is a huge effort for the IT organization. In addition, many IT organizations are hesitant to upgrade their entire company's desktop operating systems because of incompatibilities that may occur with other applications. This could make it hard for their customers to keep up with the latest releases of ProChannel. For Intelic to have to support multiple, old, out-of-date versions of ProChannel would take more resources, a cost the fledgling start-up could not afford.

HTML and JavaScript were also industry client standards and could provide nearly the same user experience with a very lightweight, standard, out-of-the-box, thin client. Using a thin client didn't require customers to upgrade their desktop operating systems, provided quicker user responsiveness, and fewer issues - resulting in better user satisfaction. None of Intelic's engineers objected. She decided to stick with HTML and JavaScript.

For the database selection, the hot new database technology in the late '90s was Object-Oriented (OO) databases. Many in the software industry believed that OO databases were the technical direction of the future, and perfect for web-based Java applications since Java is an object-oriented language.

Jan was interested in more than just using cool technology, so she probed the maintenance and production aspects of these new OO databases. She discovered that none of the OO databases had tools to easily interact with them. They also didn't support the standard query language (SQL), which was available for all relational databases, or anything similar, to enable system administrators to easily load data or interrogate the contents of the database. Using an OO database, the Intelic developers would need to write special Java programs to read and write to the database. In addition, the OO databases had no backup tools. It would be up to the Intelic developers to develop backup utilities. To Jan, having her small team develop database load, query, and backup tools didn't make any sense. ProChannel was going to be an enterprise application and needed a robust, production-worthy database underneath it. It became an even easier decision when they researched performance comparisons – OO databases definitely performed much slower than relational databases. One thing Jan knew for sure – if this product was going to go global, through the internet, to users in Europe and Asia, sales users who are impatient and always on-the-go, the software had to be quick, responsive, and intuitive. Performance was key.

Oracle was the only real choice for relational databases in the late '90s after Ingres had been acquired by Computer Associates and when Sybase was struggling with customer dissatisfaction. Oracle it was.

That made Vimal, one of the new contractors, happy since he was an Oracle guru. Oracle was an easy sell to customers, because most IT organizations were already supporting Oracle as the database for their ERP and other back office systems. Oracle was also the database that all of the developers, including Jan, had the most experience with. Jan negotiated a reseller agreement with Oracle to obtain free developer copies of Oracle's database software.

Oracle had two separate divisions: their database software division and an ERP offering. Intelic would actually be competing against some of the modules in the Oracle ERP solution. But Oracle's database business and ERP business were separate. Even

SAP, Oracle ERP's biggest competitor, ran on Oracle databases.

Besides selecting a database, there were a couple of other third party software choices to be made. Frank had been staying in-touch via email to keep abreast of architectural decisions prior to coming on-board. Frank recommended Oracle's Application Server (OAS) as their Java application server, which was the "winner" in a wide technical evaluation that had been conducted at eMarket.com. OAS was from a proven vendor (Oracle), had extensive features, and included a robust Object-to-Relational layer to handle the translation from Java objects to the Oracle relational database.

Freeman had read reports that OAS had performance issues and had a very "heavy" footprint. Freeman wanted to write his own Java servlet from scratch, which he said would be easy because the way he was designing the components didn't rely heavily on the servlet engine. Stephen was pushing them to use as much off-the-shelf software as possible. Most CEOs believed that the smart approach was to focus efforts on the main product and buy third party tools, where possible.

Freeman read about JRun, a lightweight, quick, and responsive application server from a small start-up, Live Software, that was recommended online by many developers. It had all of the capabilities needed for their product. When Freeman tested both on his computer, JRun was nimble and quick. OAS was sluggish. Freeman said JRun worked great. Jan decided to go with Freeman's quick and nimble approach. JRun was also much cheaper.

However, with this approach, they would need a separate Object-to-Relational (OR) layer. Vimal recommended an OR vendor named ObjectMatter that was inexpensive and that he had experience with. After reviewing the alternatives, ObjectMatter was chosen.

With the first two contractors and Freeman on-board, development commenced. Oracle was slow to deliver the developer version they'd promised, so to speed up the process, Jan called Elizabeth, a contact of hers who now worked at Oracle. Elizabeth coordinated inside Oracle to get Intelic a disk. Martin drove to Oracle's offices in Redwood Shores to pick it up. He returned with one of Oracle's gold product disks (disks typically restricted for Oracle internal use). Martin and Freeman soon had a copy of the database loaded on all of the servers and workstations.

Jan loved databases and database design. She felt that for good software, the design needed to consider both the user experience (which was obvious) but also the underlying database. She designed the database tables to map cleanly to the transactional objects and added simple, high-speed mapping tables to identify the many-to-many linkages between objects. She had contemplated designing the database structures the way the senior architect from Sun had advocated at their prior company. He championed implementing "meta data tables," where the table design is generic and expandable. Jan felt that some software architects work so hard to produce elegant, expandable designs that the end result isn't practical, and instead is slow, difficult to work with, and difficult to maintain. It didn't seem logical and clean to her. Besides, having a business-relatable database schema would mean it would be much easier for the developers to use, and easier for the customer system administrators to query the data for reporting or trouble-shooting.

Meanwhile, Freeman was developing the basic Java library of HTML components. He wrote a Java style guide to insure clean, consistent code was being developed. Freeman also began monitoring the software the contractors were developing. He was acting more like an experienced software professional than a developer with less than two years software development experience.

As part of the standard utilities, since they were going to be a global software company, their software had to handle global time. At Varian, Fred, the director of operations, was very focused on "global time."

Jan had never given the issues surrounding global time much thought, having previously built aerospace and defense software that didn't have a complex time component.

Fred had worked on software with worldwide users and knew of the many issues that needed to be solved to insure the software managed time correctly.

For example, there is the time zone where the company is physically located. Typically that is the time zone they conduct their business in. If a business was located in California, it would do business in PDT/PST. If a contract was negotiated in California to begin on 1/1/1998 and expire on 12/31/1998, then if a user in Japan accessed the system and it was already 1/1/1998 in Japan but in California it was still 12/31/1997, the Japanese user should not be able to quote against that yet-to-be-opened contract. Normally when talking about transactions, their start and expire date fields don't have time associated with them, only a day. In discussing a contract, people usually say a contract starts on a specific day, such as January 1. However, to have the contract used correctly worldwide, the software would need to say the contract actually starts at the beginning of the business day on January 1 which is midnight or 12:00:00 a.m. in the business's chosen time zone. Similarly, contracts would expire at 11:59:59 p.m. All date fields in the databases needed to include timestamps.

When looking at activity-based information, such as a list of emails, each user should see the email time-stamped in his or her time zone, regardless of where in the world the email was sent from. Activities that occur that do have time associated, a user action such as when email is sent, would use the current time stamp in the user's time zone.

The rules and software components to display and track global time were quite complicated. The trick Jan learned from Fred at Varian was that all dates should be converted from the transaction or activity time zone into GMT time zone before being stored in the database. When used or viewed, they would then be converted back to the appropriate time zone. Storing in GMT (Greenwich Mean Time, also referred to as UTC or Coordinated Universal Time) also ensured consistency by avoiding the need to calculate for daylight savings time being on or off. That is particularly important since not all states, like Arizona, use daylight savings time, nor all countries.

Freeman stepped up to the challenge and created a library of consistent components to enforce the correct tracking and display of global time.

Soon Frank, the senior engineer, was also on-board.

At times, technical debates arose among the team members – from the basic development approach and styles to architectural design decisions.

Martin said he was not yet an experienced Java coder, having more experience with C and C++, and wanted the team to make the architectural design decisions.

Jan was very technical, and even though her strength wasn't coding in Java, core software design and architecture concepts remain consistent over the years. Time after time she found herself agreeing with the logic and consistency in Freeman's arguments over anyone else's, even though Freeman was inexperienced, young, and unproven as an architect.

Freeman liked to keep things simple.

Jan believed that software companies often tended to do what she considered "over architecting:" Choosing too complex of an infrastructure or building features into products to cover all possible future combinations. Adding complexity that ends up never being used results in slower performance, lower reliability, and unnecessary memory overhead. Often, perhaps just a coincidence, she found that the most over-architected systems were designed by PhDs or by senior engineers who had more university training that practical experience.

Jan wasn't opposed to education, she herself had a Master's degree in Mathematics. In addition, because she had worked on aerospace programs, Stephen would joke that she was a rocket scientist. However, Jan didn't believe in overly complex software. The PhDs would claim it was "elegant" code. Jan called it "big and bulky."

Basic development and style decisions also needed to be made early to insure clean, consistent code: coding style, file folder structure, and other choices. Jan once again found herself more and more liking Freeman's clean, simplistic approach.

Jan completed the requirements specification and top level design document for the first release which she then split into tasks in a spreadsheet. The tasks were divided among the team and they were off and running.

As the product started to come together, Jan accessed the software every day and knew what she liked: A convenient placement of input boxes and action buttons so that the steps to complete a function took the minimal number of mouse movements and keyboard clicks, a minimal number of pages, and navigation that followed an intuitive flow so that the user would not need to study the screen to figure out what he or she should do to complete their activity.

It should be as easy for users to use the system to get their job done as any other normal daily task, like putting the cream and sugar in their coffee or paging through an interesting book. She hated unnecessary pop-ups, multiple layers of drill-downs, or multiple clicks to do a single task which slowed the user down in completing their work. Users needed to be able to complete the task quickly and easily. The key to success was performance, performance, performance.

She and Freeman were in one hundred percent agreement about the main driver in software architecture. Some in software referred to it as "KISS" (Keep it Simple, Stupid). She thought of it as clean and practical.

STARTING WITH THE BASICS

"Technology is nothing. What's important is that you have a faith in people, that they're basically good and smart, and if you give them tools, they'll do wonderful things with them." - Steve Jobs

It was time for the first board meeting. The board planned to arrive at 10 a.m. Jan arrived early at 8 a.m. and found Stephen was already there, looking harried as he rushed around his office to the copy machine and back to print out and prepare the board packets. Jan had prepared a few engineering slides which he'd already incorporated into the packets along with John's sales update and Stephen's own financial and marketing reports. Jan asked what she could do to help and Stephen asked her to monitor the developer cubicles to make sure they looked clean and presentable. She made sure the developers knew the board members would be coming through – no surfing the web! She had previously caught one of their contractors spending way too much time on an India entertainment website.

John arrived and was carrying a large metal object through the front door. He struggled to get it into the warehouse. As Jan followed him into the warehouse it was immediately clear what the issue was. It was freezing cold! The warehouse was the area of the facility with no heat or air conditioning. In the summer, they had opened up the full-wall-sized roll-up garage door to bring a cooling breeze (and traffic noise) into the conference room. It was now late November and the temperature outside had dropped. The "conference room" wasn't bearable without ski jackets and gloves. John set down something that looked like a jet engine. He plugged it in and it sounded like a jet engine. Whoosh. In five minutes, the warehouse was a toasty 80 degrees.

"That works!" smiled John, pleased his idea worked so well.

The board members began arriving. Julie had the coffee and donuts ready and led them to the warm and toasty warehouse. John had just turned off the noisy propane heater.

The board was impressed both by Stephen's elaborate handouts and Intelic's progress to-date. After an hour, the warehouse had cooled down so they took a coffee break, and John turned the propane heater back on. Whoosh.

"Wow," said Keith. "Sounds like we're at the race-track."

After the morning's meeting, the board left satisfied and happy with their investments.

As the developers began the detailed code design, Frank had assigned himself one of the more complex structures. Freeman had documented a style guide for all of the developers to use and had built the library of basic components. Freeman trained the team quickly on the coding style and began mentoring Sanjiv, the junior contractor. Freeman found that Sanjiv needed a lot of help. Freeman offered to do peer code reviews with the other engineers and Frank offered to peer review Freeman's code. Sanjiv appreciated it. Vimal was older than the other developers and balked at anyone, particularly young Freeman, reviewing his efforts. Martin asked for some coding assignments to get up-to-speed on the hands-on side of the effort, since there was not as much "management" of the team needed during this early timeframe. Freeman assigned him to code the user login function.

Periodically, John or Julie would return from a customer meeting with some refinement needed for the product. Together they all would decide if the change was needed for this initial release, or if it would be better to wait for the next release. For changes the team wanted to include in the early modules, Jan revised the spreadsheet and specs to match the changes. But the process was quickly becoming unmanageable.

Jan asked Freeman to download the GNU GNATS bug tracking tool that they'd used at their prior company. The GNU Project is a collaborative group of developers that produces free open source software. She wanted to use GNATS not only to track bugs, but also new enhancement requests as well. However, Freeman found it was built for UNIX computers and wouldn't install on their Windows systems.

Freeman had an idea.

"We already have a basic transaction framework for our own product. I could add a bug tracker screen like GNATS really quickly using the components we have. You design the database and what screens you want and I'll code it up. With our framework and HTML components, it will be a quick project."

"I don't want this to eat into your time though."

"It will take less time than I've already spent on GNATS," Freeman retorted.

"Point taken – carry on."

Many managers think spending any time building internal tools is a waste of developer energy and just an example of the NIH (Not Invented Here) syndrome. Jan knew Stephen would typically be opposed to spending any time building internal tools, but knew this situation was different. First, free, open-source software isn't ever really "free." As Freeman pointed out, it took developer time and energy to get it downloaded and set up. Then it never quite meets the need, so more developer time is spent learning the tool's code and adding necessary features and customizations.

A side benefit to Freeman's idea was that if they built it on their own software framework, any developer could add new features and functionality easily. In addition, the developers, testers, and she herself would be using it daily to run their own business. What better way to improve their product's usability and shake out low-level bugs than to have the team using the software themselves?

Moreover, she'd already spent a significant amount of time in the past designing and thinking about what would be valuable as an internal tracking tool. She and her friend Sandy had thought about starting their own company years before and wrote software design specs for CRM software centered around tracking tools. It would be quick and easy for Jan to come up with what she wanted for the screens and process flow needed to manage the development process. Having a clean development process was one of Jan's primary goals.

The first 20 years of Jan's experience was in the aerospace industry. During that time frame, the government had strict rules about software processes used and strictly followed the "Waterfall" Methodology. The Waterfall Methodology starts with gathering requirements. For government projects, the requirements are provided by the government and are bid on by the prospective aerospace companies. Then system designers take the requirements and derive detailed design documents. Next software designers decompose the project to create software design objects while the hardware designers design hardware components. Completed, signed-off software design specifications were then given to the software developers who coded to spec and only to spec, regardless of whether there was a better, cleaner approach or new state-of-the-art ideas. After all of the software was coded and checked into a code management system or library, the QA organization's testers would test to the original requirements. Between each phase, as the software cycle moved from requirements to design to development and to test, a formal review and sign-off occurred. The strict formality made the process very structured.

The good thing about using the Waterfall Methodology was the government knew exactly what the end product would look like. Also, because of the rigid process, resulting quality was high. Especially for software that was truly mission-critical – the software in a satellite or battle field front-line software – the amount of time and effort spent on the testing cycles was very high and not considered completed until all requirements had been tested and the government signed off on the end result.

The bad thing about using a Waterfall Methodology was that there was less innovation and development cycles were long. In addition, significant time was spent producing extensive, complete documentation at the start of the project and then methodically tracking all activity back to the extensive requirements specifications.

Jan had a dream: To take the lessons learned from what was successful in the big government projects producing high quality, complex software, strip it down to the basics, add in the ability for agility and innovation, and develop a software process that would be appropriate for a start-up. The process would need to be light-weight yet have the right amount of tracking and control to ensure high-quality code, and to support Intelic's evolution over time from a small start-up into a large company producing enterprise software.

In a developer team meeting, Jan said they needed to get a code management system to check their code into, but Freeman was ahead of her and had already downloaded a free copy of the open source Concurrent Versions System (CVS) tool and had it ready for their first code check-ins.

Jan had learned about the importance of configuration management the hard way, when she was a new developer at Ford Aerospace.

In the 1970's, Ford had decided to start a new division in Charlotte, North Carolina. Ford had designed a laser scanner system to scan car windshields and check for flaws before the windshields were installed on the automobiles. The scanner had recently been modified to search for flaws in broadcloth and other textiles. The new goal was to sell the scanners to textile companies in the South.

Jan's husband, Mike, who also worked at Ford Aerospace, was offered a promotion as the Financial Manager for the start-up division to be located in Charlotte, North Carolina. Jan was offered the one and only software position. Jan's boss would be Jack, a systems engineer. All of the other members of the engineering department were hardware designers or analog engineers.

The software ran on a very small Digital Equipment Corporation (DEC) computer. The computer had so little memory that the "Cloth" program was written in assembly language. One of the ongoing challenges was to add all of the features they needed in only 2 MB of memory. Programming tricks, like using one 8-bit software byte to house 8 different variables, were common. At one point she had to restructure subroutines and replace subroutine call statements with "Go To" statements, because a subroutine call statement took up four bytes and a Go To only required two bytes.

One day, working in the small building that housed the little company, Jack had been working on the software and had meant to remove the big eight inch floppy disk containing the software and put it back in the file shelf, but something distracted him and he left the floppy disk containing the software on his chair. A few minutes later he said, "Oops!" He'd sat on the floppy disk.

This was the only copy of the latest version of the software, and it was now not readable by the computer. It could be a disaster. It took Jan several hours, but fortunately she was able to rebuild the disk's directory at the bit level and recover the software. Whew. Immediately she put in place a written process for backups, version tracking, and disk management.

Upon returning to Ford Aerospace in California in the late '70s, Jan learned that there is an entire software discipline devoted to tracking releases, called "Configuration Management." In fact, her first Supervisory job, was to manage the Corporate Configuration Management team.

It was in the era when companies no longer had "Secretaries," and instead, similar jobs were titled "Admins." Moving to a Configuration Management position was an opportunity for upward mobility for the secretarial/admin employees.

Previously, secretaries were given salary grades and money solely based on the rank of the person they worked for. The higher the manager was in the organization, the more his secretary would earn.

Jan was well aware of the stigma and lack of upward mobility associated to a secretary title. In the 1950's when her mother, Clarice, decided to go back to work, not having had a college education due to having to work during the Great Depression, the only business positions available were secretarial. But Clarice didn't have the skills to be a secretary. She was extremely intelligent though, and figured out how to get one of those jobs. She taught herself shorthand, improved her typing skills, and even read the dictionary front to back to have a demonstrable command of English. Soon she found a good job. She continued to move into more responsible positions and applied for, and was hired, to be Secretary to the VP Treasurer of Utah Power and Light Company. Clarice was much more than a Secretary, though. She confided to Jan she actually composed all of the correspondence from the treasurer's office with customers herself, and handled much of the financial accounting. When she retired, the company hired two MBAs to replace her, each at a significantly higher salary.

Jan's manager at Ford Aerospace, Sharon, was surprised when Jan volunteered to take the Configuration Management Supervisor position, because CM was not a very technical role and Sharon thought Jan would soon be bored and want more technical challenges. Since Jan had demonstrated an ability to manage multiple tasks, and Sharon wanted to keep Jan engaged, they agreed that her new responsibilities would include managing the CM team, the UNIX system administrators, and the company's database technologists.

When Jan took over the CM team at Ford Aerospace, software versions and releases were tracked manually, taking the latest software release on a reel-to-reel tape, labeling it, putting it in a tape library, and creating a file card with the software version, date, and location in a file box for quick look-up.

Jan was surprised that Ford Aerospace was tracking their software releases in such a manual way.

She obtained agreement from her manager to add a bright engineer to her team who wrote a software tool to do the configuration management tracking, thus bringing automation to what had previously been an administrative job, and giving the configuration administrators even more job advancement possibilities.

In 1998, when Intelic was starting up, any reasonable software company had access to open source CM tools such as CVS, and used a process for carefully managing releases. When developers completed a set of new code, they would "check it into" the code management system. Then the latest set of code could be "checked out," or "pulled" to put on an integration server. After the developers verified the code functioned correctly, the code would be moved to the QA server for QA testing.

Freeman set up the directory structure for CVS and added the steps for checking the code into CVS in the developer handbook he was creating.

The next day Jan gave the screen mockups and database design for their bug tracking tool to Freeman.

The following morning Freeman came into Jan's office and said "Type http://sdtracker.intelic.com." Jan opened a browser window which was labeled "SD Tracker" with user login and password input boxes. Freeman said enter "jan" for your user id and "greatleader" for the password.

"Very funny," she said as she typed in the login information.

There it was. A summary screen with the spreadsheet list of tasks to be done. When she clicked on one she viewed a detail screen matching what she had designed. "Cool," said Jan (reverting to her 60's talking mode).

"What does 'SD Tracker' stand for?" Jan asked. "Something to do with San Diego?"

She thought it was likely that he'd named it after his hometown,

San Diego, where he'd been hoping for years to move back to.

"No, actually, Slick Daddy. See the stick figure? – that's a Slick Daddy." Freeman replied.

"Huh?" Jan said pondering the little clip art stick figure at the bottom of the screen.

She didn't have a better idea. She didn't want to call it just "Bug Tracker" because they were going to track every task using the tool including enhancements, demo projects, data loading, and documentation in addition to bug reports. She decided she would refer to it as their "Software Development Tracker."

"Well OK then. 'SD Tracker' it is." She clicked back to the summary screen.

"Look at that task list - we've got work to do!"

SOME THINGS IN LIFE SHOULDN'T BE FREE

"Price is what you pay, value is what you get." - Warren Buffet

Vimal had taken on the complex Pricing Engine. He was the senior contractor who felt he should have less oversight and more independence. He seemed to quickly and thoroughly understand the design, and asked thoughtful and appropriate questions. He was strangely secretive about his work, though.

Jan asked to review his progress, and he showed her, on his system, that the pricing engine was accurately returning the expected price according to the various pricing rules. Yet he continued to have excuses why he hadn't checked his code into the code management system yet. Jan let Vimal carry on and focused on Martin, who was struggling with his assignment. Freeman was concerned. Freeman had completed his own work and had it checked in, so Jan approached Martin and suggested they let Freeman wrap up the user admin code so Martin could start setting up integration and test servers in the warehouse. Martin was relieved.

Soon all the code was checked in. On moving from the developers' environments to the integration server, Freeman immediately encountered an issue. Vimal's code wasn't in the right folders and wasn't loading correctly. Jan heard the discussion becoming argumentative and Vimal's tone became defensive, so she went to see what the problem was.

Vimal had accurately completed the pricing engine, but the product requirement was to code in Java. Vimal, an Oracle expert, had coded the pricing engine as an Oracle Stored Procedure – a non-Java, Oracle proprietary language. He explained that the Stored Procedure would be faster and, in his opinion, was the right language to use for this type of engine. He expounded that he was an expert in Oracle, so was able to do a much better job developing code as an Oracle Stored Procedure than Java.

"That wasn't your call," fumed Jan. "This needs to be a Java application so it can be portable to non-Oracle databases if we need it to be. More importantly, the assignment was Java. I only want to train Java developers and maintain one language. If you'd wanted to propose an alternative implementation language, the time to propose that would have been when we started. Now we don't have time to re-do it which puts us in a real bind."

"There's no problem," Vimal retorted. "It will work fine."

Jan was kicking herself for allowing him to bypass the early design review process just because he was more experienced than Freeman, and because Vimal acted like he knew what he was doing. Now it was too late. The Pricing Engine would remain an Oracle Stored Procedure for the time being.

What had been a cost effective use of a fairly inexpensive but senior contractor would instead end up costing much more. Eventually, the Pricing Engine would need to be ported to Java. In addition, in the interim, maintenance would need to be done by a developer with Oracle Stored Procedure expertise.

From now on, peer code reviews would be mandatory for all developers - junior and senior.

In parallel with development efforts, Julie and Jan were working with QuickLogic to obtain spreadsheets of the data they wanted loaded for their production system.

In addition, the IT representative from Vantus, their first, albeit free, customer came into the Intelic office to get advice about how to best prepare their company's data for the initial data load. Jan and the rep spent time together, but then the rep returned to Vantus and didn't ask any more questions or return Jan's calls.

It ended up that the Vantus representative had little support from her management to spend time getting ProChannel installed. Everyone from Vantus had been very excited at the meeting in the hotel conference room, but when they left, they went back to their normal day-jobs and more pressing issues.

The Intelic team learned a valuable lesson. Software is considered to only be worth what the customer pays for it. If the price is free, there is no risk or any cost issues if it is never installed.

Intelic never gave away free software again.

BUILDING CAMARADERIE

"Telling an introvert to go to a party is like telling a Saint to go to Hell." - Criss Jami, Killosophy

Intelic's contract company had been able to free up developers from other contracts to supply Intelic with more of the engineering talent they sought. Originally Jan had approval for six developers and now needed only one more. But since they'd been running under staffed the first few months, Stephen agreed let her grab two consultants while they had a chance. Arun arrived, and quickly became one of the key engineers. He was obviously well-educated, intelligent, had strong Java experience, and he and Freeman quickly hit it off. Arun's young roommate Rajiv was also assigned to the project. Rajiv had experience working at Sun Microsystems and, although more junior, was extremely fast, efficient, and fun.

At first, Jan struggled to learn how to pronounce "Arun." She'd never known an Arun before. She thought she had it right and greeted him the first day with, "Hi Arun," pronouncing it like Aaron.

After a couple of days, Freeman came to her and said, "You know you're saying Arun wrong, right?"

"It's not Aaron?"

"It's Arun," he pronounced it differently. Jan repeated it. Now she had it.

When Arun came in the next day she thought she had it down. "Hi Arun," but she pronounced it like saying "A" then "run" with the accent on the "A." It rhymed with their new third party webserver tool JRun. Arun didn't correct her so she thought she had it right now.

A couple of days later, Arun came into her office with a smirky smile.

"Hi, A-run. How are you?"

"I'm good," he smiled, "but I thought your email was funny."

"Which email?" she asked.

"The one where you spell my name like JRun."

Her email tool was running, and he pointed to the last email she'd sent him. Sure enough, in the email she'd typed, "ARun," with a capital "R."

"Am I still saying your name wrong also?" she worried.

"Well, yes," he admitted.

She sighed. "Oh, dear. I'm sorry. Tell me again."

She finally got it. Arun. Like "a" (little a) then "rune" (accent on the rune). She was embarrassed. It seemed so obvious once it sunk in.

Freeman had a different name for Arun, though. A few years prior Freeman had developed a game to play on the network he called Robot. Sometimes during lunch two or three developers would sit at their desktops and interact playing Robot.

Freeman was so impressed by Arun, not only his mad software skills, but his speed and success winning Robot matches, that, because Arun's last name was Bhat, Freeman nicknamed him "Robhat."

Jan could tell that Arun liked that nickname. From then she saw it often when developers addressed Arun in emails.

One day Jan was in her cubicle and Arun emailed something that answered a question she had been having.

"Thanks Arun! That 'splains it," Jan quickly replied.

Arun was open enough to express himself and sent back a hurt email saying, "Are you making fun of my English?"

Jan was taken aback. Not only was Arun's English very good (he came from a technology institute that taught British English so, although some of the pronunciation made him sound like a

Londoner, he was easy to understand), she would never want to hurt his feelings. Before she could even get up to go talk to Arun she saw an email reply from Freeman.

"Dude – didn't you ever watch 'I Love Lucy?' Ricky always said, 'That 'splains it, Lucy.' She just meant you explained the question."

Arun quickly sent back an email apologizing for assuming that.

"Whew," thought Jan. She emailed to both, "Right, Freeman. 'I Love Lucy.' "

Jan told herself she'd better be more attentive to how the Indian engineers could take off-the-cuff remarks the wrong way.

"We've been at it several months now," said John during one of the co-founders' lunches at the local hamburger joint John loved. "We should have a party for morale. We haven't had an event since before the company officially started."

Stephen always tried to build morale and camaraderie. He would periodically take Jan and her engineers (direct hires and consultants) out to lunch and laugh, joke, and carry on with them. At first the Indian engineers weren't sure what to make of him. In India they were more formal with their managers, especially the President/CEO. Stephen would do outrageous pranks, like pretending to lick Freeman's plate when he wasn't looking (or perhaps he really licked it). At first the Indian engineers seemed taken aback by his silliness, yet Jan caught a twinkle in their eyes. Pretty soon, everyone was laughing, teasing each other, and getting into the relaxed spirit of the lunch.

"What kind of party?" said Stephen. "How much would it cost?"

"It could be simple. Mainly to get everyone involved," John mused. "Jan – what kind of event would the Indian developers come to?"

"Tell you the truth, I don't know." Said Jan. "Most of my career was with developers who needed security clearances. Not H-1 Visa developers from India. I admit this is new for me. Let me check it out."

A couple of days later they met again.

"Well?" said John.

"Well...," said Jan. "I'm not getting any warm fuzzies that Vimal or Sanjiv would attend anything. Arun and Rajiv seemed game, but the other two seemed embarrassed or surprised by the question. They don't bowl or play bocce ball, they don't go to baseball games. They are busy with family on weekends. I think maybe if we went somewhere on a work night, rather than weekend, and it was low key, I might get them to come."

Stephen was adamant that when building a team atmosphere it needed to include the entire team, even the contractors.

It took a lot of coaxing and special effort, including help from Julie, Freeman, and Arun, to find a venue where Vimal and Sanjiv would agree to attend.

They decided to make it on a Thursday night, going somewhere where they could have appetizers, including of course, vegetarian appetizers. They picked a location where the team could play pool, shuffle board, and other low-key games to get to know each other and build camaraderie.

A week later they had their outing planned. They headed to a cozy Los Gatos billiard bar/pub where they had reserved the upstairs billiards room, complete with appetizers and casual atmosphere. Surprisingly, every employee showed up, including all of the Indian contractors.

Everyone had fun. They played, they ate, and they got to know each other. Freeman organized competitions. Stephen took them all on. It was frivolous and only pseudo-competitive. Everyone was smiling and, at the end, they felt even more like a team than they had before.

In addition to arranged team-building events, the small group enjoyed a happy atmosphere while they worked hard.

They had decided when SD Tracker was built to use a different term than calling everything entered a "bug," because enhancement requests and other tasks would be tracked in the system. They wanted something more generic. They chose "SDR," which could mean both Software Defect Request (a bug) and Software Design Request (an enhancement request). Since other types of requests would also be tracked (such as data loading or system administration), Jan thought "SDR" could be thought of simply as an <u>SD</u> Tracker <u>R</u>equest.

Jan laughed the first time she submitted a new SDR and upon saving saw a screen that said, "Raiders Suck. Plain and simple. - Common Sense." Below that was the standard message: "SDR #101 has been saved," plus action buttons.

Each time someone entered a new SDR, another random quote appeared at the top of the "SDR has been saved" screen.

"Long Live the SD Chargers."

"The engineering staff will fix this once they sober up."

"Go back to surfing the web and stop creating extra work for development."

"Yeah right....that'll get fixed!!"

"Surely you could be helping to fix SDRs instead of creating them."

Even if Freeman hadn't written SD Tracker, Jan would have known he was the one to put in the quotes.

Then one day she entered an SDR and "Jan loves Steve Young" popped up.

While it was true that Jan loved the 49ers and their current quarterback from Utah in an "I love football" kind of way, she wasn't sure she wanted that showing up on everyone's screens. She networked to the SD Tracker computer and saw a text file titled "quotableQuotes.txt." She edited the offending item out, put "Freeman needs to work harder" in its place, and had it fixed in a matter of minutes.

Freeman entered her office later that day. "Aw," he said. "I work hard. I fixed it though," and he winked.

Two days later, up popped "Jan loves Steve Young" again. Jan went to edit file again and the file wasn't there. "Humm," she thought. "He's hidden it."

That created a challenge. So Jan checked the code base for SD

Tracker (easy to find in a folder named "/bugs"), she quickly figured out what java file Freeman would have embedded the quotable quote function in based on the filename most likely to contain the "Save" function, and voila. The list of quotes were there. Jan loved the way Freeman organized everything, including code folders and filenames, in such a logical and easy to understand way. She removed "Jan loves Steve Young," but didn't add any new ones.

When Freeman discovered the change, he came into her office. "I'm impressed," he said. "I didn't think you knew how to write Java."

"I am a software developer, you know," she said and gave him a wink.

With SD Tracker up and running, everyone started using the tool to enter enhancement ideas and bugs they'd found. They all loved the concept of the quotable quotes. Jan especially liked the one, "Let me think about that.....NO!!! - Stephen, Everyday."

That was one of Stephen's famous retorts to almost everything, leaving less than a second between the "Let me think about that" and the "NO."

Stephen laughed when he ended up with that quote on his screen.

At one of their developer team meetings, they had an idea. Whenever someone said anything "quotable," particularly if it was something that, when taken out of context, would be hilarious, it should be added to the "quotable quotes" list.

Now during meetings, when something came out funny or if taken out of context meant something else, you'd hear "quotable quote!" and see someone jotting it down in their notes to add to the growing quotable quote list.

Over the years, new quotable quotes were regularly added to the list.

"Everything takes time. - Pushpa, filling in those of us unclear on the concept"

"If we do it right, it will work. - Gary"

"They are not real people. - Edwin, concerning the rights of Americans under the age of 5."

No one was off-limits.

TESTING, TESTING, TESTING

"Testing leads to failure, and failure leads to understanding." - Burt Rutan

The code was ready to begin more formal testing.

A separate integration server was used so that code checked out of the their code management system was first loaded onto the integration server. It took several tries to resolve missing files and other process issues. Then the updated code would be checked out and loaded on the QA test server, and soon official testing began.

The primary test team consisted of Ed, Julie, and Jan; but John and Stephen also participated when they could. Jan had already been using the system periodically from the beginning, asking developers if she could network into their computers now and again. They would caution her it was still in development, but she liked to see how the product was progressing.

Now the software was solid enough to integrate the various functions together. Built into the process was the requirement to enter a comment including the SDR number in the code itself right above the code changes. SDR numbers were also included in the tag when checking updates into CVS. Adding those steps to the process didn't add any burden to the developer's effort, especially once they got into the habit. It ended up being extremely useful later for testing and for everyone researching problems to look at the SDR and quickly track down what code was impacted and why.

SD Tracker was central to the test efforts. The team had entered every change into the system, and now could go through each individual enhancement and subsequent change and evaluate if the developer had made the change according to the requirements. In addition, any issues found would be logged in SD Tracker for the developers to address quickly.

After thoroughly testing all of the pricing rules, Ed began testing all of the boundary conditions. He was quickly annoying Julie and Jan by putting in extra long data, such as entering long names like "abcdefghijklmnopqrstuvwxwyz1234567890need80charactersxxx…" in order to test the database 80 character field-size requirement, even though in business practice, names would be restricted to a more reasonable size by a business property. However, in doing so, Ed was making all the screens stretch out wider than the browser window, looking awful and hard to use. Ed did, however, find issues and problems that otherwise would have gone unnoticed, so Julie and Jan couldn't get too mad at him. Once Ed was satisfied, Julie and Jan did go in and shorten the data in the fields for easier ongoing testing.

Julie was also meticulous. Her B.S. degree in Electrical Engineering from prestigious Santa Clara University, gave her the ability to focus on the detail. Her business background and years at Silicon Valley semiconductor companies gave her the insight into the users and use cases. She was complete and thorough.

Stephen found details missing, such as the cursor not automatically initializing in the first field for data entry. He requested that the return key should act the same an "Enter" key and searches where the fields are blank should return all data instead of nothing.

John wasn't in the office much. He was always out on sales calls and customer visits. But he also found time to test the system and identified navigation and life cycle issues by testing the system as different types of users or putting transactions in different stages.

Jan was quick and found errors in places the developers didn't know existed. She tested combinations and permutations, performance, and function.

Jan loved working on a brand new product – learning the entire product from top to bottom. From the top, being able to use HTML herself to design screens; to the bottom, where she had designed the database schema and was able to manipulate the data and set up test cases herself to thoroughly test the product.

Then she encountered a pop-up error:

"When Jan tells me what to put here I'll add it in."

"Freeeeeeman!!" Jan yelled over the cubicle walls. Freeman showed up in the doorway.

"Yeh?"

"What's this?" She growled showing him the pop-up message.

"Oops. It was an exception I thought we should be catching, but wasn't in the design yet. I was going to ask you what the message should be, but you weren't in your office and then I forgot."

"Any more of these?"

"Well, er, I don't *think* so," he stammered. She gave him the appropriate message text and he quickly exited her cube.

"I'd better not run into any more of these!" she ranted to the empty doorway.

Soon Jan started noticing new SDRs in the system besides the bugs found while testing and new feature requests. All of the developers had started to use SD Tracker to make sure there weren't tasks left to do that may otherwise be forgotten. Jan thought it was probably a new process Freeman had instigated. Developers would either create a new SDR, or put a comment in an existing SDR not to resolve the open task until such-and-such was completed.

SD Tracker was now tightly integrated into the development process to help insure there would be no more loose ends.

As they all exercised their new software, they learned a lot more about navigation and transaction phases than they had been able to realize from using the HTML demo. The developers were happy to have such quick feedback, and each day they would do a new pull (check out the latest version of code from their code management system) and put the latest software on the test system.

Soon the code was looking very polished and complete. They would have a good release for QuickLogic on schedule, if not earlier.

'TIS THE SEASON TO BE MERRY

"If I were a medical man, I should prescribe a holiday to any patient who considered his work important." - Bertrand Russell

Jan was sitting in a developer cubicle downstairs when she heard Stephen calling out from the upstairs window that looked down on the developer cubicles, "Ho, ho, ho!"

Stephen had on a big red velvet Santa hat, and came down the stairs with a huge green velvet sack flung over his shoulder. He began passing presents out to each employee. He had purchased a nice crystal clock as a company gift for each. John and Jan hadn't been aware of his Christmas plan and were surprised, since Stephen was the Jewish member of the triad. When they were forming the company, John joked, "How did a Catholic, a Mormon, and a Jew get together to form a company?"

Stephen had begun a tradition of holiday cheer that grew through the years.

The next year Stephen told Jan, "Come on, we need to get a tree." Stephen was like a kid in a candy shop as he jumped out of his van at the tree lot, grabbed a saw, and hurried to just the right tree. He had driven the van he usually left at home for their nanny to use. Stephen and Jan each took an end of the tree and loaded it into the van.

When they returned to the office, everyone took part in decorating the tree in the lobby.

The following year Julie had an idea, "How about if we add a

Hanukkah candle on the reception desk." Julie was a staunch Catholic, but wanted everyone to feel included in the holiday festivities. Ashraf brought in a Muslim shrine to also add on the reception desk. Julie extended the invitation to all employees to display items showing how they celebrated this time of year. The Chinese engineers hung red envelopes behind the desk in honor of Chinese New Year, and the Indian engineers added colored strings of paper celebrating Pancha Ganapati, the Hindu alternative to Christmas.

As the company grew in size, next to the tree in the lobby was added "Giving Barrels" (one for toys, one for food). The employees enjoyed going to the Salvation Army one evening each year and volunteering to pack gift packages for needy families.

The company enjoyed adding charitable activities to its list of important endeavors.

In December of their first year, to top off the holiday season, Stephen suggested a company party at his Ruby Hills home. Ruby Hills was one of the most prestigious gated communities in the East Bay. Although Stephen had spent the last few years on a start-up salary, he'd owned and sold several businesses in his career, and he and his wife Mary were able to afford a beautiful home in the hills.

The managers spent time encouraging all of the direct employees and contractors to attend the party. It had been hard to get Vimal and Sanjiv to the social events before, and this would be on a Friday night and require at least a forty-five minute drive, but Stephen really wanted the entire company to take part in the fun.

When Jan and her husband Mike arrived, Stephen's house was lit up with blue Hanukkah lights. Inside, Stephen's wife Mary had extensive decorations and candles. Stephen had brought in a caterer and there were food stations in various spots throughout the kitchen and dining room. At first Sanjiv and Vimal stood around and looked nervous, but they soon relaxed and joined in the fun.

Jan had planned a white elephant gift exchange, and the gifts people brought were piled up on the fireplace, since there was no

Christmas tree to put them under. Jan loved white elephant exchanges. Jan learned about them at Ford Aerospace Christmas parties. Jan later instigated having them at ASK. The only guideline was the gifts were to be inexpensive (under $10), but could contain anything, good or bad, new or not. No one knew if they would end up with something nice or something atrocious. And with the two practical jokesters in attendance, Stephen and Freeman, it was sure to be fun.

To play, everyone first chose a paper from a pile of paper scraps that Mary had passed out, each with a number from 1 to 20. Jan was the M.C., explaining the rules and organizing the activity. Stephen kept track of the current the number. First, the person with number 1 had the chance to pick a gift from the gift pile Thereafter, each person had the choice of picking from the gift pile or stealing a previously chosen gift. The Intelic version of the game was to leave the presents unwrapped until the end, so people were fighting over presents based on the wrapping or shape, and would not know until the end if they had fought for something nice or not.

One of the favorite presents being stolen was a large, heavy gift. When it was Freeman's turn he stole it, and it ended up his at the end of the game. As everyone opened their gifts, Freeman moaned, "A tub of lard?" Someone had packaged a 5 pound tub of lard for their white elephant gift.

After an evening of fun and friendship, the party ended.

Stephen was dismayed to find the tub of lard in his pantry the next morning. Of course, it showed up at the next year's holiday party.

The holiday party at Stephen's house became an annual event, growing larger each year as the number of employees grew.

One year, near the end of the gift exchange, Stephen counted the remaining gifts and realized they were one gift short. One couple admitted that they thought they were supposed to bring one gift as a couple, but were each handed out numbers and, being new and not knowing how the exchange worked, had each taken a gift. They offered to return one.

"No problem," said Stephen. He dashed into another room and quickly returned with a fancily wrapped package. Mary, his wife, had a quizzical look on her face, but the gift exchange continued. Julie was next and snatched up the new package and, luckily for her, when the exchange ended she still had possession of it. When the packages were opened she exclaimed, "Wow, a bottle of good Cognac!"

Jan heard Mary hiss at Stephen, "That $150 bottle that was going to your relatives!"

"Lucky Julie," he smiled, nonplussed.

As the company matured and grew, the parties grew larger, even more elaborate, and continued to have great attendance. Jan's favorite year was when all of the Indian engineers and their spouses arrived in their traditional formal garb: The men in Nehru jackets made of silk brocade with matching silk pajama-like pants and traditional foot ware; the women in beautiful saris with high starched collars or soft flowing satins in vibrant orange, purple, and turquoise. They all looked very regal. The co-founders were very pleased that they all attended and, even more so, that they felt comfortable enough to attend in their traditional fancy wear.

They were one big family.

THE FIRST RELEASE 0.5

"Individuals play the game, but teams beat the odds." - SEAL Team Saying

The week after Intelic's first Christmas, QuickLogic asked for a demo. QuickLogic was also a start-up and didn't have a company shut-down between Christmas and New Years. The first shipment of ProChannel 0.5 to QuickLogic was scheduled for mid-January, but QuickLogic wanted to preview it earlier.

Jan was on her first vacation in over a year, and was in Tahoe on a ski trip with her family when the QuickLogic request came up. Stephen called Jan in the morning Monday while she was still in the ski cabin, and Jan recommended Stephen ask Martin to set up the demo. Martin was planning on working that week and was in charge of the systems.

When Jan got back to the cabin after a day of skiing Monday evening, Stephen called in a panic. The line into the Tahoe cabin was scratchy so it was hard to tell what Stephen was saying, but Jan got the gist of it. The system wasn't set up. He put Martin on the line.

"I can't figure out how to start the system," Martin said concerned.

"Where are you running it?" Jan asked.

"We needed to set up a different computer. The QA systems are all in-use, so Stephen asked me to load the software on one of the spare servers. It took me a long time to load everything, but ProChannel doesn't start up."

"Are you sure you followed all of the steps? Does that computer have the database loaded?"

"The database? I don't know."

"Has Oracle been loaded? Oracle is needed for it to run," said Jan. "Go back and install Oracle and then re-install the software."

"How do I install Oracle?" Martin asked.

"Didn't you install Oracle on all of the systems originally?" asked Jan.

"I had Freeman help me," confessed Martin.

"Have you ever started up the system yourself?"

After some hemming and hawing, "Actually no."

Jan realized there was a bigger problem here than she thought. After the first few Java assignments Freeman had given Martin, Freeman had told her that he didn't think it was a good idea to give Martin more Java to do. Martin wasn't catching on, and Freeman had to redo his coding, which wasted Freeman's time. Jan thought the world of Martin and had hoped he could take care of the system management, help with testing, and run through the demo until he ramped up more on the technical side. But now she saw he didn't even know the basics about how to install the system. She had a sick feeling in the pit of her stomach. The other engineers had left the office by now.

"OK," Jan said. "You'd better call Freeman and ask him to come in tonight to do the setup for the demo tomorrow."

Stephen got back on the line. "I think you know what we need to do when you get back to the office," Stephen said in a low voice. She could tell Martin had left the room. "We don't have enough money to pay for someone who isn't contributing."

"Unfortunately, yes," she admitted. She felt sick about needing to let Martin go. He was such a great, energetic person and wanted so much to be part of the group, but the small little company could not support a full-time development manager yet, which she now felt was his only applicable expertise. Plus to be an effective development manager, he needed to have a better understanding of Java and the database to earn the engineers' respect.

Freeman drove back to into work, loaded the software, and

Stephen was able to give a successful demo to QuickLogic the next day.

In January, the first mini-release (they'd named it Release 0.5 because it was only half of the planned first release) was installed at QuickLogic. The release contained 21,000 lines of code and was installed on one of QuickLogic's Microsoft Windows servers.

Whenever John was in the office and had spare time, he would test out ProChannel while thinking about the next features and functions customers wanted. Suddenly, he went into Jan's cubicle upstairs office next to his.

"I think we have a problem," John said. The software isn't handling the sales org correctly. Remember I said it needed to allow companies to set up a TARDZ sales org?" which John pronounced like tardoz. "It isn't working."

Jan remembered at first being confused by the acronym, but John had explained it as dividing the org first into geographical territories, such a Asia, Americas and Europe. Next splitting each territory into an area. Then sales regions, districts, and finally by zip code.

"Yes," Jan replied, "I remember. ProChannel can create a sales org with the five levels for territory, area, and down to zip codes. You can set up as many levels as you want. The org tree is a true hierarchy with parent-child relationships, so it is totally flexible."

"It's wrong," complained John.

"What isn't working?" she said, completely lost as to what the problem might be. She thought the org structure was quite nice and flexible. There were no limitations as to how it could be implemented. As soon as a sales rep created a transaction, then his or her manager, and any others above him or her in the org structure, could view the transaction as well. Basic Management 101. There were no screens yet to manage the organization. That would come in the next release. However the data model was, she thought, correct.

Stephen overheard frustration in her voice and came into Jan's area. Stephen asked John to explain to him what the problem was and they went into John's office to look at the computer screens.

John had to go out on a sales call so left, and Stephen came into Jan's office.

"I get what John's talking about," said Stephen.

"OK, can you explain it to me?"

"What the software is now doing is mapping transactions to sales users and then uses the organization hierarchy for managing the transactions, right?" Stephen said.

"Yes, that's it," Jan said, thinking that was going to be the end of the discussion.

"What John wanted the software to do was to map customers to organizations. He wanted to be able to assign zip codes to the bottom level sales org and automatically link the customers to the organization based on zip code. That's what he meant by TARDZ. Using the geographical responsibilities of the organization to determine who can see which customers and their transactions."

"Oh, my gosh," exclaimed Jan. "I never heard anything like that. I thought TARDZ just meant he wanted to be sure we supported at least five levels of organizational hierarchy."

"He's been in the business so long," explained Stephen, "he assumed you understood how it worked."

"There's one other part of the picture," Stephen continued. "Not all customers are assigned to organization by zip code. Some of the big customers, like IBM or Cisco, get assigned to a named organization. Typically these customers are the big accounts that the manufacturer wants their own internal sales reps to manage. They don't give those customers to the Rep Firms that work for them. Sometimes they refer to the big customers as 'House Accounts.' The zip code mapping is for most customers. The big ones are taken out of the territory mapping algorithm and directly assigned."

"Wow," said Jan. "That is almost completely opposite of how it works now."

"Good thing we've got another release coming up," Stephen smiled.

Jan had never heard of a company managing their customer base that way, but John was the expert. She sat down and began a redesign of the data tables so that instead of a table to link the sales rep to the customer, the SALES_CUST_MAPPING table, she needed a new linkage, ORG_ZIP_MAPPING, to add zip codes to orgs and then another, ORG_CUST_MAPPING, to map orgs to customers based on the zips mapped to the orgs and the customer's address zip code. She also needed a way to flag which customers would be directly assigned to a sales org instead of mapped based on their territory.

Jan needed to work out more details and spent several meetings with Stephen until she thought she had it right. Then she sat down with the developers to walk them through the changes that were needed.

QuickLogic was small enough that they were happy with the original structure and didn't relish a major change to their sales org and customer data. But once Julie briefed Jean, their QuickLogic contact, on the upcoming change and its business advantages, Jean, and the QuickLogic sales team, supported the new structure.

It was a fairly substantial change but one that, through the years, proved to be the way all of the semiconductor manufacturers wanted to manage their customer relationships, and one of the differentiators for Intelic's software versus Intelic's competitors.

When Intelic was doing the Release 0.5 installation at QuickLogic, the software didn't contain any user admin screens to add new users. The user information was pre-loaded directly into the system using scripts. Jean had asked Intelic to add the usernames and passwords for all of their sales team as part of the original data load, even though Jean was initially rolling the system out only to select sales users at Corporate. Jean planned to train everyone and do an orderly rollout over the next six months.

In March, Jean called the support line.

Julie was also customer support at that time and answered the phone.

"I think we're in trouble," Jean said.

"What's wrong?" asked Julie.

"Someone distributed all of the sales team's usernames and passwords. Everyone started jumping on the system to try it out. What should I do?" she asked, concerned.

"How's it working?" Julie asked.

"Well," thought Jean, "it actually seems to be fine. In fact I'm getting emails that the sales reps love it - even those in Europe and Asia. It's so easy to use and intuitive. But they haven't had training. Was it ready for a large user load? I thought it was a pre-release."

"Of course it's ready," said Julie confidently. "It's been thoroughly tested. Give me a call if anyone runs into trouble, but I'm sure you're good to go!"

"Well then," Jean signed in relief, "we've just gone worldwide!"

Intelic celebrated their first worldwide customer.

Since only the transactional modules, catalog search, and customer management modules were live, there were no management screens to add more parts, manage users, or make pricing changes. Intelic offered to do database updates for QuickLogic as part of their maintenance agreement until Release 1.0 was ready. Jan preferred not to have the customer make changes directly to the database via SQL, which could cause data consistency problems. Thus they would bridge the gap until either GUI screens or interface routines were available. Then customers could use the GUI or upload spreadsheets, and the software would take care of the error checking.

Jean asked Intelic to add a set of new parts to the part catalog. Jan didn't want to divert any of the developers from their Release 1.0 tasks so she took the assignment on herself. It was a fairly small task. But one thing Jan had learned at Ford Aerospace was how easily even a small, seemingly harmless change could result in a catastrophe.

While at Ford Aerospace, Jan had been assigned to manage a department comprised of five software development organizations. Each organization was working on software for a different government program and different agency. Jan's boss, Sharon, had taken her through the building where she would be working to meet various members of her new department.

Each of her new areas of responsibility was building software for a very unique program. One program was building a softcopy XRay system for Army hospitals. One was a program in the early stages of design to provide an upload/download modem as part of a larger Army program. The third was a joint project with Apple developing the first Apple laptop computer, a hardened version that could be carried in an Army ALICE pack. The fourth program dealt with building helicopter training software. The fifth program was a maintenance contract for the Army for software operational in the Middle East.

Later that day Sharon called Jan and said, "The Lt. Colonel in charge of your Army maintenance program is in town. He is going to pass out awards to your new team at 4 p.m. today after the testing is complete. Why don't you come with me. It will give you an opportunity to meet one of your customers."

They walked across the campus to the other building where Jan would be working. As they started up the steps, the front doors opened and young men and women, the developers and testers, came streaming out and down the front steps with tears in their eyes or outright sobs.

"What's going on?" Sharon asked one of the young female engineers.

She shook her head, couldn't answer, and ran by. The company's General Manager was hurriedly entering the building. He saw Sharon and said sternly, "I was just called to a meeting with the Lt. Colonel. You'd better come with me."

The three went upstairs into a warehouse room where an impromptu meeting was being held. The head of Systems Engineering, Ray (Sharon's boss) was already there with the Lt. Colonel. The Lt. Colonel was a tall man in full army combat fatigues and boots. Red hair with a face as red as his hair. He was livid.

"I normally only give companies one chance. For you," he said glaring at the GM, "this is your third strike."

He saw Jan and said, "Who's this?"

Sharon told him Jan was the manager of the software team. He glared at Jan and said, "How are you going to remedy these problems?" Sharon, to Jan's relief, quickly let him know it was Jan's first day as the manager. He redirected his glare to Sharon and barked at her to find out what was wrong and get it fixed that night, or Ford Aerospace would never have another contract with his division of the Army. However, he said, if they fix it and want to re-run the test scenarios, he was willing to spend the night. But he had to be on a plane, with the verified software, by 8 a.m. in the morning.

Sharon said they'd find the problem and run the tests.

Jan and Sharon hurried to the office of the supervisor in charge of that program. The supervisor, although she was a tough, seasoned, ex-Marine used to conflict and discourse, lost all composure and said, through tears brimming in her eyes, "This is it. I'm through. I quit. The Lt. Colonel is and always has been impossible to work for."

"What happened?" Sharon asked.

"We started the test scenarios and the first test was simply adding a new user. There was a system error. We're trying to find out why. The SETA [Systems Engineering and Technical Assistance] contractor quickly jumped to the conclusion that the code wasn't complete, and that we must be hiding problems and issues. The Lt. Colonel blew up, yelled at everyone, and they left in tears. I don't understand it. We worked long and hard on this release, and the tests we ran were perfect."

A senior programmer, one of Ford's best, appeared in the doorway. "Excuse me," he stammered. "I'm afraid I know what is wrong."

He admitted that at the last minute he had noticed a small issue in the software. Although he was well aware that the process was to first notify the Configuration Manager (CM) before changing anything, and although this change wasn't even needed for this delivery, just a "nice-to-have" fix, he thought since it was just a simple quick fix and, he thought, safe, he'd just do it. Unfortunately, he failed to realize that that the code was shared by a newly implemented user registration function which his change broke, hence the user login had failed. He had already reverted the code to the prior version and checked that in, and was sure it would now pass the tests.

The team was rounded back up, and all were more than willing to spend the night re-verifying the tests to exonerate themselves.

In the morning the tests had all been passed with glowing colors. The Lt. Colonel left at 7 a.m., leaving the awards to be passed out to the team later in the day.

Ironically, the senior programmer who caused the issue was the one who was scheduled to travel with the Lt. Colonel to install the software in Saudi Arabia. The Lt. Colonel now knew about how the error had occurred, and seemed to take pleasure in telling the programmer, before they left, that he'd need to shave his beard. The programmer had a full, red beard.

"What?" the programmer complained.

"Well, it's up to you," the Lt. Colonel shrugged, "but gas masks don't work well over beards. They tend to leak." He smirked.

They were headed to Desert Storm. The programmer shaved.

Jan had learned a valuable lesson that day. All changes to the software need to be handled with care, even quick small safe ones.

Today, although all Jan would be doing is loading a few new parts on the QuickLogic computer, it was their production system, and she was not about to take any chances and mistakenly crash their live system. The customer was a little start-up themselves and were in the process of purchasing a test server, but it was not yet available.

In her developer cubicle downstairs, first Jan created the SQL scripts that would populate the new data records, and tested them out on her own desktop computer that had a copy of the software and QuickLogic's data. Then she wrote up step-by-step procedures for uploading the new data and for verifying it. She saved the procedures and the SQL scripts on a small floppy disk, and printed out a copy of the procedures for her to use. She ejected the disk and walked over to one of the computers in the central "computer room" (i.e., closet) where she loaded the disk onto the central server and followed her procedures. There was a minor step missing in her procedure that was needed on the central server, so she went back to her computer and did it all again. Once she was satisfied the data loaded correctly, she drove to QuickLogic with the disk and instructions in hand.

The small company, QuickLogic, had only a two-person IT organization consisting of the IT manager and an administrator, a young woman named Mary. Mary met Jan at the reception desk and led her to the cubicle where the ProChannel software had been running. To their surprise, the computer wasn't there. The cubicle was empty!

Mary and Jan walked to the IT Manager's office and asked him where the computer was. He said he didn't know. Someone asked him if they could move it, but he couldn't remember where they put it.

This was perplexing. The system was up and running, but the IT team didn't know where it was! After poking around a few cubicles, Mary found the production computer in an otherwise unused cubicle with a sign on top: "ProChannel. Do not unplug!"

Jan sat at the workstation, loaded in the floppy, followed her own written procedures, and was done in a jiffy.

As she left, she asked Mary how long it had been since she had to do anything with the computer to maintain it. Mary said, "I haven't done anything since your team installed it three months ago."

"I guess it doesn't need much maintenance!" Jan said with a grin.

In the spring, Vimal, the pricing engine contractor, came to Jan's office to say good-bye. Vimal had given notice to the contract company in order to take a position with Oracle. The contract company had sent Madhu to Intelic a few weeks earlier to learn from Vimal and take over his pricing engine tasks. Oracle experience was highly valued in India, and Vimal reasoned that working at Oracle in the U.S. was a path to more easily return to India, his ultimate goal.

"I wanted to let you know how different this contract has been from any of my other contracts while in America."

"In what way?" asked Jan.

"I've never worked anywhere before where contractors were treated like regular employees. I appreciated it greatly. This was a great company to work for."

"Thank you." Jan was deeply touched. She hadn't realized what it must be like to come to a foreign country and be treated like an outsider by the companies you worked for. She hoped he would be successful in his long-term goals, and was glad the partners' efforts were meeting with success in building a team spirit.

HOW TO BUILD A GOOD INSTALLER

"For the things we have to learn before we can do them, we learn by doing them."
- Aristotle

They had successfully completed their Release 1.0 in April, which was now 125K lines of code and included new Design Registrations, Direct and Channel Contracts modules, plus included part, pricing and user management GUI screens. Release 1.0 had been delivered to QuickLogic in April. Intelic was now working on the next release, Release 1.1, which would add interfaces to the back office ERP system to track Purchase Orders. This would allow the users to see the complete picture from opportunity to quote to order, including the shipments sent from the semiconductor manufacturer to their end customers.

Meanwhile Stephen had been meeting with a long-time business acquaintance in the L.A. area, Mark, who was the VP of Sales for Diodes. Stephen was successful and the sale to Diodes was complete.

Diodes' back office system was a little-known ERP product from a small vendor, which wasn't working very well. The Diodes team hoped to use ProChannel to manage a portion of their direct inventory and order management. Having ProChannel take on ERP functions was not a role that Intelic had envisioned for their software, which was more in the Sales Force Automation arena, but Stephen agreed to build what Diodes wanted to close the deal. Mark knew he could trust Stephen to deliver.

The Diodes team traveled to Intelic's office in San Jose to attend a kick-off meeting that Julie conducted. Julie walked through the demo, and they jointly discussed how the ProChannel software would map into Diodes' business processes. The week of meetings was also spent to identify the core data that would need to be prepared and loaded for the system's use, and where the Diode's team could obtain their core data.

A few weeks later, Madhu was prepping for the upcoming installation she would be doing at Diodes. Madhu was the contractor brought in to replace Vimal. Her strong database background, systems expertise, and willingness to jump in and get any job done quickly made her a great asset to the team. Madhu was also the only female Indian engineer Jan had met who came to the U.S. on her own, without first having had an arranged marriage. She was independent and fun. She would be travelling to L.A. in a week to do the install.

Diodes would initially install Release 1.0 for their quoting and pricing needs while Intelic built the more robust direct inventory and order management modules.

Jan was sitting in her cubicle in the developer area listening to Madhu and Freeman discussing the upcoming install over the cubicle walls.

Madhu asked, "Freeman – how does ProChannel know the host name for the server we're installing on?"

"It's a property – update the properties.txt file," Freeman replied.

"What about the port?"

"Change the common.txt file in /bin."

"And the database user and password?"

"obProperties.txt file."

Jan interrupted. "Freeman – what would you think about going on the install trip with Madhu. Just in case there are any unanticipated issues."

"Sure," said Freeman. "It's an easy install so I'm sure Madhu can handle it, but I don't mind a trip to Southern California. I may swing by San Diego afterwards for a visit with my folks."

From Jan's lessons learned at Varian doing SAP upgrades, she wanted the install function to be as push-button as possible. In the 1990's, a fully automated install was not the norm as in 2015, when iPhone apps could be easily downloaded and automatically upgraded. At Varian, the installation of SAP was so complex that in order to complete the process over the weekend, two of the IT engineers rented a hotel room next door to the company. They had previously run through test installs and calculated the timing exactly. All Sunday night was spent setting the alarm clock based on their timing calculations and taking turns waking up and going next door to Varian to push a button or answer a question in order to move the upgrade process on to the next step.

Jan believed that customers deserved a better way to install and upgrade their software.

Madhu and Freeman arrived back at the office the next week.

"How did the install go?" Jan asked, although she'd already heard from Stephen that Diodes was happy with the process.

"It went fine," said Freeman, "but it wasn't as easy as I thought. There were a lot of system variables and other information we needed, and we didn't have an easy way to gather it from the IT group. It was a bit of a struggle, in fact. You know what we need? We need an automated installer!"

At that point, Freeman quickly created a new SDR and Jan gladly assigned it to him. Freeman sat down and began to write an installer.

If you want your software to have a good installer, Jan thought, put the best engineer on the job.

Besides installing the software, the installer was later upgraded to run their RunScript utility, to automatically convert the database on-the-fly when new releases were installed. The Intelic team built into their development process the requirement to check a database script into the code management system when any new or changed feature in the code required a database change. This process saved the developers from having to worry about keeping their own development database up-to-date with each code change. As the developers took a new pull from the code management system and updated their own systems with the latest code base, they would run the RunScript program and their databases would be updated appropriately. In that way all scripts were tested by every developer as they worked on the release, insuring the end result was correct data. If a later change occurred affecting the same database table, rather than go back and change the first script, a second script would be added. The RunScript utility kept track of what scripts had been run on the current database and only ran the new scripts.

Over the years, customer feedback often included how they appreciated how easy the software was to install and upgrade.

As the company grew, the support team could proudly say "Yes, installations/upgrades are easy and typically take only a couple of hours for a full install and upgrade."

Even by 2015, many on-premise enterprise application owners continued to struggle with costly, difficult upgrades. Some areas of software, such as smart phone applications and cloud applications, had mastered the art of easy installation and upgrade tools.

Jan's philosophy was that for every type of software, it never hurts to put your best developers on the low-level functions your customers will need, so all developers gain an appreciation of how customers perceive your software.

Now that there was a complete release and installer, Julie decided it was time to start using the real ProChannel software for sales demos instead of the old HTML prototype.

Freeman ran her through the installation process to install Oracle, webserver, and a version of the ProChannel software on her laptop. Jan asked Jean if they could use QuickLogic's data as the basis for their sales demo and, if so, what data would she want modified or disguised. Jean agreed and discussed the guidelines with Jan. Jan and Julie had decided their sales demo would be for a semiconductor company named Intelic, so Jan renamed the QuickLogic parts, changing the first two letters from QL to IN. Jan then went about modifying QuickLogic's pricing data in a logical fashion, maintaining similar relationships but changing all prices, while Julie removed some existing customer names and added others to the database. Julie then loaded phony users with industry-sounding roles working for various actual rep firms and distributors that their potential customers would relate to. Julie then started the task of adding transactions – design registrations, samples, quotes, debits, and orders.

They had their first real sales demo.

STAR WARS COUNTDOWN

"May the Force be with you." - Yoda

"Hey," Freeman said standing outside Jan's cubicle. "Did you realize the new Star Wars is coming out?"

"Star Wars is old – like before my kids were born," retorted Jan.

"Not the old Star Wars, a new one. Star Wars 1."

"Huh? Star Wars 1 was in the 70's."

"Where have you been?" Freeman asked. "That was Star Wars 4. They couldn't produce the first three with the '70s old antiquated computer graphics. Lucas had to start with 4, 5, then 6. Now he can finally produce the first one."

All the developers were listening now. It had been a constant buzz even among the Indian engineers.

"What are you proposing?" Jan asked.

"Close the office and go to the movies of course!" Freeman exclaimed.

One of the initial discussions John, Stephen, and Jan had was about the company calendar. Stephen proposed that five days per year should be sufficient for vacations, holidays, and sick leave. Both Jan and John moaned and said he was being unreasonably stingy.

"But we're a start-up," Stephen defended.

Jan and John didn't give in and Stephen relented to 7 holidays and five personal time off (PTO) days to be used for either vacation or sick leave. With Stephen's tight control on the funding, Jan was sure he would never agree to a movie in the middle of the day, but he surprised her when he walked up to them, having overheard the conversation, and said, "Great idea. A company outing!"

If Stephen agreed, it was done.

Freeman promptly added a "Star Wars Countdown" function on SD Tracker that each day let the users know "N days to Star Wars!" until finally the day arrived.

Stephen said they needed to go to the 9 a.m. movie. At first there was moaning, since developers barely get to work by 9 a.m. Stephen figured that that would get them through the movie without losing much developer time. He always had a trick up his sleeve. They were happy to be able to go, though, and arrived at work by 8:30 a.m. so they could carpool over to the movie theater. Stephen locked up the building behind them.

Stephen was 100 percent involved. He had sent Ed over to the theater early in case there was a crowd, since it was just the second day the movie was out, and had Ed stake out the front rows in the second section just behind the railing. There hadn't been a need – the 9 a.m. show time discouraged most techies from attending. As soon as Stephen arrived, he started taking orders for hot dogs, pop corn, and drinks, and shuttled trays of food and tossed bags of chips to all of the employees before the show began. He then sat down to enjoy the movie with the team. Everyone loved Star Wars 1.

Afterwards, as everyone pulled into the company parking lot, they saw a note on the front door. Stephen was the first one to the door, glanced at it, and handed it to John.

"Oh, no," moaned John. "I forgot this was Deb's first day!"

Deb was a new sales rep, and John hadn't connected that her first day of work was Star Wars day. She had arrived at work to find a locked office.

John called her immediately, apologized profusely, and she showed up an hour later laughing.

"Well, I'm glad you are still in business!" she exclaimed. "When I saw the locked door and no one home, I figured that maybe my first start-up folded before I got a chance to even work one day!"

It made for a good story.

Besides hiring Deb, John hired Jay to be the Intelic Eastern Sales Rep. John and Stephen had known Jay for years. Jay lived in Indianapolis and had years of semiconductor experience, plus had sold software to semiconductor companies before.

One day Jay was in California to meet the Intelic team and learn the product. Jan was working in her upstairs office when she heard an awful grinding sound coming from Stephen's office area. She went over to see what was happening but Stephen shooed her away. "Private!"

Later that day, Jan was walking by the bulletin board downstairs in the developer's area and saw something new. There was a sign posted that said, "This evidence was found at the scene of a crime." And stapled to it were what was left of two shredded socks. Stephen had been shredding someone's socks in the paper shredder upstairs!

Jan coerced the story from Freeman. Freeman had had a box under his desk for a while that contained the leftover packing material from his computer. Over the months he continued to collect any of the white peanut-shaped Styrofoam packing material for a yet unknown purpose.

Then Jay arrived. As he passed Freeman's desk on his way to the warehouse conference room, Freeman heard Jay ask Stephen, who was in the conference room, if he could borrow Stephen's car keys to put his luggage in the trunk. Jay had taken a taxi from the airport and was going to spend the night at Stephen's house. That was just the opportunity Freeman had been hoping for. He quietly followed Jay out of the office with his box in his arms. As Jay opened the trunk and put in his luggage, Freeman emptied all the Styrofoam peanuts into Stephen's trunk. Jay laughed, but said nothing to Stephen.

Stephen had gone to take his car to a meeting, and opened the trunk to put in his briefcase, when he saw the disaster. He had to drive to a car wash to use a vacuum to clean it out. He thought it was obvious that Jay had been the culprit, since sales was always playing practical jokes on each other. So he got into Jay's luggage, garnered a pair of socks, and shredded them as the "evidence."

Jay pledged to Stephen that he wasn't the culprit, but that he couldn't say who was.

Jan was glad Stephen never thought to ask her if she knew anything. She would have had trouble keeping it in.

In May, Jan was sitting in her office when the phone rang. She picked up the receiver and heard what sounded like terrorized screaming! She thought someone was dying in a car crash. It was like the garbage compactor scene in the old Star Wars 4 movie where the walls were collapsing and C-3PO hears screams and thinks Princess Leia, Luke, and Hans Solo are dying. But instead, they are yelling in joy because the walls are retreating.

It was Stephen and Deb on the phone. They had just won a contract with PMC-Sierra in Vancouver, Canada and were screaming their success!

Successes come more easily when the Force is with you.

MOVING DAY (JUNE 1999)

"Don't put all your eggs in one basket." - proverb

Stephen decided the company was ready to grow beyond their current office space. He and John found a new office on Ringwood Avenue in San Jose near a prospective customer, Fairchild. Although they had sufficient funding for the move and related expenses, Stephen did not want to spend anything on professional movers.

"We don't have much to move and have plenty of strong bodies here," Stephen exclaimed. "We can easily do it ourselves."

The team jumped into the project, boxing their offices, shutting down and disassembling their computers, the QA computers, CVS, Integration systems, and central servers. There were only a few "that's not my job description" grumbles, but soon everyone was participating. The last system to be shut down would be their internet server. Best to stay online as long as possible. Jan had already notified the internet provider of their new location. Stephen had coordinated to keep the same phone numbers to minimize disruption.

Moving day arrived, and the employees were all ready to load the U-Haul truck. They didn't have much furniture. The cubicle walls and desks would all remain – the new office space was already equipped with cubicles, plus included large conference room tables and chairs, and furniture for the hard offices which Stephen, John, Jan, and Julie would be moving into.

After the truck was loaded, Freeman, dressed in grubby levis and a bandana tied around his now curly, longer-length hair, volunteered to drive the truck. Jan and Arun jumped into Jan's red Volvo wagon and followed the truck.

Suddenly Jan got a sinking feeling in the pit of her stomach. "Arun," she said, "do you realize that everything we own as a company is right there in that truck: All of our software, everything? And Freeman is driving it!"

"I know," said Arun, "I wondered if you were all crazy."

Jan had been careful to ensure they had a CVS code management system, separate QA systems, and other effective processes, and then loaded everything together with young Freeman in one truck.

Fortunately, Freeman, the truck, the equipment, and the employees all arrived at the new building without incident. Jan vowed to herself to never put all her eggs in one basket again.

The realization must have hit Stephen as well. He immediately dictated an off-site backup tape storage policy. "Off site" ended up being at Jan's house.

WHEN TO BUILD IT YOURSELF

"The NIH syndrome is a disease." - Linus Torvalds, the inventor of LINUX

As you entered their new office building, there was a nice large lobby. One of the first things Stephen did was take Jan with him to various furniture stores to help in picking out two black leather couches to decorate the lobby area.

There was budget and a need to decorate the building. This time, instead of red, yellow, and blue banners, Stephen, John, and Jan headed over to Costco. Jan had never been in a Costco before, which amazed both Stephen and John. Quickly they found what had brought them here. Costco was having a sale on large oil paintings complete with frame. Jan wasn't enamored with them. The frames were gold and scrolled which made them look old fashioned to Jan, who favored more modern furniture. However, the paintings included a set of different golf course scenes which seemed appropriate since they, and their board members, were all golfers. The paintings were also a good size for the office, real oil paintings (or good copies), and good quality. They picked out one for Stephen's office, one for John's office, and two for the visitor conference room they were calling the Board Room. Jan said she'd bring in her own decorations for her office.

John found a couple of artificial Ficus trees and added them to their cart. They'd come in Jan's Volvo wagon to use it for hauling. Stephen took some tie-down string Costco provided, since the trees hung out the back, and he used the tie-downs to secure the back hatch door.

The new office building had two separate wings. The wing on the left was the largest. It was a large room with hard offices around the outside and cubicles in the center. Jan was assigned the first office entering the wing. Next to her was a small conference room. The corner office was Stephen's. There were two offices on the far left, one Julie took since she was performing as Customer Support Manager and needed to be able to shut the door to close out the noise from the cubicles when taking customer calls. There was another office that was empty next to Julie's and a computer room.

On the back wall was another empty office, and a good-sized lunch room.

The right-side wing was smaller – no cubicles and just hard offices on each side of a nice wide hallway. On the right side was one office (empty for now), the Board Room, and John's office. On the left was a larger training space and a spare office.

Because she was in the first office off the lobby, Jan ended up having to handle every delivery and visitor as they entered the building. Originally Stephen's plan was to have Starr, their Office/Accounting Manager, sit at the reception desk. But because most of Starr's time dealt with working on financial and personnel files, she needed to be in a more private area most of the day.

Because no one was typically at the reception desk in the lobby, delivery people and visitors naturally headed towards the wing that had the most noise and activity going on, and poked their head in the first office, Jan's. John currently was the only one with an office in the right wing, and he was rarely in the building. They had a lot of deliveries.

Jan lobbied Stephen to have a full-time receptionist but, of course, he said "No." After several days of deliveries and visitors, Jan eventually succeeded in building a case that the trade-off for her time was worth something, and Stephen relented. They hired a very inexpensive college student to cover the desk during the summer –

Jan's daughter Kristin.

"Just don't say, 'Mom will be right here,' " Jan requested when showing Kristin around on her first day. "It's bad enough I'm old enough to be every developer's mom," she teased. "I don't want the customers calling me 'Mom,' too."

The team had been busy getting the training room set up for an preview demo of the new Release 1.1. Five representatives from Diodes were traveling up from L.A. to try ProChannel configured for their business processes "hands on" to see how big a project it would be to train their sales force.

For the past few days the entire company had been running a final shake-down on the latest release. Today they were doing a trash-a-thon where everyone in the building got on the system and ran as many transactions and business scenarios as possible.

Suddenly John yelled from the developer cubicle he was sitting in for testing, "What's wrong?"

At the same time Stephen walked out of his office, "Did I do something wrong? My system stopped!"

Suddenly everyone was in an uproar. Some developers ran to the main server to review the system console messages, others started looking at the system logs to see if they could see what had happened to cause the crash. Within an hour they thought they identified at least the problem, but not the "why."

"It looks like both John and Stephen were preparing a quote and both hit the 'Quote' button at exactly the same time," reported Arun.

"That shouldn't be an issue," said Jan. "This is a web-based application on web application layer third party software! Everything is built for multiple users to do everything at the same time."

"That's true," replied Arun, "but that's what we're seeing."

They moved into the training room, where computers were set up for the demo, to try to replicate the issue. Julie stood up front and as many people who could use the training systems sat at the ready.

"OK," Julie said to get their attention, "everyone create a new quote. But wait before clicking the 'Quote' button. When I say 'Click

Quote,' click the 'Quote' button."

The first time Julie said "Click Quote," nothing happened.

"They must not have hit it at exactly the same time," said Arun.

"Let's try again," said Jan.

Julie said, "Everybody create a quote, then wait." A few seconds later she said, "Click Quote."

Still the system was working fine.

Third times' a charm. On the third try, the system crashed.

"Good," said Arun. He and Freeman took off. "Let's check the logs."

Everyone else went back to work. At 5 p.m. Arun & Freeman came into Jan's office.

"We isolated the problem. It's a 'race' condition in ObjectMatter," Arun said. ObjectMatter was their third party object-to-relational (OR) layer. Apparently ObjectMatter had a bug.

Freeman was concerned that he only had a couple of hours and then was supposed to spend the evening in traffic school. "I've already skipped traffic school once. I'm not sure what would happen if I skipped again!"

"This is a very important demo, Freeman," said Jan. "But it's up to you. I don't want to get you thrown into jail!"

Arun and Freeman went into the computer room to work on the problem, then both approached Jan a half hour later.

"We have an idea," said Arun. "Freeman has been working on an OR layer off hours that he was going to use for his personal use. He always thought that the OR layer could be done better and easier to meet the specific needs of transactional processing. It isn't complete yet, but if we both work on it tonight, we think there's a good chance we can complete it by early morning, test it out, and we're sure it wouldn't have this problem."

Freeman was willing to skip traffic school again to save the company.

While their idea for solving the bug was very appealing, Jan thought the risk was still too high.

"What are our alternatives?" Jan pondered. "I'm thinking that the problem is with the database, so it's in the shared server. What if we set up each demo system on its own database. That way the ObjectMatter bug wouldn't affect any of the training systems."

"Well," pondered Arun, "that would work. But it would mean that the Diodes users and Julie would have no shared data during the demo. So if someone entered a new customer, the other systems wouldn't see it."

"I think we could work around that during training," offered Julie, who was going to be conducting the training session."

"Seems less risky," said Jan.

The team minus Freeman, who went off to traffic school, worked several more hours to set up a separate Oracle database instance for each of the training systems while Julie modified her training plan and tested to make sure there wouldn't be any new issues with separate databases for each training workstation. Julie was always thorough and didn't want to encounter any unexpected issues during the training session in front of the customer.

The Diodes visitors showed up the next morning and went into the new training room. Before starting the hands-on portion of the training, Julie gave an overview demo of the software. She was running the current version of the software which was fairly stable, but still in development. Kim asked her, "Wait – could you go back to that prior screen? I missed something."

Julie out of habit using basic websites, hit the browser back button, and a system error popped up. She was trying to think of some witty remark to cover her embarrassment that the system had a bug, when Kim exclaimed, "Wow – you mean this is real software? I thought it was just another demo. That's wonderful."

Julie breathed a sigh of relief. She clicked "OK" to the error message which returned her to the prior screen, and she continued the overview, but the Diodes team, instead of paying attention, were already trying things out on the training desktops in front of them.

Kim exclaimed, "It's so intuitive! I get it! I don't even think we need to conduct any training for the sales team!"

What the visitors didn't know was that one of ProChannel's

main software layers had a huge bug.

The software issue had illustrated an important architecture consideration for Jan that remained one of the key design drivers for ProChannel. The software they were building was not something that would be used by one or a handful of users in the back office. The internet gave all of the customer's extended sales network access to ProChannel, including the sales reps and distributor users who worked outside the manufacturer's offices and who were located worldwide.

Although some users, such as pricing managers and higher level sales managers, accessed the software from within the company's network, "behind the four walls" as it was called, the external users, the sales reps and distributor users, were the most important users.

It is true that internal users - the pricing managers and higher level sales managers - would use the system the most. They would be the power users who would have all of the software's features at their fingertips to do the management and analytical functions. However, if the sales and distributor users didn't put data in the system, there would be no transactions for the managers to approve and no data for them to analyze.

One of the struggles Intelic's key competitor, Seibel, was facing, was that while Siebel as a company was very effective at selling the Siebel software to a manufacturer's managers, after the software was installed, the manufacturer's sales reps refused to use it. Sales users found it difficult to use and slow. Sales users are impatient, and will find the quickest way to get their job done. Instead of trying to work using a slow or hard-to-use system, they would pick up the phone and call marketing for better pricing and better packaging deals, or call their managers for approval of a new deal. The sales users went around the software when it was slow or difficult to use.

When the sales reps didn't use the software and used manual methods instead, the value proposition behind why the company purchased the software was impacted.

To counteract the situation, the manufacturer would assign

admins to enter the quote and pricing information into the software after-the-fact. This was error-prone. Plus the sales users didn't realize any value from the software. It was just in their way.

In any industry, software could only be valuable if it was used. That meant the software had to be intuitive and very quick to respond, especially when it needed to be used by sales users.

Intelic prioritized performance and ease-of-use high on the list of requirements to meet.

A few days later, Freeman had completed his own OR layer which he named "ObjectBridge." He and Arun tested it out extensively with the product. It passed with flying colors.

At first, Stephen was opposed to using Freeman's layer and pressed Jan to find an off-the-shelf replacement. A well-known guideline for software CEOs is to avoid building their own tools or software layers if it isn't part of their core product, especially if third party off-the-shelf software is available. The rule many CEOs follow is that in a "Build" versus "Buy" decision, the weight should always be on "Buy." The team had already built their own bug tracking software, SD Tracker, and Stephen didn't want to continue down that path. Freeman had also originally recommended they build their own database and web server layers, so Stephen was wary.

However, Jan reasoned, there are times when the decision should be to build it yourself. In this case, Freeman had built ObjectBridge to fit exactly with Intelic's architecture, which he had also designed. That made ObjectBridge an exact match for their requirements without needing the extra code and performance overhead of features that other companies might need but ProChannel didn't.

In the end, they agreed on ObjectBridge. Stephen, of course, negotiated a sweetheart deal for Intelic, but Freeman did get some cash out of it.

Jan was glad QuickLogic hadn't encountered the bug. Madhu went to the QuickLogic site to upgrade their server to ObjectBridge.

ObjectBridge became the OR layer for ProChannel. Time

proved that using ObjectBridge was a good decision.

Years later the VP of Engineering at another software company confided to Jan, "Our software is like yours. We built our own OR layer. I'm sure you would agree that was a mistake. In retrospect," he said, "I would have converted to Hibernate," [the leading off-the-shelf OR tool at the time]. "It's easier to hire people trained in the Hibernate software than to maintain your own, and developers love to work where they can improve their resumes using the latest, greatest technology."

Jan didn't agree. She would have never given up ObjectBridge because of its simplicity, high performance, and zero errors. It exactly fit their need. In addition, she reasoned, why focus on having your developers build their resumes when they all want to stay at your company for the long haul? Intelic developers loved working on ProChannel.

THE MYSTERY OF THE SHRINKING SOFTWARE

"Less is More." - Ludwig Mies van der Rohe

One of the measurements regarding software that Stephen liked to track was the number of lines of source code in the product as a measurement of the team's accomplishment. In January, he had asked Freeman how many lines of code were in Release 0.5. It contained 21,000 lines of code. Then, three months later in April, Release 1.0 contained 120,000 lines of code. Stephen was very excited about the productivity with only six developers.

As soon as Release 1.1 was released in July 1999, Stephen came to Jan to ask how many lines of code were in the new release. Jan asked Freeman to give her the line of code count for Release 1.1.

"100,000 lines of code," Freeman reported.

"That's a lot less than Release 1.0," Jan noted.

"That's interesting, isn't it," retorted Freeman who was pleased with the reduced number of code lines. "We cleaned up some modules. We re-wrote how customers are associated to users. We improved the catalog architecture when we added the "External Catalog" feature for Diodes. We also cleaned out some code that came as part of the Java libraries that we didn't need," he beamed.

"So," said Jan, "we significantly increased functionality with more efficient code! Outstanding!"

Jan had always thought software metrics other than lines of code were more important measurements of productivity, like function points or the growing feature list.

Stephen wasn't happy with that answer, though. He had wanted to report to the board how many more lines of code were now in the product.

Eventually Jan and Freeman convinced Stephen that less is better – less code requires less maintenance, and there's less code to have bugs.

Stephen being Stephen, his board packet had his special type of marketing spin to be sure to sell the board on the concept of more efficient code. Stephen didn't like leaving anything to chance. Even with something as basic as software metrics, he didn't want to give the board any reason to question Intelic's progress.

Creating efficient, lean code was part of the team's on-going effort to build high quality software.

Intelic began having cross-functional weekly SDRB meetings. Jan had borrowed the acronym "SDRB" from aerospace where it meant Software Development Review Board. For the Intelic process, Jan included concepts from ASK Computer's very effective Product Life Cycle (PLC) team approach to create Intelic's own version of an SDRB. Jan thought the acronym at Intelic could mean SD Tracker Review Board or SDR Review Board. Both worked.

Intelic's SDRB team consisted of a member from each product-related discipline. Gregg, the new QA Manager, led the meetings. Jan and Arun attended representing the product. (Freeman was invited, but meetings were not his idea of time well spent). Julie represented the customer. Stephen was very hands-on and wanted to stay abreast of the development efforts. In addition, he was still handling the marketing role. He attended whenever he was in the office.

At each SDRB meeting, the cross-functional team sat down and reviewed all newly entered SDRs to decide when each had to be done and to assigned them to either the current release, an upcoming release, or "Future."

Some they would find were duplicates, and would resolve as a "Dupl." Some couldn't be replicated, so were closed as "Can't Dup." Some were just bad ideas or not really bugs (e.g., operator errors).

For those, Stephen came up with the resolution of "No Fix Warranted" or "NFW." He thought it was funny that it had a double meaning.

One day during the SDRB meeting, Stephen received a call and said he needed to duck out of the meeting for a few minutes. A photographer had arrived to take his picture for an upcoming interview for an important business magazine.

When he returned, someone asked how the photo session went, excited that the company and product were getting publicity.

Stephen said, "I asked the photographer if he could make me look thinner. He said, 'No problem.' I asked him if he could make me look taller. He said, 'No problem.' So I asked him if he could make me look more intelligent. He said, 'Sorry - there's only so much I can do.' "

Stephen had the team laughing in stitches.

Once Release 1.1 was declared complete, besides upgrading QuickLogic to the new version, the new customer, Diodes, was eager to get it installed. Release 1.1 contained the new External Catalog feature Diodes wanted to attach to their website to allow anyone to search for products and view product datasheets. In addition, Release 1.1 contained a more complete order capture function and the order integration to the back office ERP systems that both Diodes and QuickLogic wanted.

WE NEED A BOAT RIDE

"Number Four: Party on Jan's boat." - Top Ten Reasons Tee Shirt

At their prior company, the CEO had created tee shirts to commemorate one of their software releases. The back of the shirts listed "Top 10 Reasons for Release 2.0" with number four being "Party on Jan's boat." Unfortunately, that party never happened.

Jan thought it was time for that party.

Jan and her husband drove to their boat berth in the California Delta about 70 miles east of San Francisco. They were joined there by Freeman, Julie, and Jan's daughter Julie Anne who helped get the two boats ready: the larger 43 foot boat, Tranquility, and the smaller ski boat that was on a hydro hoist in the same berth. The rest of the company were going to board Tranquility at the Sugar Barge Restaurant and Marina on Bethel Island, where there was ample parking plus coffee or breakfast for any who wanted to arrive early.

It took about 15 minutes to motor Tranquility from its berth to Sugar Barge. Meanwhile Julie Anne took Freeman and Julie out in the ski boat, which gave Freeman an opportunity to take a few wakeboard runs while waiting for the arrival of the big boat. Julie Anne was a skilled ski boat driver, and Julie was designated as the flagger.

Few people know about the California Delta area. The Delta is formed by the confluence of two major rivers: The Sacramento River and the San Joaquin River. After the gold rush, idle laborers were put to work in the Delta area to build levees and reclaim rich peat farmland, much like what was done in Holland. Today the Delta consists of over one hundred productive farm islands surrounded by one thousand miles of meandering waterways. The many tule-lined sloughs are ideal for water sports, such as water skiing and wake boarding. Over the years, some island levee walls have broken, flooding the farm tract, and resulting in larger bodies of water. One is Franks Tract just east of Bethel Island, known for its fishing. It has been designated a state recreational park. Another, a few miles south, is Mildred Island, which flooded in the '80s. It also was never reclaimed as farmland and now serves as a favorite anchorage for many boaters that spend weekends anchored out.

It was a beautiful August day, warm and sunny, with clear blue skies. A perfect day for a boat ride and water activities.

The first thing Jan did upon arriving at the Sugar Barge docks, after securing the boat, was to take various life jackets up the ramp before the group headed to the boat. There were four children coming. Starr, their office manager, brought her two boys, and Stephen and his wife Mary brought their young daughter and son. Jan had also discovered that the two Indian engineers, Arun and Ketan, who were part of the group, didn't swim at all. She didn't want to risk losing them into the muddy Delta waters!

Everyone embarked. Mike and Jan did their captain and first mate duties to leave the dock and begin their short voyage.

Many of the employees had never been on a boat before. As they were under way, Jan went from the command bridge down the ladder to check on people in the cockpit and the salon to make sure everyone was feeling fine and enjoying the trip. As she reached the cockpit she gasped. Ketan was taking Arun's picture, but to do so he'd had Arun step out on the swim platform. The boat was traveling fifteen knots so the swim platform was covered in churning water and the boat was slightly raised in the bow, dipping down in the stern. She grabbed Arun's life jacket and pulled him into the cockpit.

"Yikes," she said. "Don't do that!" She admonished everyone to stay in the cockpit during the ride.

"Even better," she said, "how would you guys like to come up top and see everything from the command bridge?"

Arun and Ketan were happy and excited to climb up to the upper helm where they could get an even better view over the slough walls to see the farmland beyond, which couldn't be viewed from water level. Mike had radioed to request the Connection Slough Bridge be opened, and the engineers were fascinated to see the large pivot bridge in action. Ketan took many more pictures.

As they got near Mildred Island, the ski boat joined them with Freeman happily wakeboarding behind, waving and doing trick maneuvers.

When they arrived at Mildred Island, they anchored the boat to spend a relaxing few hours there, and side-tied the ski boat. The children immediately jumped into the water to swim and play. Jan, Starr, and Julie set up lunch. After lunch, Freeman rallied a group to sit around the large dinette and play a game of Pictionary. Freeman said he would be on one team, Chaiya, a junior engineer Jan had recently hired to be part-time IT and part-time developer, would be on the other. Freeman then started to assign teams. He was going to put each of the Julies on a different team and started by saying, "The young Julie," motioning to Jan's 23 year old daughter, "on Chaiya's team and ..." He looked at Intelic's Julie who was glaring at him.

"So which Julie am I?" she asked.

Freeman stammered, since clearly Julie wasn't going to take "the old Julie" well at all, since she was also a young, very attractive woman.

"Um, um, ... the other Julie?" he asked tentatively. Everyone in the room burst into laughter seeing Freeman's red face, including both Julies.

Meanwhile Ketan had ventured into the water with his life jacket on and was happily floating around. He'd never been in a river, lake, or even a swimming pool before. Neither had Arun, but Arun wasn't eager to try it out. Freeman was calling out from the salon, teasing Arun that he needed to just jump in. Jan was happier with Arun safe on board. Finally Freeman yelled, "If you don't jump in, I'm going to come push you in."

Immediately, Arun took a step off the swim platform, into the water. He went completely under water and came up coughing and choking. Before Jan could do anything, Freeman came flying out of the salon, jumped onto the swim platform, and grabbed Arun's life jacket to raise him up out of the water so he could cough out the water and catch his breath.

"Hey man," Freeman said, "I didn't mean to drown you!"

"I thought I'd better jump in before you pushed me in," Arun sputtered.

Freeman tried to help Arun to the swim ladder, but Arun said, "No – I'm going to stay in. I want to try to figure this out."

Arun took one hand and held on the anchor line to try to find his balance, but kept rolling into the water face first. Buoyancy was such a new feeling he had no idea how to balance. Ketan was taking to it naturally, but it would be a few years before Arun ventured into the water again.

A few years later, Arun and his wife traveled to Hawaii. At that time, Jan's daughter Kristin was working on a Pacific Whale Foundation boat in Maui. Kristin arranged for Arun and his wife to have complimentary whale watch passes. Jan admonished Kristin, "They want to try out snorkeling. Your job is to be sure they both survive the adventure. Arun doesn't swim!"

Kristin surrounded them both with swim noodles and made sure they were safe and having fun. They all enjoyed the outing.

Mike took a group out to water ski and wake board. Jan stayed on the big boat to clean up after lunch. Stephen and Jan were astonished when they saw Ketan skiing by waving.

"Oh, great," muttered Jan. "He can't even swim and they have him going 30 miles per hour behind the ski boat! Hope if he falls his life jacket stays on!"

The ski group returned, having had fun, and the next group to go out on the ski boat started to assemble. Jan thought she should stay with the big boat, but everyone convinced her to go out and, since she loved to water ski, she wasn't that hard to convince. Mike drove the ski boat past the anchored boat so Jan could wave and show off her slalom ski turns.

Tired and happy, the group headed back to Sugar Barge then home, having had a great team building experience.

FOCUS ON THE CUSTOMER

"Customer service represents the heart of a brand in the hearts of its customers." -
Kate Nasser

Julie was needing to spend more time as Customer Support Manager now. One day she had an urgent call from Diodes. Gregg, the QA Manager, and Arun were within hearing distance of her office and heard the concern in her voice. Apparently there was a big problem with the system. Suddenly the user sign-on mechanism was failing, and users were unable to log in. Just before the problem happened, the system administrator had uploaded some new user information.

Gregg and Arun immediately dropped what they were working on and went into Julie's office to offer help. Jan and Stephen were having a meeting in Stephen's corner office, and Madhu came in to alert them that there was a big customer issue and gave them a quick synopsis. Stephen, being very technical, was aware of how ProChannel's user login process worked and threw out an idea about what the problem could be. They immediately got up and the three of them headed into Julie's office. Soon Jan, Stephen, Gregg, Arun, and Madhu were all brainstorming on the white board and were coming up with a viable reason for the problem and the solution. It ended up that Stephen's idea was right on-the-mark. Just then Julie's phone rang. It was the Diodes contact. He asked her if she wanted him to escalate the problem to his upper management to be sure she had Intelic's focus on the problem.

Julie looked around her small office, filled with the CEO on down, and smiled. "No," she said, "there's no need to escalate. I think I have all the help I need."

Julie quickly gave the Diodes contact the step-by-step instructions how to view the data to see if their conjecture was valid. They quickly found that it was a data issue, as Stephen suspected, and within a few minutes Diodes was back up and running.

Jan was glad the entire company cared about the needs of the customer.

Years before, Jan had worked for Ingres in a Director position reporting to the President. She had only been at Ingres a short time when the yearly Ingres User Group was to be held in Florida. The President asked Jan to attend.

At the end of one of the coffee breaks set up outside where attendees could mill about on the lawn in the shade of big trees, the meetings were about to resume. As everyone headed up the stairs into the building, Jan was followed by two customer attendees. She overheard their discussion.

"We're getting horrible support from Ingres," one said. "We can't get any information about the status of our bugs and no one can provide us any updates."

"We don't have that problem," said the other. "I know a number you can call that will get you action right away. Just call the main number and ask for extension 4372."

Jan hurried into the building and saw the President sitting on a bench in the hall.

"Dennis," she said. "I think we have a problem with customer support!"

"Why is that?" he asked.

"One of our customers just told another the number to call for support."

"What's wrong with that?" he asked.

"It was the private phone number of the direct line to your desk!" she exclaimed.

Obviously, if a company offers good customer support, customers won't start calling the President directly.

Good customer support is important for gaining and maintaining the customer base.

One day Madhu approached Jan and asked her if she could make her an employee.

This was the second time this situation had occurred. Late in 1999, Arun had given notice to the contract company that he was leaving, and joining another company. Freeman went to Jan to give her the bad news.

"What?" exclaimed Jan, and rushed in to see Arun.

"Arun, why are you leaving us? We really need you," she implored. Arun had become invaluable to the engineering efforts, and she was panicked at the thought of losing him.

"I'm sorry," he said, "but as you know, my contract is written so that you can't hire me. I want to start working directly for a company, not through the contracting firm, so that I can achieve promotions and job growth. I knew I couldn't approach you, and I needed to find a company willing to sponsor my H-1 Visa."

"What if I could work something out with your contract company to let us hire you. Would you be willing to stay?" she implored. "I'll match whatever the other company offered you, or more if you need it."

Arun smiled, "I would much rather stay here. I love working for you and with Freeman and the team. I just know the owner. It isn't possible. But yes, if you could get his agreement, I'd definitely prefer to stay here. It would need to include how to bridge my H-1 Visa – those take several months to transfer. In addition, the new company offered me a Green Card. Could you do that?"

"If I can, I will," she promised. "Let me talk to Stephen about the Green Card, and if that's possible for us to do, then I'll call Rajiv."

Jan quickly made sure Stephen was in agreement to pay for the H-1 Visa processing now and start Arun's Green Card as the next step. He was.

The contract company was co-owned. The co-owner Jan had worked with from the beginning was the second partner, Rajiv, not the engineer she had worked with at the dot.com and who had been adamant about the no-hire clause.

She called Rajiv and explained the situation which, of course, he was already aware of. "But," she implored, "what good is it if we both lose Arun to another company? Intelic didn't solicit him because of the contract provisions, and now we both lose out. I was afraid that clause would give us trouble, and now it has. I don't see how I can continue to use engineers from your company unless you help us find a way to keep Arun. He is too vital to our efforts."

After some hemming and hawing, Rajiv relented.

"All right," he said, "but you'd better not start converting all our contractors to your employees!"

"Thank you," she sighed and promised him that stealing his contractors was not her intent.

"Your company will also be able to keep Arun longer this way," she said.

"What do you mean?" Rajiv asked.

"We'll start his H-1 Visa right away, but it will take a couple of months to process. In the interim, he will need to remain a contractor with you. So, you see, you'll have a few extra months of taking your share out of what we pay you for his salary."

Rajiv agreed, and soon Arun became an Intelic employee.

Now a year later, Madhu was wanting to leave the contract company and join Intelic directly. She knew Arun had done it, and wanted to follow in his footsteps.

Jan called Rajiv again. She assured him that she had not approached Madhu, but that since Madhu was working at the contract company when Arun transferred, Madhu knew it was possible.

"This is not the start of any mass migration," she assured Rajiv. "Less than one per year is probably your normal attrition rate of contractors you lose to other companies. Can we make an exception one more time? Besides, Madhu is the only other of your contractors that has become vital to our efforts."

Rajiv said he thought that would be fine. He had worked long enough with Jan now to know she meant what she said, and it wasn't her intent to steal all of their engineers. Intelic had, since the start, used many of their contractors.

Jan was relieved and pleased, and gave Madhu the good news.

A few days later Stephen came into Jan's office. "The contract company is suing us," he informed her.

"What?" she said. "Rajiv said it was fine."

"Well, seems his co-owner doesn't agree. He called me on the phone and yelled. He's livid."

"What do you want to do?" she asked. "Should we just let Madhu go to find another job somewhere?"

"No," said Stephen. "We'll counter sue!"

Stephen wasn't one to be messed with and he was furious with the company's owner.

Besides Madhu, Intelic at that time had only one other contractor from the contract company, and she was fairly junior. Jan had been having success hiring directly, so all of the other engineers were employees. Absolving the relationship with the contract company would not cause them any hardship, except for losing Madhu. Madhu would need to keep working for the contract company until Intelic could get Madhu's H-1 transferred, if the contract company would even keep her on after approaching Intelic to hire her. Else Madhu would have no choice but to return to India.

Ketan had already made that choice. He had gotten tired of working for the contract company a few months earlier, and had returned to India.

After two rounds between the contract company's lawyer and Intelic's, with the case Stephen had built including calculating the cost impact of the Pricing Engine fiasco, where the code had to be re-written from Oracle SP to Java, and the injury it would cost Intelic to suddenly lose Madhu, Intelic's suit was for a higher dollar value than the contract company's lawsuit. The contract company backed off. They dropped their lawsuit, so Intelic did the same. The contract company allowed Intelic to hire Madhu, and held her H-1 Visa until it transferred to Intelic.

Jan decided the contract company wasn't focused on Intelic as their customer. Jan immediately started recruiting efforts to replace their other contractor with a direct employee, so that as soon as Madhu was on-board, she terminated the contract company.

That's what happens when you don't focus on your customers. You lose their business.

To win PMC-Sierra as a customer, a small but fast growing semiconductor company headquartered in Canada, Intelic agreed to work with two local San Jose PMC sales managers to design a new "Opportunity" module. It would be similar to the Design Registrations used by distributors, but PMC (and most other manufacturers) also wanted to have their sales reps track promising opportunities that their direct sales team identified. PMC sent two of their sales managers to Intelic's office for several long design sessions, where they worked with Intelic to review screen designs and flow, and suggested additional features.

Jan enjoyed working with actual customers. Most of the product requirements and design previously had come from John and Stephen, who both knew the industry and had definite product ideas. Sometimes, though, it's useful to get information directly from the customers' mouths.

Jan had learned the importance of listening to the customer while at Ford Aerospace. On the same Army maintenance contract where the red headed Lt. Colonel had left with Ford's software to install for use during Desert Storm, months later the Lt. Colonel was back in town with some of his young Army engineers to meet with the Ford Aerospace team to provide input on the requirements for the next maintenance release.

The list of the requested maintenance changes was written on the whiteboard at the front of the conference room. One of the young Army engineers stood up, and wrote priorities on the board next to each list item indicating, by priority, what the highest priority items were to the lowest.

One of the items on the list was to change the queuing algorithm.

Jan, when reviewing the requirements list in preparation for the meeting, had seen the queuing change item, and thought it would be low priority.

The system ran on two computers. The front-end smaller DEC PDP computer received communications from the battlefield from various sources, and put them in a queue.

The PDP was networked to a larger, DEC VAX computer which then took each message out of the queue, in a first in, first out priority, and processed it to display on the operator's workstation along with any other matching important information.

The system was used far behind enemy lines for intelligence processing only. It was not involved in front-line activities.

Jan was surprised that changing the queuing algorithm from first in, first out to last in, first out would make it into the number one priority position over larger issues and bug fixes. So she asked the Army engineer to elaborate.

"Well," he said, "let me give you an example."

"Two weeks ago we were sitting at the operator workstations analyzing data when the area's internal network cables stopped passing data. This is not an unusual occurrence," he stated.

The systems were housed in army trucks and networks set up using mobile antennas and wires housed in big cables between the trucks in the dirt.

"Several systems were impacted, including the traffic between the PDP and the VAX. The PDP continued to receive messages, but the VAX was unable to process them. It took a half hour for the technicians to fix the network cable and get the VAX back online," he continued.

"After they were back online, after processing for another half an hour, the message that displayed on the screen, the last message that had been received, was, 'Incoming SCUD.' It would have been really nice if that was the first message in instead of the last."

"Ah," said Jan. "I see your point. Change the queuing algorithm. Priority 1."

In addition to customer support, Julie often helped Jan in designing new product functionality, leveraging her semiconductor and engineering background. Julie knew the two PMC reps that were supporting the new Opportunity Form design and was also thoroughly aware of the process since she, as a sales rep in her prior company, had also had to manage a new sales opportunity process. Both her friendliness with the PMC reps and her background were extremely valuable.

A couple of times when the office environment became too busy to focus, Julie and Jan slipped off to a local hotel and sat by the pool working to add more detail behind the design specs. Most of the time they just tried to carve out a little quiet time in the office to work together.

One afternoon while they were working in Jan's office on the PMC enhancements, Frank and Freeman knocked on Jan's door.

"We're heading out a little early today – 49ers opening day game! We already asked Stephen. He said we could take a couple of hours off," they grinned. Then, before Jan could say much, they vanished.

"Wish we weren't so busy," Julie lamented. "My sister had two extra tickets for the game today, but I told her there was no way I could get the time off."

"It's too bad you couldn't use those tickets, but I'm sure glad you're here. I don't think I could get the PMC design work done that we need for tomorrow's meeting without your help. I appreciate it!" said Jan, trying to make her feel better.

Fifteen minutes later, John and Stephen were in Jan's doorway. "See you tomorrow," John said. "49ers game. Got to run." And they were gone.

"What is this?" Jan said. Stephen, in particular, was always a workhorse and put long hours in.

Julie went out to get some coffee and returned.

"Do you believe this?" she exclaimed. "We're the only people in this building!"

"Can you still get those tickets?" Jan asked. "I couldn't go but you should."

"Nah," said Julie. "My sister already sold them."

"That's too bad," said Jan.

"Well," said Julie. "If everyone else is at the game, we could at least take a short break. I remember there's some wine in the lunch room leftover from a customer event. Let's treat ourselves to a glass."

"We deserve it," exclaimed Jan.

They went to the lunch room and found a nice bottle of wine so began to look in the drawers for a cork screw. But there was none to be found.

"I'll bet Frank has one and, since he was the first to leave, I have no issues with riffling through his desk drawer," teased Julie. But neither Frank nor Freeman had a cork screw that they could find.

"Darn," said Jan.

"Let's see if there's anything else in the lunch room."

They found three bottles of Corona beer but again, alas, no bottle opener. There was one can of Budweiser.

"Oh great," said Jan. "All we can do is share a Bud."

There also weren't any glasses to be found, so they went back to Jan's office and Julie poured half the Bud into Jan's clean coffee cup and drank the other half from the can.

"Cheers," Julie said.

John was in the office testing out the new features and became very excited about the new PMC Sales Opportunity Form.

"This is great!" John exclaimed. "We should be using this to track our own sales opportunities."

John asked Freeman to set up a separate server with ProChannel on it. He told Freeman the labels he wanted and other configuration changes. John decided to call it "Coaches" denoting it was the coach for the sales team. Besides renaming the screen "Coaches," John had Freeman change MPN (Manufacturer Part Number) to Software Module and other label changes to denote selling software. Jan had been working with Stephen on the sales bundles so she volunteered to add the software modules into the Product Catalog tables. Julie helped load the current and in-process customer names and set up the sales team as ProChannel users.

During sales meetings with prospective customers, John would get out his laptop and enter their data - what modules they were interested in, key contacts, important upcoming dates such as when they would like a demo and when they would make a "buy" decision, and other relevant data.

As the customer rep saw John filling out the form, they'd ask, "What sales opportunity software do you use?"

John would beam, "This is ProChannel, of course. Configured to match our software sales business."

"Really?" they would ask, typically surprised. "You use your own software?"

"Of course, it's the best!" John would let them know.

Stephen heard of the exchanges between John and the customers, and quickly added the fact that Intelic used its own software to track its sales opportunities to his marketing pitch. Or, as Stephen would say, "We eat our own dog food."

Customers loved that, and it gave them even more confidence in buying the product.

When the release that included PMC's new Sales Opportunity Module was ready for customers, PMC scheduled their implementation kick-off. The first week, meetings were held at Intelic. Later meetings would be held at PMC's Corporate offices in Vancouver, Canada. The VP of Sales that had been instrumental in purchasing the software, and his two reps that helped on the opportunity design, were located in San Jose. PMC's President and his Vancouver team flew to California for the initial kick-off sessions.

After Stephen welcomed them, PMC's President gave motivating opening remarks about how important the new ProChannel initiative was for the success of PMC. They then spent the week getting an overview of the system from Julie, and reviewing the data gathering steps needed.

In Vancouver, starting the next week, Julie led the multi-week implementation effort. Jan traveled with her part of the time to provide support. Their favorite flight was an Alaskan Airlines from San Jose directly to Vancouver.

On the first trip, when returning home, they were in the Vancouver airport and found that their flight had been delayed.

"Well," said Julie. "Let's get a bite to eat while we wait. I saw a sign that said smoked salmon. That sounds wonderful."

They went to the small airy seafood bar and sat down.

The waiter behind the bar waved to acknowledge them and said, "Just a minute. I'm shucking oysters. Then I'll be right with you."

Julie and Jan had ordered oysters a couple of nights before in downtown Vancouver and found Canadian oysters to be fresh and wonderful.

"He's just now shucking oysters! Let's split a half dozen oysters too." Jan suggested.

When the waiter came to take their order, Julie ordered oysters and the smoked salmon.

"We don't have the smoked salmon here," he said and could see the disappointment in Julie's eyes. "But it's just across the building, over there." He pointed to a shop across the terminal. "I'll run and get a package for you. Do you know what would go good with oysters and smoked salmon? How about a glass of Chardonnay while you wait?"

They didn't need to be sold. From then on when leaving Vancouver, they made sure they got to the Vancouver airport early enough to enjoy their oysters, smoked salmon, and Chardonnay.

The PMC implementation went smoothly. Due to Jan's prior SAP experience, she had designed the software to be easy to install and easy to upgrade.

Unlike Intelic's software, it was well known that big ERP "gorilla" software required a multi-year implementation effort, extensive amount of work, and typically resulted in huge cost overruns. There were horror stories repeated at IT conventions about companies who paid $2 million for software and ended up spending another $5 million in implementation services. The cost of Oracle software purchased by the State of California and the resulting $41 million overrun was one of the reasons for California Governor Gray Davis' recall as governor.

In comparison, Intelic implementations could be completed in a couple of months' time at a fraction of the cost. While Jan reasoned that it would be nice to get millions of dollars above and beyond the cost of the software itself simply for installing the software and loading the initial data sets, charging companies for "no added value" services seemed unconscionable. Companies should only pay for value added, she reasoned. The way she had designed the software architecture made it easy to customize and configure, and easy to install and upgrade. It didn't cost the little company any more to build software with ease of installation and upgrade as a key requirement, so it seemed an obvious decision to Jan. And one their customers' appreciated.

GROWING PAINS

"In the business world, the rearview mirror is always clearer than the windshield."
- Warren Buffett

For QuickLogic, Diodes, and PMC, Julie and Jan had been the hands-on implementation team. But as Intelic grew, Stephen wanted to create a separate Professional Services Organization and searched for a skilled professional from one of the larger ERP companies. He found Rebecca, a tall slim redhead from a fairly large ERP vendor where she ran a department with 35 service consultants. Her resume was good – she had co-created the project methodology used for rapid implementations. Her background seemed perfect.

Both Julie and Jan were excited to bring Rebecca on. Rebecca would report to Jan, at least until she was up-to-speed on the product and implementation processes. Julie would help her spin up-to-speed on the product and current implementation methodology.

Julie had developed a set of "Implementation Guidelines" that had been effectively used during the intensive one-week kick-off that started each of the implementation efforts with a new customer. The week began with the customer's full implementation team in attendance including their CEO, President, or other high-ranking official who was the "owner" of the project. To make sure each team member was committed to the project's success, the project owner was requested to give opening remarks, instilling in the team the importance of this implementation project and the benefits (cost and productivity improvements) their company hoped to obtain. Then

Julie would give a demo reviewing all of the modules (User Administration, Quoting, Pricing, etc.) to give the team members a basic understanding of ProChannel. Then the team reviewed each module in more depth to understand what data needed to be collected and initially loaded into the system: product catalog, user list, pricing, current customers, etc. The team would also decide company-specific setup options such as naming conventions, categories to track (such as their customer segments and how to categorize customers), and other business options.

After the customer's implementation team was trained, a two to three month effort began, where the team gathered their company's data in spreadsheets or exported data from their ERP or legacy systems.

In parallel, the customer's IT team ordered the new hardware. Once the hardware arrived, the customer's IT team, with help from Intelic, installed the database, web server, and Intelic software on their new computers. Meanwhile, Julie and Jan worked to upload data into the customer's new ProChannel system as the data sets became available, and to verify everything was working as it should.

The process had worked well for their first few customers and Julie and Jan assumed it would be the basis for expanding the implementation process for larger and more numerous customer implementations.

However, something changed between the time Rebecca was made an offer and when she came on-board. Rebecca had convinced Stephen that Intelic's current implementation services were below par, and that Julie and Jan were doing it all wrong. Stephen was eager for a world-class company and, since Rebecca's background was services, he bent to her suggestions. One of Rebecca's suggestions was that she report directly to Stephen, instead of to Jan.

While Jan was glad to have less to worry about – product marketing, designing and developing the product, and running their IT center was more than a full-time job – she was concerned that Rebecca didn't know anything about their product. As time went on, Jan's concerns grew.

First, Rebecca not only didn't want to learn anything about the current implementation methodology, she was aloof and separate. She had requested a hard office and spent most of the day in her office, alone. She made it especially clear that she wanted no suggestions or input from Julie. Rebecca was less outspoken with Jan, since Jan was one of the co-founders. However, Julie became very distraught, and talked to Stephen about her concerns.

Stephen thought it was just female bickering. He didn't dare say that to Jan, since he was smart enough to know that would rankle her. Instead, he decided that a team building exercise was needed off-site, and planned an outing for Julie, Jan, Rebecca, and himself to play golf at the lush, private, Ruby Hills golf course where he lived.

On the afternoon of the off-site, Julie and Jan rode to Ruby Hills together, but Rebecca had a customer appointment and planned to arrive separately. Since Stephen would remain in Ruby Hills after the golf game, he also drove separately.

Since Rebecca had made it a point to interact at work with Julie and Jan as little as possible, they hadn't had any discussions about the golf game prior to when they all arrived at the golf club. Julie and Jan were in the pro shop when Rebecca arrived. The Golf Pro saw her and said, "I'm sorry, you can't golf here dressed like that!"

Rebecca had changed from her work close into dressy blue denim shorts for golf. Ruby Hills, like most private golf clubs, had a "No Denim" policy. She looked through the shorts in the Pro Shop and only saw one pair in her size. One look at the price tag, and she wasn't about to buy them. She changed back into an above-the-knee gingham jumper she had worn to work, which passed the golf club dress code, but she felt very out-of-place and embarrassed.

Stephen laughed it off and spent the afternoon working to build camaraderie amongst the team. As always, Stephen had fun. At one point, Jan was looking for her ball. She was fairly certain it had landed on the right side of the fairway, in the rough. There were no trees or other obstructions in the area, but the ball wasn't in sight. Just then Jan saw her ball, plugged down in some gushy mud, almost totally underground.

"Yuck," she said as she reached down and lifted it up to place it on some grass.

Just then Stephen came roaring up in his cart, with Rebecca hanging on tightly in the passenger seat. Stephen began yelling at Jan as he rapidly approached. "I saw that! That's cheating! You can't pick up the ball!"

Jan was very embarrassed. Although she had played golf as a child, she only recently picked golf up again, and had not refreshed herself on the many rules of golf.

"I'm sorry," she stammered feeling very chagrined. "What should I do now?"

Then Stephen broke out in a roaring laugh.

"What?" said Jan.

Rebecca was chuckling now too. "Stephen saw your ball and he ran over it with his cart," she explained.

So that was why it was stuck down in the mud. Jan rolled her eyes at Stephen, shook her head and cleaned off her ball to continue the game.

"Men!" she muttered to Julie, smiling.

Jan and Julie loved having a day off, and loved playing the beautiful Ruby Hills golf course. While Jan, Julie, and Stephen were having fun – laughing and carrying on and trying to encourage Rebecca to join in the fun – Rebecca maintained a more somber mood. Unfortunately, she had never played very much golf. Both Jan and Julie had long impressive drives (although not close to the length of Stephen's drives), and both played a good game. The contrast made Rebecca feel even more uncomfortable and singled-out.

The day didn't make much headway on the "team building" front.

Over the next few weeks, Rebecca hired a couple of team members as part of her first steps to building a top-notch professional services team.

As Halloween approached, Julie got into the spirit of the season and suggested a pumpkin-carving contest. Stephen liked the idea, as he was always looking for ways to improve team camaraderie. The developers typically brought their lunch to work, but to be sure Sales and others could do their best at arranging to be in the office, Julie sent out email notices to everyone ahead of time announcing the event. She bought several large pumpkins, and assigned teams based on organization. As the fun was underway, she looked around, and one pumpkin station was empty – professional services. She went out and found Nancy in her cubicle and said, "Hey – we're having the pumpkin carving contest now. Come on in the lunch room."

Nancy shook her head. "Rebecca said we need to finish up a briefing we're working on, and need to meet in 15 minutes in the conference room to go over it."

Just then Rebecca was walking by on her way to her own office.

"Hi there," Julie said brightly, smiling. "Come on in for the pumpkin carving contest! Everyone else has started on theirs!"

Rebecca slowed her pace down only slightly then, without a word, stared straight ahead, head up, and marched stoically by Julie, into her office, and shut the door.

Julie was trembling and came into the lunch room to grab Jan to come out in the hall with her. Jan could see the tears brimming in Julie's eyes. "I can't believe her!" Julie whispered so no one else would hear. "She hates me and she won't do anything to help build this company's team spirit!"

Jan tried to comfort her. She smiled at Julie and said, "You're doing a great job at that though! Don't let her ruin the event. Come on back in. You're the pumpkin-carving judge, after all."

Julie wiped her tears, put on a brave smile, and went in to try to get back in the mood and enjoy the fun.

Freeman and Chaiya's pumpkin won. It was definitely the most creative, although the idea of putting the large butcher knife through the pumpkin's head and running ketchup down the side like blood was a bit unnerving. Definitely macabre enough for Halloween.

Julie remained concerned that Rebecca was not good for team Intelic, and brought it up again to Stephen. Finally, tired of the conflict, Stephen brought John and Jan into his office for a discussion. Stephen's concern was that Julie was over-protective of what had been her responsibility, and may never let someone new come in and revise the process.

Stephen said, "Do I need to make a choice between Rebecca and Julie?" Stephen expressed his belief in Rebecca's experience and background, and that she had the credentials he needed to take the company to the next level in professional services.

Jan was astounded.

"What?" she said. "That wouldn't even be a choice! Julie is one of the most valuable employees we have. And I happen to agree with her. True, Julie is extremely passionate about the company, and at times that could come across as her trying to control everything. But that isn't what is happening here. I'm not sure what Rebecca has accomplished yet, and she is not helping maintain the company atmosphere we want. On the other hand, Julie is invaluable to me in product design. I don't think I can get the new features done without her industry knowledge, unless one of you two want to devote a lot of time to the design over the next few months."

Of course, neither Stephen or John had any extra bandwidth to help Jan with the product industry experience she needed to complete product design, and they could tell it was important to Jan to keep Julie on-board. Stephen started to ponder whether he was coming to the right conclusions, if Jan was as adamant as she was.

Whether Rebecca also came to the conclusion she was inadequate for the job, or if there were other circumstances, she only stayed with the company a few months. Early the next year, January 2000, she told Stephen she had decided a start-up wasn't for her, and she was returning to her prior company, taking Nancy with her.

Rebecca had made little progress during her few months at Intelic. That meant Julie had a lot more work to do to complete upcoming implementations as well as handling the customer support desk, but she was so relieved that Rebecca was gone that she quickly swung into high gear and managed to stay abreast of all the activities. Julie dusted off her Implementation Guide and processes, and was ready for the next customer implementation.

There were also struggles going on within the development group. Sales had done very well the first year, and with each sale came the need for additional product features. The workload for the developers was increasing quickly.

Work was underway on the more advanced direct inventory and order management features Diodes desired. In addition, the PMC opportunity form design work and implementation was underway.

Linear Technology had purchased the software and had negotiated displaying more information during the quoting process to allow sales reps and their managers to compare past quote pricing before determining if they should meet a customer's price request. Pop-up screens were needed displaying a searchable Quote Log containing prior quotes. In addition, increasing the types of available pricing rules was on their list.

Although the development workload was growing, Intelic had not secured another round of funding yet. Stephen remained cautious, and required strong justification on why more resources were needed before agreeing to add anyone. Stephen was of the belief that companies that hire more people than they really need never recognize they have over-hired, because employees always find work to do.

However, with all of the active customer engagements and new product development going on, Jan was able to convinced Stephen that the little development team needed to expand to meet the customers' needs.

Jan hired more developers and testers. Two new hires included Dwayne and Ling, two software engineers from Sun Microsystems.

Dwayne thought that the "right" way to develop software was to have the teams segmented so that some developers would be responsible solely for the front-end graphical presentation layer, some would focus solely on the back-end database, and some on the performance of the object-layer. He thought that application developers, like he and Ling, shouldn't have to worry about the database performance; that the database developers should be solely responsible for the database performance, so he and Ling wouldn't need to have any database expertise.

Dwayne also was convinced that the ProChannel architecture was lacking. He felt Intelic should be converting from ObjectBridge as their OR layer to "Enterprise JavaBeans" (EJBs), a new technology from Sun. Dwayne believed that converting the architecture to EJBs would leave developers like he and Ling to be free to concentrate on the business problem at hand. EJBs were rapidly being adopted for enterprise applications.

Jan disagreed for multiple reasons.

First, she felt that Intelic's success was tied to the fact that every developer was in-tune with the big picture. That they all worried about top-to-bottom performance. Yes, it meant that each of the Intelic developers needed to be smarter and better trained across-the-board, but she thought that segmentation of responsibilities gave people "outs" and let them point fingers at others. She wanted every developer to feel fully responsible for their area, and that included their screens and database performance.

Second, EJBs were new and unproven. Until EJBs had more time to be a proven architecture, Jan didn't want to drastically alter the architecture.

The other developers agreed with Jan. Before long, both Dwayne and Ling decided to return to Sun. With their departure, the development team relaxed and made more progress, all being on the same page.

Ultimately it ended up being the correct decision. As is the case for many new architectures, problems quickly appeared in the initial versions of the EJBs. Developers began finding that implementing the EJB standard was far more complex than originally thought, and returned to object-relational mapping approaches, like Intelic's. In addition, enterprise applications using EJBs incurred a performance penalty, which would have been the worst case scenario for ProChannel, where performance was key.

The use of EJBs fell out of favor quickly within the software industry. Jan was glad they had not migrated off ObjectBridge.

GROWING THE BUSINESS (1999/2000)

"Rule No. 1: Never lose money. Rule No. 2: Never forget Rule No. 1." -
Warren Buffett

With the growing number of developers, Jan convinced Stephen it was time to bring on a more senior engineering manager to help her with the development and with their internal computer systems. She was able to convince Gary to join their little company as Director of Engineering. Gary had worked with Jan at several prior companies. Gary, like Jan, had been trained as a software manager at Ford Aerospace, which gave him the same background as Jan in strong processes and effective software development techniques. At Ford Aerospace, trainers from the parent company, Ford Motor, were actively involved in their aerospace company's widespread training in Process Improvement, Employee Involvement, Supervisor Skills, and Quality.

While Jan and Gary were both at Ford Aerospace, the software industry was struggling with quality and on-time deliveries. As a result, in the mid-1980's, DARPA commissioned Carnegie Mellon to work on how to improve software. William Sweet, from the Carnegie Mellon Software Engineering Institute (SEI), worked with Ford Aerospace managers and other companies, to develop early versions of SEI's Capability Maturity Matrix (CMM). The goal of the CMM was to optimize software processes. Both Jan and Gary had worked extensively using the SEI CMM model. Jan believed that the core of the CMM model was very valuable, but for a start-up it would need to be streamlined down to the bare minimum, and made very efficient.

In addition to managing using the same methods and techniques, Gary had extensive experience building what was called "Trusted Software." Trusted Software was a requirement in highly classified systems. Building Trusted Software incorporated processes and techniques to insure multi-level data management based on "Access Control List" (ACL) concepts. The result was assurance that only the people who are supposed to see certain data could see it. Jan had managed a team of PhDs working on research projects building A-Level Secure systems, but Gary had actual hands-on experience building secure software delivered to the Air Force.

This proved invaluable in building a web-based system, where many users would be accessing the software, but not all users should view the same data. For example, semiconductor companies wanted their distributors to access the system for design registrations and quoting. However, a distributor user from Arrow should never be able to see transactions (quotes, registrations, etc.) for a different distributor company, such as Avnet. In addition, distributors worked with many manufacturers, including those carrying competing products. Thus, in addition to being a partner of the manufacturer, they were also a competitor. Strict, trusted security was needed to insure that a distributor user had very limited access to what he/she could view. Sales reps (users working for independent rep firms) had more access, but could not access (view) all data and definitely could not edit pricing, commissions, and other data. Even sales managers who worked directly for the manufacturer would be restricted based on geography and role.

The complicated security model the software used quickly differentiated it from any potential competitors, and was one of the key reasons the start-up was having success with its early sales.

Gary quickly became very proficient in complex Java coding, in addition to his management and technology skills.

John had convinced an acquaintance of his, Rich, to join the company in the customer support role. John had known Rich for years. Rich had strong semiconductor experience, having worked for several years for Avnet and Arrow. Rich, like John, Ed, and several board members, was also a prior racecar driver. In addition, Ed, their original pricing expert and one of the first employees at Intelic, was Rich's father-in-law. Ed had since retired.

Rich reported to Julie at first, but Rich quickly ramped up. Soon Julie was able to focus more on professional services and product design, which she loved. Rich became the Manager of Customer Support.

As part of the Sales effort, Jan, John, and Stephen traveled to the East Coast. Both John and Stephen traveled so extensively they were able to upgrade both themselves and Jan to First Class seats. Jan and Stephen sat behind John. Stephen whispered to Jan, "Watch this!" Then he proceeded to talk in a fairly loud but muffled voice, making sure only a few random words could actually be heard by John.

"Did you know [mumble, mumble, mumble] John [mumble, mumble, mumble]. I was very surprised but they said [mumble, mumble, mumble], and John [mumble, mumble, mumble] …"

It was hilarious. Jan could see John go from not paying attention at all, to starting to lean back to hear more. He then became more rigid, as he strained to hear. Then he caught on that it was one of Stephen's typical jokes, and turned around to yell (in fun) at Stephen. They were all in an uproar, laughing.

They landed in Boston. John had arranged for a rental car, and the three drove to Portland, Maine. Jan had never been to Maine before. It was icy and cold. They stopped for dinner at DiMillo's On the Water - an old, large boat that had been turned into a floating restaurant.

The next morning they headed to Fairchild's offices for a sales call. Fairchild had hired a third party consultant to help with the software purchase decision. One of Fairchild's requirements was to run the system on Sun Unix computers. While ProChannel currently only ran on Windows, because Jan had known other companies would want other options, the software was Java-based. Java was not only a portable language, but was a language originally developed by Sun. In addition, all third party tools their system needed were selected for their ability to run cross-platform. She was confident that running on Sun Unix would pose no major issues.

In reviewing the recommended hardware configuration, she thought that the consultant firm was proposing hardware requirements much larger than Fairchild would actually need. But Jan knew many IT managers go overboard on equipment rather than needing to potentially upgrade later when data sets and users increased. If Intelic won Fairchild, Intelic would need to purchase and install Sun computers, to verify the software worked as planned and potentially make some minor porting changes before delivering it to Fairchild.

The meeting went well, but Fairchild was very early in their decision-making process.

After the Fairchild meeting, Stephen, John, and Jan drove back to Boston, where John had arranged for them to go to the Boston Celtics game versus the Miami Heat that evening. The stadium was close enough that they could walk to the game from their hotel. Prior to the start of the game, there was a moving ceremony, honoring the Boston fireman lost in a recent tragedy.

The next day, they drove to the office of Analog Devices Inc., outside Boston. There was a large meeting with many ADI personnel in attendance. Stephen was an outstanding presenter, and painted a picture of the value Intelic could bring to ADI's business. As he did his sales presentation, John watched from the back of the room to determine "buy-signs," and watch for any concerns.

One major item ADI was interested in was mobile use of the system. Although ProChannel was a web-based system, thus accessible from anywhere, ADI's current legacy system had the ability for the sales rep to download a copy of the Design Registration form, so the rep could update it using his/her laptop while traveling, off the Internet. This was an era before wireless WiFi was prevalent and before WiFi was available on airplanes.

Both John and Stephen were in "Sales Mode." Jan had joined Intelic because John had proven what he often said, "My word is my bond." She had also found in dealing with Stephen, that he was always open and honest.

However, salesmen tend to leverage fuzziness to their advantage. Not to mislead, but to avoid slowing down a sale for minor reasons, which could most likely be addressed later. Jan could also tell that, because ProChannel was a web-based application, the answer to the stated question, "Can the system be used remotely?" could be answered by Stephen, "Yes." Because "remote" can also mean out-of-the-office at home on your modem.

However, Jan knew that what ADI was looking for was the ability to make off-line updates, then synchronize back to the main server when the sales rep was again online.

To-date, the company had been very successful selling what actually existed, not selling "vaporware" like other software companies. Vaporware is software that has not yet been built, but sales pitches it as if it already exists. Vaporware is different from the sale to QuickLogic, because QuickLogic knew the software was being built. Similarly Diodes knew the inventory and other features they wanted were not yet in the release. With vaporware, the customer believes the feature being touted is currently in the available release.

Also, mobility seemed to be an important point for ADI, not one that they would accept a quick "Yes" or "No," and then move on. Jan was worried that if a "Yes" answer were given too hastily, the ADI team would ask the more detailed questions anyway, which would put the Intelic team in a bind.

So Jan quickly jumped in and said, "I'd like to answer that, but first can you describe in more detail how your legacy system operates remotely?"

An ADI representative gave them a quick run-down of their "Mobility" module. It was what Jan thought, and while it was a feature they did not have in the product, it didn't sound like too big a stretch to build. The ProChannel software was so clean, with such a small footprint, that the entire system plus a small database could be loaded on the Intelic sales reps laptops to run stand-alone for demo purposes. The trick would be to have a download system that would filter out a large company like ADI's huge dataset to just what that sales rep needed, and then have a synchronization process to merge changes back into the main system when the sales rep returned.

"Would you be willing to share with us your current legacy software as a model?" She didn't plan on reusing their software, since it was built on a Microsoft Access Database and was not written in Java, but she thought that would give them a good start in learning what tricks the ADI developers had already learned in building their version. ADI was more than willing to accommodate that arrangement.

The Intelic team asked for a quick break and brainstormed their options. Jan had a pretty good idea about how long it would take to build it. Based on the size of the ADI deal, the cost was a good trade-off. Stephen was worried that, with their other commitments, Jan thought it would take six months before it could be made available. Stephen fretted that her forthrightness could slow down the deal. But Jan thought it was much better to take that risk than win the deal and then have ADI find out they were only talking about standard web-based access, not a real off-line solution.

After the break, the ADI group re-assembled. "We can definitely build a mobile solution for you," Stephen began. "What would your timing be on needing that?"

The ADI team was ecstatic. "We don't need it right away," their representative shared. "We can use ours in the interim since we plan to interface our legacy system with yours until we can update and train all of our reps. That will take at least a year. So with your commitment to build our mobility solution, the Intelic product will satisfy all of our needs, and we can phase out our legacy software over the next year."

Jan breathed a sigh of relief, happy her forthrightness had not jeopardized the sale, but instead had improved their chances.

The last hurdle was to pass the scrutiny of ADI's IT security experts. When discussing security with ADI's security experts, Jan was able to leverage her experience at Ford Aerospace managing the research of four PhDs building secure systems and analyzing complex security issues. In addition, with Gary on-board, who had managed building government multi-level secure software, although ProChannel was not "formally" multi-level secure, it was designed to provide the best state-of-the-art security that commercial internet systems required. She felt comfortable discussing security with the IT gurus, and was able to convince them there was little or no security risk to adding ProChannel into their suite of IT software.

The ADI deal was soon signed, including the new software module, Mobility.

Stephen and John were sometimes worried that putting Jan, an engineer, in front of customers would give customers too much information and slow down their sales process. Jan remained confident that being open with the customer is the best policy, and that the sales can be aggressive as long as the engineering team knows they can deliver what the customer is expecting – the features and the schedule.

With more customers coming online, Rich had hired Lei for database support and Ashraf to help with customer calls. As his team became busier, Rich suggested that instead of making the customers call in their issues and concerns on the telephone, or interface by email, Intelic would be providing better customer support if customers had access to an online tool to report issues and enhancement requests. With such a tool, Rich's team could provide more rapid feedback than using voicemail and email.

Rich felt Intelic was getting a lot of value from using SD Tracker as an internal tool. He proposed a new SD Tracker module to be used for customer calls. Using ProChannel's security filter, the new Call Tracker would be secure. Each customer contact could view only their company's calls. Rich also suggested adding an internal comments feature where only Intelic employees could see internal comments as well as the external comments that all, including the customer, could see. Rich felt that such a tool would let customers track and view online all of their requests, including a history of discussions – all of the same benefits the Intelic was getting from SD Tracker.

Everyone thought it was a great idea. Because it would leverage the features of SD Tracker and ProChannel, it would not take a lot of time to build. They had a new summer intern, Micah, who needed to learn the ProChannel architecture, and working on the new Call Tracker would give him that training. Besides, their summer intern was inexpensive and quick. Stephen agreed.

Rich immediately wrote down requirements while Micah worked to make a clone of the SD Tracker module to modify into a new Call Tracker module.

In addition to the Call Tracker screens, Micah added an FTP (File Transfer Protocol) site for QA to post new releases of the software and related documentation that the customers could download. The FTP Download site was filtered to let the customers view and access only the software and documentation they had purchased. In addition, the customers could upload copies of their database, logs, and other files to give to customer support when trouble-shooting issues.

Rich and his support team also worked on an FAQ feature for frequently asked questions.

Micah soon had the new Call Tracker ready for customers to use. After Rich and his team tested it thoroughly, they put it online for customers. Thorough testing of anything that the customer would see, whether product or tool, was important for maintaining Intelic's professional image. Intelic might still be a small company, but their customers were huge semiconductor manufacturers who assumed Intelic was much larger than it was, based on the breadth of the product and professionalism of its support and services teams.

The customers loved Call Tracker and their new ability to log issues, enhancement requests, and questions online.

Jan liked the improvements for customer support, and knew

customer support was an important part of winning new sales.

When Jan worked at ASK Computers, a Gartner analyst was talking to the ASK CEO and management team. ASK had acquired the Ingres relational database company a few years earlier. Jan had loved using Ingres when she was at Ford Aerospace, and considered it far superior technology to any of the other, then-popular, relational databases. However, the ASK/Ingres division was not making its sales numbers, so Amal, the ASK CEO, had asked the Gartner consultant to review the sales history and give them advice.

"It's an interesting situation," the Gartner consultant reported to the ASK management team. "In vendor evaluation situations, time after time, when companies are comparing Ingres against Oracle, the Ingres technology wins hands down."

"However," he continued, "when it comes to customer support, Ingres fails and the customer ends up buying Oracle."

In parallel to acquiring new customers, Stephen and John had been working on obtaining Series B financing. As with Series A, the goal was to raise money solely from Angel Investors, and not approach any VCs. They were successful, raising $2 million from Angel Investors by November 1999.

In December, Release 2.0 was completed, which contained the additional Order Management and Inventory Tracking upgrades Diodes wanted. Diodes quickly upgraded to Release 2.0.

Release 2.0 also included the PMC Opportunity Form, and PMC went live on Release 2.0 in February 2000. It was now only a year and a half since Intelic first opened its doors. The company had been able to hire, deliver four releases (0.5, 1.0, 1.1, and 2.0), and had three customers live and several other customer deals closed or in process. Each of the four releases had expanded the footprint in accordance with John's original product vision, plus incorporated customer needs and suggestions to evolve the product even further. The clean and simple architecture was proving itself to be robust, scalable, and maintainable.

The Linear Technology enhancements were made available in

Release 2.2 and Linear Tech went live on 2.2 in March. By June, ADI went live on Design Registrations, knowing their Mobility module would be available in the next major release.

Early in 2000, Intelic signed another new customer, SaRonix, a manufacturer of crystal and clock chips. Jan, Julie, and Malcolm, a new services lead, went to the SaRonix offices for their first discussion prior to starting the implementation meetings.

As the three of them were waiting in the SaRonix conference room, Malcolm noticed in the center of the large oak conference table, a velvet box with several crystal chips. He was fascinated, and picked one up to get a closer look. SNAP! It broke in half. Just then the SaRonix team came into the conference room. Malcolm looked up with a terrified look on his face, holding the two halves of the chip in separate hands.

"I broke it," he stammered. "How expensive is it?"

"Oh," the SaRonix lead smiled, "just a couple of hundred dollars."

"I'll pay for it," offered Malcolm quickly.

The SaRonix team laughed. "That's $200 to buy one. They only cost us a few dollars to make. Don't worry about it."

"Whew," Malcolm breathed out a sigh of relief.

The meeting proceeded well. Julie gave an overview of the implementation process, what types of SaRonix representatives should be part of the implementation team, and other information.

During the initial meetings, Claire, one of the SaRonix team members, asked about the options for displaying inventory in ProChannel. When SAP had been implemented at SaRonix a year earlier, the implementation project overran the budget and the complex SAP Inventory Module was not fully implemented. SAP tracked the number of parts in the warehouse, and a report of the inventory was generated nightly. But there was no real-time available-to-promise (ATP) function. Jan described the possible ProChannel options. If the ATP function was working in SAP, ProChannel had an ATP interface to allow a user to view the SAP ATP data real-time.

Or they could upload and display the nightly SAP inventory report in ProChannel. One other option was to upload the nightly report and then use ProChannel to calculate inventory on-the-fly during the day based on new shipments and any manual adjustments, the feature Intelic had built for Diodes. Claire thought SaRonix users could benefit by turning on the ProChannel calculations to view more accurate inventory on-line.

Two weeks later the formal implementation team meetings began. They had been discussing the Order Management module and the option of using ProChannel to calculate inventory independent of SAP.

"What?" their IT Manager exploded. "What do you mean that your system calculates inventory ATP? That would be just stupid. That's the job of the ERP, our SAP system."

Jan agreed with him in theory that the ProChannel CRM software should not try to do the job of major ERP modules, particularly for large manufacturing companies. She was about to explain that the feature was developed for a customer whose older back office couldn't manage their inventory, and could provide useful information for SaRonix users since SAP ATP was not available, when the IT Manager interrupted. "What's the matter with you people! Don't you know anything about enterprise systems?" he yelled.

Jan was both infuriated at his tirade and embarrassed by his attack. She was even more embarrassed for the Claire, who had brought up the suggestion, and was getting the brunt of his tirade. Jan and Claire had already discussed that ProChannel could support SAP ATP if SAP were complete. There was no reason for his bullishness.

Fortunately, the IT Manager was a short-term consultant and not part of the full-time implementation team. SaRonix management did not want to invest any more in SAP functionality, and decided to simply display the nightly inventory snapshot in ProChannel. The rest of the implementation went smoothly, and SaRonix was happy with the final result.

EXPANDING THE TEAM

"Talent wins games, but teamwork and intelligence win championships." -
Michael Jordan

Freeman had always wanted to move back to San Diego. He'd told Jan that was his dream when she first hired him out of college. He reiterated it when she was trying to convince him to join Intelic. To sweeten the deal, she had told Freeman if he stayed long enough at Intelic to get the product and development underway, she would work on getting him relocated.

Jan had gotten permission from Stephen to start a remote development lab in San Diego, and Freeman was promoted to be the manager of a small 4-person development team. It was a win-win. Besides making Freeman happy, they had been having trouble finding engineers in Silicon Valley, and there were available engineers in San Diego for less pay.

Jan was impressed how quickly Freeman set up the office in San Diego, since he had no prior experience doing so. He had found a small office space that met Stephen's cost guidelines. He brought in second-hand cubicle walls and installed them. He rented a copier, central networking equipment, central server, and other office necessities. He hired two engineers from San Diego, and was bringing them up-to-speed.

Stephen and Jan decided to pay him a visit and check out their new remote office.

They flew to San Diego. Stephen rented a car and they drove to the new office. Freeman walked down to the carport area to greet them as they were pulling in.

"Park here," he motioned to an empty space.

Stephen and Jan got out of the car when Stephen noticed that while the space they were parked in was unlabeled, some spaces had company names painted on the entrance to the stalls. Then he raised his eyebrows and motioned to one of the parking stalls.

One of the parking stalls had "FREEMAN" written in bold white letters.

"I didn't know the landlord was going to have a stall painted for us or I would have given him the name of the company," Freeman quickly explained.

"You've got your own parking spot, eh?" Stephen joked.

They went up to the office area Freeman had rented. It was cute with its own little lunch area, network and fax equipment on a counter, and there was a small room with six cubicles.

"Looks great," commended Stephen.

Freeman was traveling from San Diego to San Jose for a week to attend engineering meetings. It was good to have Freeman back in town. He was going to be arriving that evening. Intelic had hired several new developers. Freeman would be giving them briefings on the system architecture, and spend time working with them.

Jan arrived early the next day and Freeman was in the lobby looking kind of bleary-eyed.

"Freeman," she said, "what are you doing here so early?"

"I slept here." Freeman said.

"What? Didn't you get a hotel?"

"I was going to, but forgot to get a reservation. I remembered that those new leather couches looked comfy, so I thought I'd just sleep here. It would have been nice if you guys had a pillow or a blanket somewhere."

"You're crazy," Jan said. But she made a mental note that they should have some blankets in the building. "Do you have a room for the rest of the week?"

"I'll get one," said Freeman. "It wasn't that comfortable in the lobby."

Freeman freshened up and went to meet the new engineers.

Stephen arrived after attending a sales call and found his desk drawer filled with popcorn. A picture of someone holding a bag of popcorn was left at the scene. The person's face was cut off so he couldn't tell who it was.

Stephen was furious. He had been out of his office the prior afternoon and thought someone had sneaked in then. At night and in the morning, his office had been locked.

Stephen saw Madhu and Chaiya in the hall. Chaiya was always quite a prankster.

"You two – into my office," he commanded.

Neither had a clue what the issue was.

He showed them the evidence - popcorn in his drawer, the photograph - but they both pleaded ignorance.

He then saw a tile in the ceiling that wasn't quite in place and suspected that someone had come in through the ceiling. He remembered that Freeman was flying up for the week and was arriving the night before.

"Freeman," he yelled.

Freeman came into the office.

"Did you do this?" he asked.

"Aw, you caught me," Freeman admitted.

"Don't you know these are private files with important company business? And some now have butter on them!" Stephen was obviously upset.

Actually, Freeman hadn't considered that. He and a friend had dinner the night before and thought it sounded fun to crawl up into the ceiling area and drop down into Stephen's office to do a little prank.

"Don't do that again!" warned Stephen.

Freeman felt he was on the verge of being fired, so there were no pranks for a while.

Freeman had wanted to ask Stephen for something, but decided to wait a few days until Stephen cooled off.

Before Freeman left town, he went in to make his pitch. He'd asked Jan, but she said he'd better go directly to Stephen with this one.

"I want to buy a foosball table," he said.

"Let me think about that – no," said Stephen.

Undaunted, Freeman continued. "It's not for me. I'm struggling with how to get my developers working together better. They bring in their own lunches, and eat in their cubicles. No one wants to go out to eat. Clara comes in, is quietly at work, and leaves at 5 p.m. every day to go home to her children. Richard and Duy have nothing in common. I thought if we had a foosball table, I could challenge them to a game during lunch, get them out of their cubicles, and start to build some team spirit."

Now he had Stephen's attention.

"How much would it cost?" asked Stephen.

Freeman handed him the paper with the ad for the used foosball table.

"OK," said Stephen. "Go build that team."

A month later Freeman reported back.

"Thanks, Steve," he said. "It's going really well now. Clara won't play very often, but Duy and Richard are really having fun, and we are all getting to know each other better. Even Clara is talking more. It's working."

Besides staffing in development and services, Stephen decided he, himself, needed to step away from the day-to-day marketing efforts since he was so busy in his CEO role. Up until now, he had participated extensively in product design and marketing. Jan was always amazed at his bandwidth and ability to handle so many roles.

George was hired as the new Marketing Director. George had a booming voice, so Jan was glad his office was in the Sales wing of the Ringwood office building where his telephone conversations were at least a little muffled.

Stephen organized the first sales offsite, held in Santa Cruz at the Pasatiempo Golf Resort. It included the sales team, new Marketing Director, and the three co-founders.

The resort had cute cabin-like rooms and an airy conference room for their sales meeting. The outing was planned to include a round of golf - a common activity for sales and marketing folks, but something Jan had just recently had the opportunity to be involved with. Engineers usually aren't invited to sales and marketing golf outings. The night they all arrived, they got together in John's cabin for poker. It was apparently the normal sales outing. Jay brought a large bag of poker chips for the event. They laughed and had fun. However, Stephen wasn't about to turn this into a "just for pleasure" outing. They were instructed to meet the next morning at 8 a.m. sharp.

George was running a little late, but Stephen started anyway. They reviewed the year's accomplishments, next year's plans, and company mission statements. As usual, Stephen was well prepared and had a wealth of information and business insight to share with the team. Jan was disappointed and a bit concerned that, in addition to being late, once George showed up, he didn't seem to be participating very much.

The next day they got up early again, and headed to the DeLaveaga Golf Course in Santa Cruz for a round of golf. Afterwards, over lunch, Stephen was giving a briefing on marketing trends and sales results when he looked over and George's head was nodding. He was fast asleep. This infuriated Stephen.

No one was surprised when George did not show up at work a few weeks later. He had been let go. Stephen was never one to keep an unproductive worker on-board.

Lesson learned – don't fall asleep during the CEO's presentation. Especially before you prove your worth to the company. Bad form.

PRACTICAL SOFTWARE

"He who is best prepared can best serve his moment of inspiration." - Samuel Taylor Coleridge

Jan and Gary entered the Conference Room to attend the SDRB.

"I'm glad there's an SDRB today," Gary said. That surprised Jan because Gary, like most engineers, didn't like meetings, but was required to attend the SDRB as Director of Engineering.

"Why are you glad?" asked Jan.

"Because one of our new developers is out of work, and I need some bugs to give him to fix," replied Gary.

The more senior developers were working on more complex features. Junior developers were typically first assigned some SD Tracker fixes or smaller ProChannel bug fixes during their first months as learning exercises while they came up-to-speed on the architecture, development principals, and guidelines used at Intelic.

As the SDRB assembled, Gregg, the QA Manager, turned on the projector to start going through the SD Tracker list of new bugs reported.

The only SDRs on their list today were a few enhancement requests and some requests to have customer support to make data updates, but no new bug reports.

"Sorry, Gary," said Jan. "Looks like the current release is now quite stable."

"Sorry we don't have any bugs for your new developer, but our customers aren't finding anything new," said Jan. Her next sentence was, of course, captured in Gary's notes, and she saw it pop up later as a new quotable quote:

"They [our customers] are all happy. This is a problem. – Jan"

Quality was very important to Jan. Maybe it came from her time and training at Ford Aerospace where the parent company, Ford Motor's motto was "Quality is Job One." Or maybe it was because Jan just thought customers deserved software that was reliable.

Intelic's process was to fix all issues found when testing the current major enhancement release in order to have a clean release. Only if a bug was found during the final few days of testing prior to the release date, so late that fixing it may jeopardize the release date, would there even be a question of whether to fix it now or fix it later. If found too late to fix without schedule impact, the team would determine if it was a bug their customers would likely encounter, in which case it still had to be fixed and the team worked overtime if needed. If it was a lower-level or obscure issue, the team would assess if it could wait to be fixed in the first maintenance release. Usually the team was able to fix all bugs found by QA in time to ship the release on time, bug-free.

To avoid getting into the situation of running out of time to fix bugs found near the end of testing, one of Jan's management approaches was that once the team was more than halfway through a release, Jan and the engineering managers would review the release to see if it was on-track.

In aerospace and defense companies, tracking time estimates occurred constantly. Developers were required to spend a great deal of time estimating their coding projects initially, and then updating schedules regularly. If developers missed their estimate, and schedules slid, some managers became hostile, and teams worked overtime.

Jan didn't want to impose that kind of rigor and burden, knowing estimates are just that, estimates. But she did want to know mid-way through if the project wasn't on-track in order to have time to make adjustments: time to either remove some features or negotiate a longer schedule. Continuing to develop and making the schedule date by squeezing time out of testing at the end wasn't an option.

The three "Fuzzy Ps" concept Jan had learned about when at Ford Aerospace (that to manage software projects, one had to balance People, Plan, and Product) had been incorporated into SD Tracker and Intelic's software process. Those three are the only viable axes in the world of software that can be controlled and still produce a quality product.

Many software companies say that besides the 3 Ps, another trade-off can be made, and that is quality.

"How can quality be a trade-off?" Jan asked when she heard that was a consideration by some managers. "Software managers know that bugs found by a customer are many times more costly to fix than bugs found during the design and development process. If an issue is found during the initial design and planning, changing the design would only take a few minutes – say it would cost $10 to fix. If it is found later in the midst of the development effort, it will cost a couple of hours to go back to the Product Manager (PM) to verify the design and fix the code, or $100 to fix. If found in the final testing, it costs $1,000 to fix - to go back to the PM to verify the design, re-code, and re-test. And the same issue found by the customer costs $10,000 to fix. Those issues found by customers need to go back to verify the design, re-code, changes are likely to cause other issues, testing needs to be re-done, manuals updated, and other customers need to be notified. It is a very expensive proposition. Not only that, it affects the customers' perception of the software vendor and its software."

Bottom line, Jan believed, the trade-off should never be quality. Good software managers need to watch their Ps and their Q.

The SD Tracker form had two fields to track the total development hours and the development hours left to complete. When starting a new release, developers would enter their total time estimates for each SDR assigned to them. These were often very rough estimates, but helped the managers determine the feature list and release date. When a release status review was needed, the engineering managers would ask their team to update their open SDRs with estimates of hours left to complete.

A "Release Status" tool had been added to SD Tracker that used the developer hours left on each SDR, plus any upcoming holiday or planned vacation time, and based on the percent confidence the manager had in the schedule, the tool would calculate the date when the code would be completed. If the schedule was calculated using 100 percent confidence, that meant the developers were able to spend 100 percent of their time on development. However, that doesn't consider unexpected meetings, illness, or unforeseen difficulty with the code. Jan had found, through the years, that using 60 percent confidence provided the most accurate estimate of when the code would be complete. Developers could give realistic but aggressive estimates rather than trying to inflate their estimates to protect themselves from any unexpected event. However, even at 60 percent, schedules were still aggressive, and at times developers needed to work long hours to make the date. They were a start-up, after all. Managing the timeline using percent confidence, plus realistic estimates, gave managers a more accurate understanding of the amount of work the team could accomplish.

Two other SD Tracker fields tracked total QA hours and QA hours left. A similar analysis for QA would determine how long it would take after the code was complete to perform final testing. This determined the expected release date.

Using 60 percent as the confidence in their Release Status tool was a fairly accurate reflection of real life. This gave Jan and her managers repeatable success meeting schedules, and gave Intelic a good track record of on-time releases.

If the release date had to be firm due to customer commitments, and if halfway through the release the Release Status tool calculated that, even with a more aggressive, higher percent confidence, they could not make the release date, Jan could be quite draconian in her use of a red pen (figuratively speaking) to cut out less important features to make sure the release schedule was met, including allowing for sufficient test time.

If the release schedule was less firm and the Release Status tool calculated a release date after the planned schedule, Intelic management would need to decide which was more important: To include all planned features (the Product "P") and accept the schedule risk (the Plan "P"), or remove some features. Those were the only options. Big companies, like Ford Aerospace, could move developers from one program to another if needed. But there wasn't an option at Intelic to bring in more resources for the current release (the People "P"). It took several months before a new developer was up-to-speed and productive. Reducing test time and releasing with known bugs (affecting quality) was not an option at Intelic. There were only two axes to work with. The only options were to remove features or to accept a potential schedule slip.

ProChannel wasn't software going into space, so unlike her aerospace projects, the budget for QA couldn't possibly guarantee that there would never, ever be any bugs. If a company is building software that will be controlling a satellite in space, then the testing required is more rigorous than earth-based software because fixing a bug in space is extraordinarily expensive, if even possible. For aerospace companies, the testing phase covers absolutely every path possible through the software. For a commercial software company, it is not feasible to test every path possible through the code. The cost of the software would be astronomically high. However, a commercial company could reasonably test the paths they knew their customer's users would take based on common business processes.

The size of the QA staff was determined by the amount of testing that was deemed reasonable to provide a consistently high product quality. A good rule-of-thumb is that the number of testers should be between 30 percent to 50 percent of the number of developers to provide high-quality commercial software. The percent can be lower the first few years. As the product grows and supports more business functions, more testers are needed to do more

IT STARTS WITH AN IDEA

regression testing. Since the Intelic developers were focused on quality, Jan never found the need for a 1:1 ratio of testers to developers that some, in the software industry, believed was needed.

Given a fixed number of testers, and using the Release Status tool, the QA manager could estimate how long it would take to test all of the new functionality in a release. He would add to that the time to regression test the important business functions by the expected release date. That was why it was so important, when the schedule was firm, to review the release status mid-way through the release cycle, to ensure confidence that software development can complete with enough time remaining for sufficient testing.

Too many software companies continue to code to complete the requested features and, at the end, cut back on the testing time. At Intelic, once code was checked in, QA needed the time to execute their test plans and close every SDR. The schedule needed to also include sufficient time for developers to fix any issues QA found.

Jan felt there were really only three options when a bug was reported in code about to be released: (1) Fix it now, (2) fix it in the first maintenance release six weeks later, but only if it was a minor issue that wouldn't impact any business process or slow down sales users, or (3) determine the item was not anything that needed to ever be fixed - not a real bug. For example, adding 100,000 daily News items (one displayed per day) caused a memory issue. But it would take 350 years before that limit was reached, so it was deemed to be not a real bug. Any SDR like that would be assigned to the "Future" release, a release the SDRB joked should be named "Not in your lifetime," or closed as NFW. The first few ProChannel releases had no bugs in "Future." Even after many years, very few of these "Bug" SDRs had accumulated in the "Future" release.

The second option (to wait and fix the bug in the first maintenance release) was rarely needed. The Intelic team preferred to get the problem fixed. In general, they all felt that any bug found during testing should be fixed before the product is shipped.

To Jan, a "no bugs" policy seemed obvious. However, many

154

companies don't follow the same policy.

At one commercial software company, each developer kept a list of bugs he or she knew existed in their code, in a folder in their desk drawer. Only the bugs customers reported were entered into the company's bug tracking system and used for quality metrics. The reported bugs were a small fraction of the bugs the developers knew existed. The unreported issues became critical when customers encountered them. Instead, Jan believed, all known bugs should be entered in the company's bug tracking system, so issues can be fixed before customers find them.

At another company, software was regularly released with a large list of "Known Bugs." The "Known Bugs" list was included in the Release Notes with each release. To Jan, that made no sense at all. If you know about the bug, fix it. If you don't fix it, then the bug list continues to grow. That company spent a great deal of ongoing engineering time sorting through the huge bug list, prioritizing the bugs, and assigning the biggest issues to maintenance releases. Meanwhile, the total number of bugs that existed in the product continued to grow. The software team was bogged down in a continually growing pile of bugs.

The company's VP of Engineering said to Jan, "I don't believe you released your software with no known bugs. That isn't possible! All software has bugs."

Unfortunately, that is one of the fallacies commonly believed in the software industry. Because of that, it is a common practice in the software industry to consider quality one of the items that can be traded-off.

Letting quality slide is a slippery slope. If no one is tracking the overall quality metrics, quality can slide without anyone noticing until the product has degraded to the point the customers rebel. Take for example the Microsoft operating system, when the "blue screen of death" was a common occurrence. That was an accepted byproduct of the belief, "All software has bugs."

A growing backlog of bugs is often caused when a software company continually tries to produce more features than their team can handle. While Intelic was very aggressive in the number of new features and modules, because of the management expertise and team commitment, they were able to release software with "No Known Bugs."

Prior to the final test period which started after all code was checked in, testing was ongoing throughout the release. Jan and, as they grew, other product designers, reviewed the product changes as new functions were developed, working with the developers throughout the release.

As soon as functions were completed and checked into the code management system, QA could also begin testing those new features. They didn't need to wait for the entire release to be completed, as was the process when using the Waterfall Methodology. The early review and testing helped find any issues during the development cycle, reducing the number that would be found in the final testing phase.

This iterative approach allowed the team to produce software faster, and more in-line with the business requirements.

Another part of the test phase was to test installation and upgrade scenarios. For each release, Jan created a "Conversion Guide," including a step-by-step walkthrough of what needed to be done for a customer to upgrade from a prior release to this new release, including any customer-specific data preparation needed for prior to the day of the upgrade. Most data would be automatically upgraded using their data migration tool, but customer-specific data may need special handling.

Several customers would provide an export of their production data for migration testing. QA, together with customer support, would take the data and run through the upgrade from a prior release to the new release using the Conversion Guide. Everything was done to make the customer experience as clean and easy as possible.

In particular, the time it took for an upgrade to occur was important. The requirement was to be able to upgrade production servers within twelve hours on the weekend. Jan didn't want her customers to have to manage through an upgrade process that ran multiple days and nights, like Varian had to do when upgrading SAP.

ProChannel was typically able to be upgraded in a much shorter timeframe than 12 hours. The team tried to obtain production databases from their largest customers to test upgrade times. If upgrade time was slow, the engineers would identify which data conversion scripts took the longest, and would optimize and streamline those scripts in order to make the conversion as quick as possible.

Near the end of each release, Jan prepared a "Release Handbook," for internal use. The handbook included the list of new features, test results, and any issues with the release. Preparing the handbook was not very time consuming, since all of the information was in SD Tracker. Jan liked adding the page in the section titled "Known Bugs" that said "None."

The Release Handbook was circulated and signed-off by the head of each Intelic organization before the release was shipped. Stephen liked the process so he could easily double-check the quality status, and so that all of his management team was cognizant of the new features and release status.

In addition, Julie and Jan prepared formal Release Notes to send to the customers.

Besides Intelic's process concerning enhancement releases, Intelic had a clear process regarding maintenance releases. As customers installed the new enhancement release or turned on new features or implemented a new business process, new issues would sometimes be found. New customer implementations invariably identified new ways of using the software that hadn't been thought of before, hence was not part of the test scenarios.

After the enhancement release was shipped, the bug backlog was kept under control by fixing all new bugs customers found in regularly scheduled maintenance releases. New bugs found by customers would typically have been introduced in the recently implemented code, hence were easier to fix sooner than later. If not fixed right away, bugs could be years old and the code may have changed significantly. Many software companies don't follow this simple process and put bugs in a pile to address sometime in the future. That is not a good process.

At Intelic, the first maintenance release would ship approximately six weeks after a major enhancement release and contain fixes for all bugs encountered. The team waited six weeks because most customers don't take the initial release immediately. Customers try to wait for other customers to go first.

Every four weeks thereafter, a maintenance release would be shipped for other newly found bugs. Typically each maintenance release had less bugs than the prior release, and after four or six maintenance releases, the software became stable.

After software stabilization, only if a new customer implementation occurred would new fixes be needed. After the stabilization release, the bug fixes could be sent as another maintenance release or, if the problem affected only the one new customer's business process, a one-off patch would be sent, since the other customers were satisfied and were not encountering any problems.

Other companies end up with piles of open bugs. Some try to address their huge bug list by dividing the engineering organization into developers who develop new code versus the teams that only do maintenance.

At Intelic, the developer who owned the module (typically the developer who broke the code) fixed his or her own bugs. To Jan, that was more efficient than having a separate maintenance team, since the developer who owned the module would be more knowledgeable about his or her code. In addition, it seemed appropriate to have a developer fix his or her bugs as a learning experience about what they had coded that had caused the breakage.

The other advantage of this approach was that it didn't create two classes of developers: prima donnas who are elite and work on only new code versus lower-level coders who do maintenance only. Every developer had the opportunity to work on new product in addition to maintaining their own code.

This approach did mean that Intelic was pickier about the developers hired, because even junior developers had to have the potential to ramp up quickly to take on the more complex development assignments and thrive. The result was the Intelic engineering team was extremely high caliber, and very committed to product quality.

When Intelic had first started having SDRB meetings, lively debates would often occur with the engineering representatives, Arun and Gary, saying, "That's not a bug – development didn't do anything wrong. Look, the code does exactly what it's supposed to do. Look at the spec!"

Jan would agree, "No one has ever wanted the code to do THAT before. We never designed for that scenario. That's not a bug – it's a new feature. The customer will have to wait for an enhancement release. We can't put enhancements in a maintenance release."

The reason for that rule was that all other customers who were currently in production that wanted bug fixes couldn't take a maintenance release that also included enhancements. Enhancement changes could alter the way their businesses functioned, and cause the customer to need to go back and redo implementation work. Customers wanted a clean and quick bug fix release requiring minimal testing.

"But," argued Rich, representing customer support, "the customer is saying that it is a common business practice, and that our software should already be supporting it. Without a code change, they will be getting the wrong information, and can't rely on the product. It's a big deal."

This typically occurred during new customer implementations, as the professional services team worked to configure the software to the new customer's business processes.

Customers who had purchased ProChannel and were now implementing, couldn't wait for the next enhancement release. That could be six to nine months away. However, the engineering rule was, "No new enhancements in a maintenance release."

But the requests being made by Rich were items most customers perceived as a bug. Because of that, all customers would also want it fixed as quickly as possible. The customer considered it a bug.

Gary and Arun were right, though. It wasn't a "bug." A bug would mean a developer made a mistake, and that would add a bad mark for quality software.

To solve the dilemma the SDRB added a third classification to the tracking system:

1) "Bug" for true defects – code that doesn't match the spec.
2) "Enh" for enhancement requests – new features to be spec'd.
3) "Gap" for issues the customers consider a bug, but items that were not in any spec or part of any discussion between the spec writer and the developers.

Having a third classification let all of the SDRB members agree on how to quickly disposition customer issues without having arguments. The SDRs that Rich (representing the customer) and Jan (representing engineering) used to fight about simply became a "Gap."

In addition, Jan found that when only true bugs are classified as "Bugs," developers readily take responsibility for fixing their bugs, resulting in better accountability. Accountability encourages better teamwork. "Gaps" were Jan's responsibility as the product designer, something she missed in gathering requirements. Developers were happy to add those to the code, without any blame.

The classifications also improved Intelic's ability to be responsive to customer requests. Depending on the extent of the fix, Gaps could be part of a maintenance release, since customers considered them a bug. If the change would affect any current customers' business processes, a property would be added defaulting to the current business process. Hence existing customers would see no change unless they decided to take advantage of the new feature.

Allowing Gaps in a maintenance release expedited the Gap's delivery more than being classified as an enhancement would since enhancements required a major release. Customer satisfaction was improved.

As Intelic grew and the engineering organization expanded, Jan obtained Stephen's approval to bring in a VP of Engineering. Jan would move to a new Chief Technical Officer (CTO) position.

Jan had two potential candidates she was looking at for the VP of Engineering. She ran the names by Gary who agreed. They were both on his short list. The candidate they decided to interview first was Anita, who had led the software engineering effort for the Sunnyvale Division of Ford Aerospace, and also had worked with Jan when they both were young software engineers at Ford Aerospace. Gary had also worked with Anita. Anita agreed to the role. Both Jan and Gary were very excited to have her come on-board.

Jan had originally proposed to Stephen that Anita would report to him directly, since typically CTOs are parallel in the organization to the VP of Engineering role. The CTO position normally does not have direct management responsibility, but instead is responsible for technology direction. Jan didn't need to spend full-time devoted to technology, but by freeing up from day-to-day engineering management duties, Jan would be able to provide more support across-the-board to product marketing and professional services. With Anita as VP of Engineering, Jan knew the day-to-day would be handled, and she could spend more time helping other organizations. However, Stephen wanted Jan to also continue to be responsible for engineering. Stephen was used to relying on Jan and didn't want any product issues to come directly to him without Jan's involvement. Jan discussed the change with Anita, and Anita didn't mind. In fact, she was happy that Jan would continue to negotiate budget and schedule with Stephen.

An advantage to hiring Anita was that Anita, like Gary and Jan, had been trained in the Ford process and quality methodology. They shared a common passion for practical software methodologies that removed any unnecessary steps in the process while ensuring quality and customer satisfaction.

Another advantage was that Anita could also run the QA organization. Currently QA reported to Jan, but would be moved to Anita along with development and IT.

Many in the software industry preach that it is vital that the QA organization be parallel to the development organization, and that both should separately report directly to the President. They say the VP of Engineering should never manage both development and QA.

The reasoning is that if the VP of Engineering manages both development and QA, he or she will not properly balance quality with the need to deliver new product functions. Too often the result is that QA loses the argument, and quality suffers.

Jan had seen that situation occur. At her prior company, Jan had managed both QA and development. Before she left, she hired two Directors of Engineering to replace herself (James wanted to split engineering between technology and applications). One of the two Directors was given QA to manage in addition to his development responsibilities. The QA Manager later confided to Jan how difficult that situation became. The developers, with knowledge of the Engineering Director, kept giving QA code late, and leaving insufficient time to test. The Engineering Director, who was the QA Manager's boss, dictated the date when the software had to ship. When software was shipped that had bugs in it, the CEO believed it was the QA Manager's fault, and the QA Manager was fired for not properly testing the code.

That was a common story. Having a Development Manager also manage QA was often fraught with peril.

Jan, however, respected both the need for product features and quality, hence was as quality-driven as any QA Manager. Anita had a similar quality focus. Jan was sure quality would be maintained with Anita at the helm.

As Anita reviewed the current software development processes and tools, she came into Jan's office, concerned.

"You're using a home grown bug tracking system?" she questioned.

"Yes," said Jan. "We all love SD Tracker. It works great."

"Really?" Anita pondered. "There are some very good tools on the market now, and then we wouldn't need to maintain our own tool and continue to add new features to it ourselves. Are you sure we don't want to reconsider buying a tool?"

Jan said, "Why don't you use SD Tracker for a few days and then come back with a recommendation."

A few days later Anita flew into Jan's office. "SD Tracker is great!" She exclaimed. "Never migrate off of it. I've never used anything as effective and complete."

During the same timeframe, their customers were requesting better reporting functions within ProChannel, instead of needing to have their system administrators run database exports. Customers wanted their users to be able to run a report themselves, via a GUI, whenever they wanted. Intelic added a Reports Module to the list of tasks for Release 4.0.

Stephen was adamant that they needed to partner with a Reporting Software vendor rather than build their own. There were many Reporting Software vendors specializing only in report writers, so Stephen reasoned it was wiser to partner than build their own. He tasked Jan to review Reporting Software vendors and select one.

When Jan told Anita about Stephen's request, Anita was in opposition. Anita's prior company had tried several times to partner with other companies as a way to quickly extend their product line. The partnerships had never been successful, so Anita thought it would be a waste of time. Jan thought they needed to make a valiant attempt at partnering, so Anita agreed to try.

They reviewed the various Reporting Software vendors. Most were viable choices from the database side. ProChannel had a very clean database design that matched what was needed to use third party reporting tools. However, the challenge was what to do about ProChannel's use of resource files.

When Jan worked at ASK computers, one of her assignments was engineering director and architect for their new MANMAN/X product. Most of the engineers at ASK had been with the company for many years, and their expertise was either DEC or HP computers running proprietary operating systems using each vendor's proprietary database. The software was written in Fortran, a popular programming language during the '70s and '80s.

MANMAN/X would be a new product, in partnership with Baan, an ERP vendor from the Netherlands. The Baan software was UNIX-based and ran on the Ingres relational database. The Baan software was written in the more modern C programming language. ASK asked Jan to lead the MANMAN/X effort since Jan had more experience than other ASK managers using UNIX, relational databases, and more modern coding languages. The others had mainly used Fortran and the non-relational databases MANMAN ran on.

While taking Baan Developer Training, one of the things that impressed Jan was how Baan was architected for global language translation. Everything that appeared on the screens, including labels and pop-up messages, was read from resource files instead of being part of the code. Using this approach, it was fairly easy for consultants to convert the system from one language to another.

When Jan was designing ProChannel, she thought that the use of resource files would be a good design approach. If every word that appeared on the screen was read from a resource file, in addition to language translations, the manufacturers buying ProChannel would have complete control of the business nomenclature displayed, so the screens would match their business processes. Intelic's customers had taken advantage of the use of resources.

However, now, when evaluating reporting systems, the question was, "Could the reporting tool use the resource files so reports would match the manufacturer's business screens and nomenclature?"

Only one reporting software vendor claimed it could step up to that requirement. The vendor said their reporting tool had flexible programmable interfaces which could be used to take the data in the resource file and use that to convert the database field name to the alternate word to display in the report. For example, if the database field was "MPN" (Manufacturer Part Number), but the customer had decided, via a resource file, to label that field "My Part Number," then the report writer should display the column "My Part Number" instead of "MPN."

After several months working with the reporting software vendor, the vendor's representative called Anita and apologized.

"We thought we were going to be able to accommodate your resource files," she said, "but our engineers have determined that we cannot meet your needs. Can we proceed without supporting resource files?"

Unfortunately, most of Intelic's customers modified resources to meet their business processes. Reports that didn't match their screens would not be understandable to the users.

Besides, the issue went beyond labels. The data in the database itself could be converted via the resource files. For example, a category list may be stored in the database as "1," "2," "3." Using resources, one manufacturer may display the categories on the user's screen as, "Gold," "Silver," "ROW" (Rest of World) whereas another manufacturer's category list might display as "Top Level," "Mid Level," "Lower Level." For either manufacturer, showing "1," "2," "3" on a report would not make any sense to their users.

Examples of how Intelic's customers leveraged the resource files were numerous and were part of the value ProChannel provided, the ability to adapt to each manufacturer's business processes.

Jan felt that this was a "No Go" for the partnership with the Reporting vendor.

Jan discussed the issue with Stephen, who concurred that the use of an outside vendor was not viable for Intelic.

Anita took ownership of designing the new Reporting module. The "Ad Hoc Reporting" feature, available in Release 4.0, gave customers the visibility into their business they had sought.

Stephen wanted to expand to new verticals, and grow the business faster than they would be able to do with another round of Angel funding. The Series C funding round brought in their first real Venture Capital company. The $5 million VC investment allowed them to expand their team more quickly than ever before.

Intelic had outgrown the Ringwood building, and found a building on Berger Drive in San Jose that was owned by someone both John and Stephen knew from the semiconductor business, who offered them a great deal. The owner also had a huge set of private artwork in his warehouse, and he was excited that they were willing to hang it on the walls for display. Jan thought the artwork was very strange – modern art on metal that portrayed various pipe joints and balls. But she had to agree, it did fill the walls and bring color to the building.

The two-story building was much larger than they could fill. One huge wing was empty and held extra cubicle walls Stephen had negotiated, but they didn't need to install yet. There was a huge training/customer area. They had their own kitchen, and in the back was a large picnic/barbeque area.

Intelic's new offices were in an industrial part of San Jose. One morning Anita arrived and quickly found Jan in her office.

"There are two homeless men in front of our offices. One is peeing in the shrubbery!" she exclaimed, offended.

They found Gery, the VP of Finance/Controller, who had taken over from Stephen the accounting and financial management responsibilities. Gery was big and tall. Jan and Anita asked him to scare the two men away. Gery wasn't excited about the assignment, but didn't want homeless men hanging around as the employees were arriving. He talked them into moving on and not doing that again.

Intelic soon discovered that their new offices were in-between the homeless encampment, under an overpass on Highway 101, and the drug needle turn-in station. Therefore, there were a lot of homeless roaming by their building in the mornings.

Other than that, it was a great building.

They hired six people to create a new professional services team. Greg, who took the new VP role, was from Arrow Distribution, and was well-versed in the industry. Greg hired five people: two senior managers and three less senior employees.

The newly hired professional services team attended several weeks of training sessions presented by Julie. One of the managers, who had significant engineering background, continually tried to "break" the system by entering data that users would never enter, such as hitting the back button multiple times as fast as possible and other unlikely scenarios.

This annoyed Jan, because she felt he was wasting time on scenarios that would never be encountered. But the developers didn't mind, and took it as a challenge to tighten up any loopholes.

Later that year, Stephen hired Frank (which he pronounced "Franc," since he was French) as the new Director of Product Marketing. As such, he was responsible for product management (product design, new specs, and the product release plan) in addition to preparing marketing collateral and information for customers. Jan was glad to have someone in the company to gather requirements and work on new module specs besides her.

One of the product changes Stephen had been lobbying for was a new Look and Feel for the product, a redesign of every screen including colors, fonts, and layout. A year before, during an SDRB meeting, Stephen had said he wanted a new Look and Feel, "Right away." Gary had said that was not a simple task, and Jan added that the current release plan was full unless Stephen wanted to change the current schedule. Stephen asked why a new look and feel would take any development time. One of the new quotable quotes became,

"We just want to change the entire look of our system...That has nothing to do with development. – Stephen."

Now that they had a new dedicated product manager, Stephen assigned Frank the task of redesigning the screens. Jan still liked the current screens that had evolved from early prototyping sessions and later were improved with colored buttons to ease navigation: Red to go back, green to continue forward in the process.

Frank recommended changing the background color to blanched almond. Blanched almond was the color used at Jan's prior dot.com, creating screens that, Jan thought, looked old and antiquated, like parchment. Jan liked fresh, clean, white screens.

Frank spent time studying competitors' screens, reviewing how Microsoft Exchange looked and other popular Microsoft tools. Jan didn't think they should be looking at Microsoft as an example of anything – Microsoft, the company that produced the "blue screen of death."

Stephen liked the different odd and even colored rows, smaller font, and consistent layout that Frank was designing, even though John complained that at his age he wanted larger fonts.

Frank wasn't deterred by the complaints. He studied popular web font styles, colors, and action button layouts. He wrote a detailed Look and Feel spec defining each screen type (summary screens, detail screens, pop-up choosers) and rules for that screen type (where the title would be, placement of buttons, and so on). Jan had to admit she was impressed by the level of detail and consistency Frank was creating. Jan's early prototype screen designs had, in retrospect, been much less consistent. Frank had chosen different colors for fonts, background, rows, buttons, etc. based on screen type rules.

Jan still hated blanched almond.

The word got out about Jan's color opinions, and Arun suggested that now would be a good time to incorporate styles, and add the color choices as properties to give their customers options. Then customers could change color schemes if they wanted, and if Stephen wanted a new look and feel in a year, they could quickly change the colors throughout.

The developers often tried out new technologies first on SD Tracker, since it was the same architecture as ProChannel and could be more freely toyed with. One day Rich yelled from his office, "Micah!" Micah was the intern they'd hired who was working on SD Tracker before ramping up into full-scale ProChannel development.

"What's wrong?" Jan asked as she went to Rich's office.

"Everything is pink!" Rich said, exasperated.

Jan looked at Rich's computer screen. Sure enough, everything on his screen was pink. All she could see was a big pink square.

"What is it?" she asked.

"SD Tracker!" said Rich.

It seemed Micah had decided to test the color properties out by randomly changing them on a user's screen on a rotating basis.

Micah strolled in. "Don't worry Rich," he said. "It will only stay pink for a few minutes.

"A few minutes?" Rich complained. "I have work to do."

Rich and his customer support team relied heavily on SD Tracker (including his Call Tracker module) to manage their customer interactions and obtain feedback from engineering on issues and questions.

Jan suggested Micah find another way of testing. However, since everything on the screen was currently pink, she and Micah could certainly tell the properties were working.

As Frank, the Director of Product Marketing, also began writing and updating Word specs, and as the number of developers increased, Anita's concerns about the spec writing process emerged.

Anita came into Jan's office.

"We really need to buy DOORs as soon as possible!" Anita exclaimed. When she came onboard, Anita had been surprised that Intelic used Microsoft Word, and the "Track Changes" function to write and update specs. At her last company, a tool called "DOORs," a requirements traceability system was used. Anita said they found DOORs extremely effective. Unfortunately, it was also very expensive.

Jan knew the value of requirements tracking tools, but wanted the readability features of a Word document. Anita said DOORs had both.

With more people writing specs and more developers providing feedback, Word documents, even with change tracking turned on, were getting very confusing, and software developers often weren't in-sync with what the spec writers were anticipating.

Because of the cost of DOORs, it was a difficult sales job for Jan, but she finally convinced Stephen that now with more people writing specs and more developers, it was necessary to purchase the expensive DOORs software. Intelic's budget could only afford five concurrent user licenses. However, that was sufficient. Only the spec writers required a DOORs license. DOORs had a feature that it could export the spec as an HTML file that any browser could read without a license. The developers, and any others who didn't need to make spec changes, but who only needed to be able to read the specs, could access the spec using a standard web browser without a license.

The DOORs purchase included one-week of training for five people. Training included more advanced features. Anita, Jan, and Frank took the training to learn how to create new specs and how to edit and manage existing specs. Arun and Gary also attended the training. As engineering managers, they weren't doing spec editing, but they wanted to learn the advanced features to fully leverage all of the functionality available with DOORs.

Each existing spec would be converted into a DOORs document. While a DOORs document looked like a Word document, DOORs also had columns to add additional tracking information to each item. In Word, there could be multiple requirements in one paragraph. In DOORs, each requirement was a separate item, so paragraphs needed to be split up. That way if the requirement changed, the change could be noted, and developers could easily keep track of any changes.

Anita created a process where a column in DOORs next to each requirement contained an SDR number (an SD Tracker task). If anyone changed a DOORs requirement, then a new SDR was required to be created in SD Tracker so the change could be assigned to a developer. The link (although maintained manually) between SDRs and requirements would ensure developers could easily find in the DOORs document all changes that were part of their SDR task.

Another DOORs column tracked the release number, where the

change would be done. Later, it would be easy to see which release contained the added features.

If the requirement was changed again in the future, the new SDR and release number would be added.

A third column (a pull-down selector) was for QA to use during testing. QA tested each SDR that was checked into the code management system. Now, for a more complete picture, QA would go through each spec and test the changes linked to the current release that were marked as "New" or "Modified," and then would change the selector to "Tested," when testing was complete.

It took quite a long time for Jan and Anita to upload the latest specs into DOORs, and to separate the paragraphs out into separate requirements. But from then on the work became very streamlined.

The use of DOORs in the Intelic process was not like spec writing using Waterfall. From Intelic's start, the product team used an iterative and collaborative approach, unlike the formal Waterfall development process. The basic design requirements and information was added to the related module DOORs spec. Then developers and the designer reviewed the request and suggested any changes. Then the developer would start working on the feature. Often the developer would return with other suggestions and improvements, which would be added to DOORs.

The developers also liked to add any of the more complex algorithms or decision matrices to DOORs. Although not typically part of requirements specs, it proved to be helpful to the developers later when modifying complex code for new features.

Because everyone was using DOORs throughout the process, the DOORs specs were always up-to-date and, at the end, reflected what both the designer and developers agreed to. Then the testers tested according to the completed DOORs spec.

In some companies, screen designs or mockups weren't allowed in specs, so that developers, not product managers, would have complete leeway into the screen design product decisions. Before the company opened its doors, Jan had written the HTML-based demo, and then wrote an initial spec based on those screens and business flow. Intelic's specs had always included prototype screens or actual HTML demo screens as a visual guideline for the developer. When the developer had a better screen idea or a better approach, the developer would discuss his or her idea with the spec writer. Hence at times the actual product diverged from the mock-up.

In traditional testing, QA ignores screen prototypes or screen shots and tests the requirements only. That means the spec writer has to put in words every screen feature and the contents of every pull-down. With a prototype, the screens provide that information so there is actually less documentation needed.

Kevin in QA was too thorough to ignore the spec graphics. He had a better approach. He took the initiative to create a Word document with a screen capture of each new product screen paired with the mockup graphic in the spec. Jan was then able to quickly and easily either copy the new screen shot to update the mockup in the spec or, if the new screen was not what was anticipated, enter an SDR to fix the screen. This new step by Kevin helped create DOORs documents that accurately reflected the final product and insured product quality.

One nice feature of DOORs was that when anyone made a change, they could "baseline" the document. That way everyone could view the way the document looked at various timeframes to see the spec for Release 4, for Release 5, and so on and view what changed for each SDR.

The only problem initially encountered with the process was when a spec writer made DOORs changes without creating a matching SDR. The developers would be working on a print-out of the previous version, where they'd made notes, and would miss that a change had occurred. Soon, though, everyone learned to enter new SDRs to keep everything in-sync. SD Tracker sent emails to all interested parties when an SDR was created or changed.

Everyone – the spec writers, developers, and QA - were pleased with the new process. The developers found it streamlined their activities significantly. In addition, there was less confusion. QA liked to have a more readable document to use to create test plans.

Gary and Arun found more advanced ways to take advantage of DOORs features. Jan wanted to track each customer and what modules they were licensed for. Arun found if they put that information in a DOORs matrix, they could used DOORs tools to export the license information into a file they could use for ProChannel's license key builder. In addition, Gary built a tool that QA could run which verified the actual customer's license key matched DOORs. Stephen liked that assurance also.

Jan decided to maintain the "properties" files in DOORs. Properties were text files that ProChannel read which controlled system parameters, business options, and import/export options. For example, system properties provided the host name of the system, where the Oracle database was residing, etc. Business properties defined what time zone their customer ran its business in, what its base currency denomination was, plus numerous business options to allow flexibility in how each customer configured their own system.

When there were only a few customers, the Intelic customer support team tracked and maintained each customer's property files for them. An export tool then created a separate customer-specific property file for each customer install. Later, as they obtained more customers, and as the ProChannel software and their customers became more savvy, customers managed their own property options. DOORs was still used to prepare the default properties files, and to track when new properties were added to the product.

DOORs soon became a resource for the entire company. Customer support found that it was easier to investigate suspected code issues by reviewing both SDRs and DOORs. If the requirement was in DOORs, they could clearly identify it as a bug, not a new enhancement request or even a gap. The professional services team also referred to the DOORs specs for information about licensing, properties, and product.

Anita and Jan thought of their streamlined methodology as "Practical Software," much different than the old "Waterfall" methodology. Practical Software had the iterative approach of the newer "Spiral Methodology" being touted at the time, but had less waste. Spiral Methodology required that the requirements be known prior to the start of development and also advocated prototypes be built and then the actual code written later. Jan didn't like the "throw-away" concept of prototypes when real code could be developed instead. In addition, in the fast-moving start-up environment, requirements were not always as well known up-front, and evolved during the project. Less rigor allowed the team to be more agile.

The keys to the Practical Software methodology were:

1. Iterative requirements resulting in online specs, used throughout the process and tested at the end, so the specs were a true and accurate reflection of the final product.

2. An easy-to-use, effective task tracker for every task being performed. SDR tasks were linked to requirements and to the code itself.

3. Use of a code management tool for code, of course, but also for database update scripts, to keep the databases up-to-date and consistent.

4. A focus on delivering software releases with no known bugs, and then quickly fixing any bugs found by customers in regular maintenance releases.

5. Cross-functional communication and collaboration using team-based, efficient processes and tools. Note: To ensure effective collaboration, the team needs to be co-located or, at a minimum, in the same time zone.

Jan liked that their software process matched their software architecture – lightweight, clean, and practical. Unlike ERP software that was big and lumbering, like a gorilla, Intelic's ProChannel was more like a chimp, able to do any tricks the customer needed while being high performance and agile.

Years later, a product manager from another software company reviewing Intelic's software methodology said, "You're 'Agile'!" Jan hadn't followed the Agile movement and replied, "Yes, we are agile."

AGILE VERSUS PRACTICAL (2001)

"Every generation laughs at the old fashions, but follows religiously the new." -
Henry David Thoreau, Walden

Unknown to Jan at the time, in February 2001, at The Lodge at Snowbird ski resort in the Wasatch mountains of Utah, seventeen men met to talk, ski, relax, and try to find common ground. What emerged was the Agile Software Development Manifesto (http://agilemanifesto.org/):

Manifesto for Agile Software Development

We are uncovering better ways of developing software by doing it and helping others do it.
Through this work we have come to value:

- **Individuals and interactions** over processes and tools
- **Working software** over comprehensive documentation
- **Customer collaboration** over contract negotiation
- **Responding to change** over following a plan

That is, while there is value in the items on the right, we value the items on the left more.

The Agile authors' goal, similar to Jan's, was to replace the Waterfall software development process with a more efficient and effective process. The second and third statements, "Customer collaboration over contract negotiation" and "Responding to change over following a plan," clearly are a rejection of Waterfall rigorous phases and the resulting inability of a software organization to adapt. Here Agile and Practical Software were in complete alignment.

When Jan took Agile training later in her career, the first thing she noticed was the many similarities between Practical Software and Agile. Obviously the early pioneers of Agile had many of the same thoughts and concepts as Jan and Anita had.

Like Practical Software, Agile was based on an interactive, collaborative approach between the product managers, developers, and testers.

Agile matured and became a popular process for developing software over the years. The Agile authors and Agile adoption generated immense improvements in the software industry; in how software was developed, managed, tested, and delivered.

By 2015, Agile had become almost a cult. Most software developers proclaimed it as the only way to create effective software. Agile bulletin board discussion groups were prevalent. A new industry of Agile training emerged.

Jan was impressed with the effectiveness of the Agile training in giving software developers and managers better tools for estimating tasks and other management aids.

However, one difference between Practical and Agile is that Agile estimates were made in "story points," instead of hours. Jan believed the motive was to move developers away from the blame-oriented processes inherent with Waterfall as practiced by big IT organizations and government projects, and the time-consuming schedule management processes. While the story points concept was interesting, the Intelic engineers were already excellent at making realistic software estimates in time-based units, having been trained for years managing software delivery and schedule as a team, without "blame." But Jan could understand why the Agile followers felt the need to move to an entirely different mode to replace bad practices in companies driven by the Waterfall methodology.

Agile then teaches the concept of tracking a team's "velocity" to manage the amount of work (story points) a specific team could accomplish within a specific time-period, for example in a two week timeframe. Tracking velocity was an interesting answer for how to manage using a non-time-based "point" system. However, the SD Tracker Release Status tool provided Jan and her engineering managers a more flexible, interactive way to manage the schedule. "Velocity" assumes that the same team stays together release after release; or at a minimum that team members code at approximately the same rate.

Jan found over the years that developer productivity varies widely. If an average developer's productivity was 100 percent productivity, then super developers, like Freeman, produce much more, around 200 percent productivity. On the other hand, even experienced developers in India were typically 60-70 percent of U.S. average developers. New hire developers in India, after a six month ramp-up, were only at 20-30 percent. (For more about why this disparity exists between U.S.-based developers versus developers based overseas, see the chapter on "The Offshoring Dilemma.") There can be a wide range within one team.

Regardless of the limitations of story points and velocity, Jan thought that any training, including Agile methods, which helps software engineers gain confidence in estimating accurately and consistently, is a plus. It was a good first step. As Agile matures further, moving into true time-based estimates would be a real plus.

Agile embraces other practices, such as continuous releases – releasing new code every two to four weeks. Jan felt that may potentially be useful in an IT organization building specific tools or an online application where users can download new versions quickly, and at will. But ProChannel's customers did not want to apply new enhancements continually, due to their internal test requirements. As cloud computing becomes more dominant, and tools and processes for releasing software in a cloud environment become more effective, continuous releases (or at least shorter releases) may become more acceptable to enterprise application customers.

One concern Jan had with Agile was that besides the 3 Ps – Product, People, and Plan – the common belief was that another trade-off can be made, and that is quality. One of the Agile tools is a "Quality Slider." Even if the Agile goal was to show that the level of quality is variable, such as the amount needed for aerospace versus mission critical business applications like ProChannel versus a less critical application, the decision about how much quality is the "right" amount is a decision that should be made by the company up-front, based on type of software being built. It is not a decision that should be made for each release based on schedule and how many features management wants to include. That distinction had not been made in Agile training or practice, and was needed. Making that trade-off, release-by-release, leads the team to include extra content, and let quality slide.

The way Agile software was most often managed was to form small "Scrum" teams, which included the product marketing/product designer (called the "product owner" or "PO"), in addition to a few developers and testers. If the code being developed required more than seven developers, more Scrum teams were formed. The product marketing representative being part of the team aided the interactivity. The Scrum team approach improved interactivity between the PO (owner of the requirements) and the developers, plus included the testers early in the process.

In addition, each Scrum team identified a "Scrum Master" who was responsible for facilitating the team and for removing any distracting influences.

This is a good approach to meet the goal of improving interaction between the product designer, the developers, and the testers. However, it is quite segmented (all the smaller teams), and in real life practice, especially where one person has the vision across multiple teams, may not be as effective.

In order to avoid the Waterfall process of product marketing working on requirements and design specifications until complete, and then passing them "over the wall" to development, Agile replaced "requirements" with "stories." Stories were constructed as a simple sentence about what the PO wants the software to do, such as, "As an admin user, I want a User Profile screen so I can add new users and update information about existing users."

According to Agile best practices, each story was written down on a yellow sticky and stuck to a board. (Yes, really. A yellow sticky). The board was then filled with stories/stickies. From there the team discussed, face-to-face, each story, gathered more information, might create diagrams or other artifacts, until the need and solution were clear. The developers did "story point" estimates for each story. The Scrum Master determined how many stories could be completed in each two to four week time box or "sprint," based on the team's past velocity. The developer was then ready to work on the code for the first sprint.

As progress occurred, the story's yellow sticky would be moved on the board from one phase to another, left to right. Interaction between the PO and developer continued, and sticky notes moved to the right until the sprint was complete.

The Agile "Individuals and interactions over processes and tools" and yellow sticky process was clearly a reaction (or an over-reaction) to overly structured Waterfall processes and rigorous tracking tools that got in the way of software development and were a burden to developers, rather than an aid.

Jan believed the "yellow sticky" process had several downfalls. First, it was not useful for any follow-on activity. At the end of the sprint, the yellow stickies end up in the garbage can. While it may be a useful process within each Scrum team during new code development, it was not useful for ongoing maintenance or later upgrades. Those activities seemed to be external to the Agile process.

Although many Agile followers eschew any Agile software

tracking tools (other than bug tracking tools), some Agile tools have emerged in the marketplace to capture stories, estimates (story points), and progress. However, none of those tools did standard bug tracking. A few Agile tools interfaced with bug tracking tools, but mainly for bugs found in the new code during the sprint. Bugs found by customers after a feature had been released, and how to best handle those bugs, was not part of the Agile process. Ongoing maintenance and upgrades were not adequately addressed in the Agile methodology.

In addition, without an effective tracking tool that tracks enhancements/stories, bugs, gaps, and future customer requests, the software engineering organization's efforts were a "black hole" to the rest of the company: customer support, professional services, and management. A board full of yellow sticky notes was not very useful to the rest of the company. Input into new features and functions was the responsibility of the PO alone. Using yellow sticky notes did not empower other organizations to interact and give feedback. If an Agile tool was used, it could improve company-wide interaction. But most Agile tools were too pricey to provide a user seat for everyone in the company. In addition, Agile tools are not secure enough to allow customers access, so customer suggestions and feedback needed to flow through the PO. Also, because Agile tools did not integrate well with bug trackers, the overall software process was disjointed.

With a centralized tool like SD Tracker, that everyone can easily access, customer support can track the progress of bugs and new feature requests, and professional services can interface with engineers on new features needed for their customers. Management can check on how everything is progressing – not to condemn the software organization or micromanage - but to effectively manage, which is management's job. Otherwise, everyone in the company outside the Scrum teams are in a "wait and see" mode.

Agile and Scrum teams are definitely a software-centric solution to the problem of, "How to improve software development."

In a prior company when Jan was on-staff to the President, she was asked to help improve customer support. In their first meeting, the Director of Customer Support said her biggest problem was lack of visibility into any issue the customer was concerned with; in particular, critical issues. Bug fix requests went into the black hole of engineering, and there was no visibility as to when, or if, the customer would receive a fix.

Jan talked to the Director of Engineering, who was shocked by customer support's perception of engineering. "There is total responsiveness by engineering to all critical issues," she claimed.

Jan asked her to describe the process. The Director of Engineering said, "When critical issues are reported, engineering immediately sends the issue to the 'triage team.' "

"What's that?" Jan asked.

"The triage team are the developers responsible that week for critical issue triage," the Director responded matter-of-factly.

"Does customer support know who is on the team?" Jan asked.

"No," said the Director. "That's internal to engineering. The members rotate weekly. That isn't customer support's business. We don't want them calling the triage members directly. The next week all open issues are handed off to the next week's triage team."

"How does customer support know when the issue will be fixed?" Jan asked.

"If it is critical, it will be fixed as soon as possible," the Director replied.

"But what should customer support tell the customer?" Jan was getting exasperated and could understand the Director of Customer Support's concerns.

"That the bug will be fixed as soon as possible," the Director repeated. "That's the best we can do, after all," she said as if it was so obvious that there should be no communication back to the customer about engineering findings or estimates, it wasn't worth discussing.

While the conversation dealt with bugs, which are not part of Agile, the result was the same feeling outside organizations have when working with an Agile team that is releasing critical product changes customers are waiting for, or that implementation teams need to complete their work. A centralized tool provides transparency and communication. Yellow sticky notes on a board in an engineering conference room do not.

Agile is a methodology focused solely on improving software engineering, and lacks perspective about how Agile affects the overall company. Besides eschewing tools, the focus on the statement "Working software over comprehensive documentation," Jan thought, was leading Agile followers astray.

The Agile authors stated, "We embrace documentation, but not hundreds of pages of never-maintained and rarely-used tomes." That made sense to Jan. Clearly the authors' concern was with the Waterfall approach of writing complete specs external to the software organization, and then throwing them "over-the-wall," with no way for the developers to give feedback. Jan had seen the detriment to that approach in large government defense software projects, where better ideas were discovered during development, yet the development organization was unable to do anything except code exactly to the spec. Clearly a more incremental approach was needed.

However, Agile training and practices went to the extreme and promoted "no specs." The Agile practice of jotting down stories on yellow sticky notes stuck to a whiteboard was as opposite from a design spec as possible.

"But," Jan asked on an online Agile discussion site, "if the only documentation is a bunch of yellow sticky 'stories,' at the end of the project, those will be scraps in a garbage can. Where do you find out what the code really does?"

The answers were, "Ask the developer," or "The code should be clear."

That may work within the development team, but what about the extended team: the product managers, customer support, and professional services? Jan didn't want everyone interrupting the developers all the time to find answers to complex questions about what the code really does and is capable of. In addition, the code doesn't describe the business problem being solved. How does the extended company know all of the business processes that the code automates? How does customer support know if the customer's request is a bug or just a gap in the design?

At Intelic, with DOORs as part of the software process, the DOORs specs were used by the developers as they coded, and were tested by QA as part of standard testing. Everyone knew DOORs accurately reflected the code. In addition, DOORs explained the business processes being automated, in a readable way.

In Agile, when discussing documentation, the question is often asked: "Who would use that documentation and why/how?"

Jan's answer was, "Everyone in the company. Accurate documents are useful for the developers - not as a replacement for training and not a static user manual - but rather as a handy reference to delve into for more detailed, complex, functional understanding and design details. Even for experienced developers, the DOORs documents are like a wiki for the product."

She continued, "For customer support (the Call Center), documentation is needed to be able to quickly identify if a customer request is a bug, a training issue, or if it should become a new feature request."

As ProChannel grew to become a huge enterprise application, when product managers needed to add new features and functions to an older module with complex business functionality, online specifications helped immensely. In addition, professional services relied on the documentation when investigating all of the business options and features that the software was able to support.

Anita had been able to easily convince Jan that having hundreds of pages of hard to maintain Word tomes was opposite to the goal, the same as the Agile authors stated.

Some companies that still believe there is some worth in documentation think they are fulfilling that need by producing incremental design documents, documenting changes only. However, after a few releases, there is no central "Bible" defining everything that is in the product.

Some say all that is needed are the resulting training manuals and user documentation. However, when creating those, the technical documentation team comes in later, after the product is complete, and tries to document what is in the product. Even if there is more rigor, and training manuals and user guides are tested, they are "after-the-fact" and are not used by the developers during development. Those documents may be accurate. But more likely, may not.

The DOORs specs were Intelic's product Bible.

The DOORs/SD Tracker combination was not ideal because their linkage was manual (the SDR number was added to the DOORs column), plus required duplicate effort to enter the requirement in DOORs and then create parallel SD Tracker tasks to track them. However, the result was that every task, every bug, enhancement/story, and gap was in one streamlined tool (SD Tracker) that could be used both for software management and customer support. The DOORs document contained the complete business processes and requirements. Admittedly, it took work and dedication. But it was worth it.

Agile tools and bug trackers alone are lacking.

Jan hoped Agile would be able to evolve, once the software industry moved completely away from Waterfall. She hoped Agile would expand beyond the software organization, to looking at how to empower all organizations. She hoped Agile proponents would move to embrace real, time-based estimates, so that managers could more effectively manage project schedules. She hoped Agile proponents would embrace the fact that quality was not a "trade-off." She hoped Agile proponents would expand the methodology beyond process, and include guidelines for clean, simple software architectures. And, Jan hoped Agile proponents would learn to embrace the right kind of documentation as part of the process. Then Agile would be Practical.

SOFTWARE 2020

"You can't connect the dots looking forward; you can only connect them looking backwards." - Steve Jobs

Years after Intelic, Freeman asked Jan, "What would you like to do that you haven't yet done?"

Jan had an "Aha Moment." She realized that an SD Tracker task is a DOORs requirement. The only difference was that in SD Tracker, users viewed tasks like a task list, like a spreadsheet. DOORs gave everyone a logical view, like separate, organized Word design documents would, with a table of contents, section headers, and logical organized flow. She realized companies didn't need a separate bug tracker tool, an Agile story tracking tool for those using Agile, and a requirements management tool like DOORs. Having multiple tools caused extra work to link them together and keep everything in-sync. All three tools were just different views of the same task/requirement object.

Jan said to Freeman, "I want to build a new engineering tool. I want one tool that combines SD Tracker and DOORs into one set of task objects, but with different views – so the user can use it like SD Tracker, but also view the finished specification like DOORs. If I ever manage another engineering organization, I want to have that tool to use."

As she thought about it more, she realized that since Agile stories are just tasks too, the tool could include a "New Story" feature, and velocity and other charts, so companies trying to use

Agile wouldn't need duplicate tools for stories and for bug tracking. Who knows, maybe she could sell it as an improved Agile tool also. The tool would also need to support time-based estimates, like the Release Status tool, for more advanced teams who have learned how to estimate in real, time-based units. Another view would show the stories organized, like a Word document, or like DOORs. Spec writers could add screen prototypes, diagrams, charts, whatever is needed to support the story. It would be an "almost automatic" spec writing tool. Users in other organizations could use the spec view to tell what the software does, like they did with DOORs. But it would be easier than DOORs because the linkage would be automatic. Agile companies might even learn the value of good specs!

Jan asked Freeman what he still wanted to do. Freeman said, "I want to build a new architecture from the ground up."

Both Jan and Freeman were only consulting a few hours per week at that time.

Jan proposed, "How about if you build your new architecture and I design a new Tracker tool to put on top that has multiple views?"

"Sounds fun," replied Freeman.

They spent the next few months and built a new tool they called Software 2020 – named because it gave managers 20/20 vision into the software process, and because it was modern enough for the year 2020. It was multi-tenant, so could be run in the cloud, but also easy to download and install on-premise. It was highly configurable, and each user had personalized configuration options.

Jan was happy with her new tool and Freeman was happy with his new architecture. Jan was relieved that if she decided to start another company, or take another VP of Engineering job, she now had an effective tool to use; an even better tool than SD Tracker, an Agile tracking tool, and DOORs combined.

People touting Agile methodology don't believe in tools, but Jan believed that just the right tools, practical tools, were necessary both for clean, consistent software, and also to give the information needed to all organizations.

"When centralized documentation is produced as a by-product of the process, and is tested and accurate," Jan would add, "why not aim for that? That seems practical to me!"

BUSINESS IS BOOMING

"The question isn't who is going to let me; it's who is going to stop me." - Ayn Rand

The reward for a very successful first three years, revenues doubling yearly, and additional funding, was to be able to hire more employees and build a more complete organizational structure. Intelic was feeling like a real company now.

Intelic had been staffing up to meet the need. Intelic was soon up to 70 employees, including 30 in engineering reporting to Anita: developers, QA test engineers, and IT support.

The professional services team that Greg led was ramping up to do the implementations. Customer support lead by Rich was managing the day-to-day support calls. Julie was doing Sales Support in addition to continuing to provide her industry expertise for product design.

Julie had also been doing customer training. With the ramp-up, John recommended hiring his daughter, Jenn, as a trainer.

Jan was opposed, but didn't want to offend John, so went to first confer with Stephen. "We already hired your nephew, Micah, as a developer," she stated. Micah had started out as an inexpensive summer intern but quickly proved his worth. They were glad he decided to work as an employee for a year to make extra money before returning to get his master's degree.

"Fortunately, Micah has been a wonderful find. However, I've had difficulty in the past when there are performance issues with relatives. We should be careful about hiring more relatives."

"We hired your daughter, Kristin, at the reception desk," Stephen noted.

"That was just for a couple of months as a summer hire. This is a full-time employee. Micah turned out great, but what if Jenn doesn't. That could cause problems between the management team."

"Jenn has a lot of experience in the semiconductor area, and I know her. Trust me," Stephen requested. "I'm sure she'll work out fine."

"All right," Jan relented, only partially convinced.

The employees were working long, hard hours, but were still making room for fun. With their own indoor lunch room plus outdoor patio for picnics, they enjoyed better camaraderie during lunchtime, plus organized special events. They would have company breakfasts, where the managers would flip the pancakes and serve the employees. Several times John arranged for a vendor to bring a barbeque truck parked next to the outdoor patio for a special lunchtime treat.

Of course, part of the fun were pranks. One prank the Intelic developers loved to pull was that when one of them took a long vacation, he or she was never sure what they would come back to.

This was the era when practical tricks were part of the start-up mentality. Sun Microsystems led the charge. It was well known in the valley that one year, Scott McNealy, who was then chief executive of Sun Microsystems, walked into his office and found it transformed into a par-four golf hole, including the removal of walls. Another year Scott McNealy's office was moved completely to the inside of a packing crate.

The Sun pranksters didn't only attack Scott. Eric Schmidt, Sun's product development chief, found a Volkswagen Beetle replacing all the furniture in his work space. For a day or two he conducted his meetings in the car. Chief Scientist Bill Joy's Porsche was disassembled and reassembled on an island in a man-made lake; he had to row out in a dinghy to retrieve it.

The Intelic pranksters did not go to the cost or expense of such elaborate pranks, but there were some good pranks regardless.

One time Shilpa returned from her vacation to find the floor of her cubicle completely covered in lawn (in small planting containers). She had to try to roll her chair over the lawn segments that day until she had time and could get help to cart them away.

One year one of the developer's cubicles was completely filled with a large weather balloon Chaiya had found. The main problem with that prank was that the huge chalky balloon looked so cool everyone came by to see it. Before the developer returned from vacation, one of the women in sales just "had to" touch it, and her nail popped the balloon. Loud! So Chaiya brought in a baby wading pool, and was about to fill it with water when Jan stopped him.

"I don't think so," said Jan. "What if it leaks? We're just renting here, and it would make a huge mess if that much water got into the carpeting."

Obviously, Jan would have been a real wet blanket at Sun Microsystems.

Chaiya only paused a moment, then got a couple of friends and they returned with a huge number of sand bags. They filled up the wading pool with sand and added small palm trees and bottles of Corona for the beach effect.

A few weeks later, Gary, the Director of Engineering, left for his first one-week vacation since coming to Intelic. Next thing Jan knew, a few developers had a door-size piece of plywood and were about to nail it over the door opening. Again, Jan thought she'd better be the voice of reason.

"Wait a minute there," Jan said. "Remember, we're renting. I'm not sure it's a good idea to be adding nail holes into the door frame. How else could we attach it?"

Just then Stephen came into the developer area. "Uh, oh," thought Jan.

Stephen walked up. "What's this?" he asked, and the developers excitedly explained their plan.

"Wait right here," Stephen said and rushed out of the area. Jan was puzzled. Stephen came back a few minutes later with his tool belt strapped around his waist, and a power drill in-hand.

"Hold it up for me," he said, motioning to the plywood board.

He fired up his drill and zing, zing, zing he ran screws into the door frame, mounting it securely.

"Well, all right then," said Jan. "He's the boss!"

When Gary returned from vacation, he stood for several minutes, looking at the piece of plywood, not sure how he'd ever get into his office. Stephen didn't offer the power drill to Gary and no one else mentioned it. Gary had to go into the computer room to re-route his phone, and sat in a cubicle that day. The next day he brought in his own power tools to regain access to his office.

Besides the pranks, there was real work to be done. Intelic had won quite a few new sales deals within a year. Rich, Julie, and Jan finished the implementation efforts at Micron, Cypress, and Micrel.

The professional services team was ready to take on the new implementations for Legerity, Pericon, Elantec, and CEL. Rich was then able to re-focus full time in the Customer Support Manager role, and was busy more than full-time supporting all of Intelic's production customers. Jan and Julie worked on new product features, while Frank ramped up by working on the Release 5.0 "Look and Feel" project.

Jenn was also up-to-speed, and had updated the training program and started giving customer training. The feedback from customers who took her training was glowing. Jan was relieved that her worries had been unfounded, and Jenn was a good find.

SELLING VAPORWARE

"Honesty is the best policy" - Benjamin Franklin

There was excitement in the office when sales closed a deal with a large semiconductor company on the East Coast.

As Jan was reviewing the details of the sale, she stopped and stared at the list of modules that had been sold. The sales rep had listed two large modules, Forecasting and Multicurrency, as being available in the upcoming release in April, in two months. Those two modules weren't in the April release plan.

Jan took the list and headed into Stephen's office.

"I'm confused about what I'm seeing here," she stated.

Stephen said, "I was surprised, too."

"But we don't have that software to deliver," argued Jan.

"I know," said Stephen, "but the sales guy claims he really thought it was in the next release, and now the contract is ready to be signed. It's a big sales deal!"

Jan said, "Those two modules were on the release plan a year ago, but you'd swapped them out for Asset Management after the economy crashed because our customers are now more interested in where their current assets are than their sales forecasts. Right?"

"Right," said Stephen.

"And you briefed Sales about the change. Right?"

"Of course," said Stephen, bristling a bit.

"Then how could the sales guy be confused?"

"Talk to him and find out," Stephen suggested.

Jan did. She returned to Stephen's office.

"He said he really thought Forecasting and Multicurrency were going to be delivered in April. Do you think he could be lying to me?"

Jan prized honesty over all other traits.

Jan was one hundred percent against selling vaporware, software that is sold as if it exists or would soon be available, but isn't actually in the release plan. She had built her professional career on being up-front with everyone, being honest. Selling vaporware didn't fit into that picture.

Intelic had had success with customers in the past by being perfectly honest, even when the software wasn't complete. QuickLogic knew the software wasn't built when they signed. At ADI, when ProChannel didn't have a Mobility solution, Intelic won the deal anyway when Jan presented a viable plan for how and when Intelic would get that new module into ADI's hands.

When Jan was at Ford Aerospace, she was responsible for procuring the capital equipment (the internal computers and workstations the engineering teams would use). Some managers would inflate their requests, so that when the finance team cut funding from their request, they would still have sufficient equipment. Jan's approach was different.

She calculated exactly what was needed, and presented that in her capital requests. If the finance team tried to cut equipment out, Jan had a justification for everything in her request. After a while, the finance team learned to trust her. Tommy, the Capital Supervisor, once confided in her, "You're the only manager that we don't cut your capital requests, you know."

"Really, why is that?" she asked.

"Because you always only ask for what you need," he replied.

That approach worked well for her throughout the years. When Ford Aerospace was sold to Loral, Jan successfully negotiated a $3 million capital project. It was by far the largest capital expenditure Loral had ever approved for a single project.

"How did you do that?" other managers asked.

"I figured out exactly what the minimum was that we needed, and that was what I went in with. There was no way they could cut my request because we absolutely needed every piece of equipment to successfully complete the program."

The same was true with software sales. If the software wasn't there, she was fine telling customers exactly what was in and not in the current release. But, being an aggressive software manager, she also was willing to let them know exactly what she believed her team could deliver by the time the customer went live, or how long thereafter it would take to deliver anything else. Customers appreciated her up-front approach.

But now, Intelic was in a position where they had a new customer who thought that when the Release 5.0 was available in April, there would be two modules available that would not exist.

Stephen said, "We will be delivering Forecasting and Multicurrency in the next release."

"That's a year away," Jan complained.

Stephen responded, "I know how you feel about this. I won't sign the contract if you don't think we should move ahead. We can always walk away. But there are many other modules they will get that will start to make a positive impact on their business as soon as they install. Also, it is a lot of money for Intelic."

Jan said, "Give me an hour and I'll get back to you."

She went to her office and tried to think of a win-win way out of this situation without ruining Intelic's credibility.

ProChannel did have some multicurrency functionality added In Release 3.0 for their big customer back east, she thought, but only for the Design Registrations module, not throughout the product. Besides, the way currency was implemented for Design Registrations was simplistic. All cost data was stored in the customer's base currency. To-date, all customers used U.S. Dollars as their base currency. True multicurrency should store the value in whatever currency the transaction is done in. The advantage of storing in base meant the software didn't need to do calculations when displaying totals on the summary screens and reports. Reporting was all in base currency. But the approach was very simplistic.

What if Intelic simply added extra currency fields in each transaction the new customer would be running: Quotes, Orders, and Debits? Then the developers could only add currency to those three modules and use the same algorithm used for Design Registrations, which simply captured the currency code for new transactions and calculated in base currency. They wouldn't then need to alter the Pricing Engine. Contracts would still be supported in base currency only. Summary screens and reports wouldn't be affected. She did a quick estimate of how long that would take.

Jan then thought about Forecasting. In a simplified approach, Forecasting could be thought of as a report. What if for this release, Intelic just wrote a new report called "Forecasting," she wondered. That wasn't as robust as their planned module but it was "something." She knew how long it would take to write a new report.

They could call the two new features, "Multicurrency Phase 1" and "Forecasting Report." Release 6.0 would then include the more complete Multicurrency and Forecasting modules.

She hurried to get Anita, Gary, and Arun together and asked them what they thought, to see if Arun thought her estimates seemed accurate, and if Anita and Gary thought there was any way to squeeze the two new features into the existing release plan.

Anita was concerned, and asked Jan if they could remove anything from the current release. Together they thought of a couple of functions that could be made lower priority, features that were changes engineering had recommended to better support customers, but were features that weren't in any sales discussions or that customers were waiting for.

With those features removed, all agreed they could add in the new functionality without impacting the release schedule.

Jan hurried back to Stephen's office.

"OK," she said, "we've figured out how to add a Multicurrency Phase 1 and a Forecasting Report into Release 5.0. However,

Multicurrency is no more than a few fields and calculations like provided now in Design Registrations. The Forecasting "feature" will just be a report. Neither will be up to our normal standards; however, maybe those new features can provide enough functionality to bridge the gap until we deliver Release 6.0."

Stephen liked the idea.

Jan still didn't like the situation they were in and added, "I'm convinced sales would have been able to close the deal if they had been up-front with the customer, and instead committed that those two modules would be in the 6.0 release. I'll leave it up to you how you think best to handle this sale. However, let sales know I'll stop any other deal that includes vaporware, no matter how good the deal looks to them! This is not a good situation to be in."

"Agreed," said Stephen.

Jan found out later that Lucy, the Intelic professional services manager doing the customer's implementation, was upset that the two features weren't as complete as other product modules. In addition, although new documentation was available, because the features weren't part of the original release plan or formal training, Lucy didn't think Intelic had provided services with sufficient information. Lucy thus decided on her own to tell the customer they had been sold vaporware, and that the modules wouldn't be available until Release 6.0. Intelic lost credibility for a period of time with that customer. In addition, the effort the Intelic engineering team invested in the work-around features, which were never used by any customer, was wasted.

Fortunately, the implementation of the complete modules a year later with Release 6.0 was a success and, after delivery of actual Forecasting and Multicurrency modules, the customer became one of Intelic's staunchest supporters.

Intelic never sold vaporware again.

ORGANIZATIONAL SILOS (2002)

"It's not whether you get knocked down, it's whether you get up." - Vince Lombardi

The new professional services team had been operational for some months when Julie talked to Jan about how the professional services organization seemed to be separate from the rest of the company. The VP, Greg, was friendly and outgoing but, in addition to Lucy deciding not to install the Forecasting and Multicurrency work-around features, Lucy and some other members of the professional services team had been complaining loudly about issues they were encountering when configuring ProChannel to work for new customer implementations.

One of the new services managers had a strong background in software engineering. Jan had hoped when he was hired, that he would lead the effort to develop a toolkit for professional services to use during implementations. However, he felt strongly that such a toolkit should have already been part of ProChannel. Jan suggested they work together to identify what else services needed, since Jan and Julie both felt the software was already very easy to configure and install. Jan wasn't sure what he felt was missing. He said he didn't have time, and that wasn't part of his job description. He took the position that a tool kit should already be in the product and, if not, it should be designed by product marketing or engineering, not professional services. Greg, his boss, agreed.

This created a different working relationship between services

197

and product development than Intelic had enjoyed during the early years when Julie, representing the customer, and Jan and her engineering team, representing the product, worked in close alignment, resulting in a customer-focused product offering. Instead, Intelic's new services team clearly gave the message that, "You are product development. You should know what we need. We are services. We don't need to be involved with the product."

Jan recognized this phenomena from her time at prior companies. The management problem was referred to as "Organizational Silos," where each organization works independently, concerned primarily for their own organization's success and not for the good of the entire company. In one company Jan had worked for in particular, the silos were very evident. Each group believed they were the only organization that was performing well. When organizational silos occur, meetings between different functional groups are contentious.

Jan believed that organizational silos were often a natural result of the Waterfall process. Following the Waterfall methodology, one organization works on a new project doing their job until their area of responsibility is complete. The project is then passed to the next organization. Each organization is responsible for a separate phase of the complete project: requirements gathering, design, development, test, implementation at the customer site, and customer support. The Waterfall process can lead to each organization focusing only on their area of responsibility, and pointing fingers at another organization if the information they receive isn't complete or accurate.

At Intelic, on the other hand, their Practical Software process was more interactive, and organizational responsibilities had not been rigid. Although VP of Engineering and then CTO, Jan had also been a requirements gatherer, designer, spec writer, and customer consultant in addition to engineering tasks such as database designer, technology lead, and engineering manager. Julie also wore multiple hats.

It went beyond the Jan and Julie, though. The developers felt responsible for requirements and design as well. When new modules were being designed, Freeman would work in partnership on screen designs. Arun would give feedback if additions were needed to help implement the software, or if new properties were needed to insure existing customers' businesses weren't impacted by new features. Every developer thought outside their box. Development didn't then throw completed code "over the wall" to QA and say "Now it's your job." Developers felt as responsible for the final quality as QA did. Everyone thought about the impacts to the customer.

The same had been true for all organizations, until now.

However, the management team had bigger problems to solve. After an outstanding 2001, where the business doubled its revenues, followed by initial success early in 2002, sales fell off. Stephen was getting concerned. They had already made the same revenues in 2002 as they had in 2001, or slightly better, but unless sales picked up again, they wouldn't be doubling their revenue this year as projected.

In general, the economy had been having difficulties. Before now, Intelic seemed impervious. In March, 2000, a recession began after the dot.com boom crashed. Then 9/11 occurred in 2001. The United States economy was in a recession. Only now, starting in 2002, was the downturn beginning to catch up to the semiconductor industry, an industry which typically lagged behind economic trends. The downturn was now reflected everywhere. Even the yearly Silicon Valley Charity Ball, a huge gala where the valley's business leaders gathered in tuxes and formals to raise money for local charities, and which had been held yearly since the 1980's, was cancelled.

By September, 2002, sales were still flat, although the company had staffed up earlier in the year. This was not the position Stephen, the savvy and fiscally cautious CEO, wanted to find himself in.

Stephen decided that the only prudent course of action was to bring the headcount down sooner than later, and only retain enough employees for important functions.

The hardest hit area was engineering. With no new sales and a depressingly empty sales funnel, the product was sufficiently robust to sell "as is" for some time.

The question wasn't "if" they needed to go through a layoff, it was how it could be handled with the minimum impact to both the employees to be retained, and the employees to be let go.

Stephen and the management team put in a significant amount of effort to plan the layoff with as much sensitivity as possible. Stephen ran the numbers and reviewed the headcount. The hit to engineering would be the highest, but there would still be cutbacks across-the-line. Included was Freeman's little remote office, but Freeman himself was, of course, spared. By previous arrangement, Intelic had agreed to relocate Duy from San Diego to San Jose when his girlfriend started college at San Jose State. Since he was highly rated, Duy was spared from being included in the San Diego layoffs, and he moved north.

The layoff day in October was the most difficult day to-date in the short history of Intelic. Excellent developers and others across-the-board needed to be let go. The management team worked hard to help the employees laid off with whatever they could to make the process as minimally painful as possible.

It was a sad day, but necessary. Now management needed to make sure they took all necessary actions to swing the pendulum the other way.

To swing the pendulum the other way, the sales team was being pushed hard to obtain new customers to re-build Intelic's revenue position and get out of the hole they were in. As their board members, Bob and Keith always said, "The best way to get out of a hole is to sell your way out." John also began looking outside their current list of target customers and began discussions with a large distributor company, Memec.

A distributor company had never before hosted ProChannel for their own internal tracking. Distributor reps used ProChannel daily, but only as an outside user accessing various manufacturers' systems. During the day, one Memec rep would log onto Diode's version of ProChannel to track activities where their customers were buying

Diode's parts. The same Memec rep would log onto QuickLogic's version of ProChannel to buy ASIC chips and also onto SaRonix' ProChannel for clock chips.

For a distributor to purchase ProChannel for their own internal tracking, ProChannel's business model would need to be reversed to meet a distributor's business process. Sales had discussed with Memec management that there needed to be changes made to ProChannel before Memec could go live on ProChannel. Release 5.5 was being planned to include, among other new Release 5.0 semiconductor-oriented modules, a new "Distributor Model Design Registration" module that modified the existing ProChannel Design Registration module to work for distributors.

Jan asked Stephen how he suggested they design the product changes that would be needed. Jan herself was not well acquainted with the business processes inside a distributor company, nor was Julie. In the past, Stephen, John, and Julie had been a ready source of input into the product design, but this project required more feedback directly from the customer.

Stephen said that Memec was going to work with Intelic on the requirements. Stephen's plan was for Lucy, the professional services manager with the strongest experience in the semiconductor industry, to spend a significant amount of time with the distributor over the next six weeks, traveling globally to visit various offices to meet with various Memec organizations to learn their processes.

While Lucy traveled, Frank was wrapping up the Look & Feel changes and Jan and Julie were jointly working with developers and test on the Release 5.0 Asset Management modules – Price Protection and Stock Rotation. When Lucy returned, the plan was that she would work with Jan and Frank on the distributor changes required, so that they could design and build the new distributor module.

However, Lucy hadn't left on her travels with the same understanding that Stephen had. After her travels, Lucy returned and complained to the other professional services team members that

Intelic had sold Memec vaporware.

Intelic had not sold vaporware, but without Lucy's support, no one else had insight into the distributor's needs. Memec had already invested many of their employees' time in working with Lucy, so would not want another Intelic employee to come in again to collect requirements. But Lucy had adopted the "professional services" philosophy that it was someone else's responsibility for product design. This, to Jan, was another example of why they needed to get rid of the "organization silo" forming around professional services.

Frank jumped in and worked hard to coerce the services team into working with he and Jan to feed Lucy's expertise into the product changes required, rather than standing on the outside complaining. Through patience and perseverance, his approach worked sufficiently enough for the product and services expectations to merge.

However, Julie had, at the same time, received feedback from other friends who worked for Intelic's customers, that the services people working on-site doing ProChannel implementations had made statements to the customers complaining about Intelic, or about lacking features they thought should have already been in the product. To Julie, the services representatives that were involved were less concerned with evolving ProChannel or maintaining Intelic's company image than with showing the customers how much they personally knew about the industry.

Julie, ever the protector of the Intelic image, was appalled. She felt the services team was throwing Intelic "under the bus."

Stephen had also heard feedback from his contacts about statements the services managers had made to a customer. He decided to pull the two senior managers into his office and have a frank discussion. That was a "wake-up call" for the two.

To help bridge the organizational silo, Jan volunteered to spend more time working with Greg to help his team with implementation handbooks and processes.

Although none of these efforts immediately removed the organization silo around professional services, as the services team became better trained on the product, and as some who were less team-oriented left Intelic (including Lucy), a better, more collaborative working relationship developed.

The new Distributor Model Design Registration was available as part of a special Release 5.5.

Fortunately Intelic's internal conflicts did not tarnish the relationship with their distributor customer. At a meeting at Intelic after the implementation, the distributor's CIO stated, "This was the most successful software implementation we've ever done! Congratulations!"

The other good news was that, although there had been struggles with professional services, the rest of the company was continuing along as a close, tight-knit team. Even though Freeman was now the sole member of Intelic working from San Diego, he was happy having his office in a bedroom in his home. He worked to stay closely connected to the activities that occurred in San Jose.

One day Duy, the prior member of the San Diego office who was now working in San Jose, was having difficulty understanding one of the requirements Jan had written in the spec he was working on. Duy emailed Jan for clarification and Jan, being busy on another effort, quickly emailed the answer back. Duy didn't understand the answer and asked the question differently. Duy, out of habit, had cc'd Freeman on all emails.

Jan saw a new email come in from Freeman to Duy.

"Dude," it said, "she's in the next office. Get up off your seat and talk to the woman."

Jan smiled, realizing that she should have taken the time to meet with Duy, and hadn't realized that his shy demeanor may make him reluctant to approach her.

Just then Duy appeared in her doorway. "Excuse me," he said quietly.

"Come in, come in," she greeted and apologized for not going out to answer his first question in person. They spent time together until she was sure he understood the requirement and had no further questions.

"Thanks for coming in, Duy," she said. "Drop in anytime."

Duy was smiling as he headed out of the office.

Even though Freeman was remote, he was still team building.

THE OFFSHORING DILEMMA (2003)

"A wise man makes his own decisions, an ignorant man follows the public opinion." - Grantland Rice

Offshoring was taking off across the country. Entrepreneurial business courses were teaching the promise of offshoring, and business magazines were reporting that the successful CEOs were following the offshoring trend.

In 1999, Stephen had emailed Jan an ad from an Indian firm advertising, "Five developers and a manager in India for the price of one US developer."

"We have the staffing need for six developers now," Stephen beamed. "Look," he said, pointing to the ad, "you can hire six quickly, get rid of the local developers, and we can save money!"

Jan pondered. "I like the price, but I don't think it would be feasible right now when we need to do very interactive development. Plus training them would take a significant amount of our small team's time without any short-term benefits. I think that we are too small to be thinking about offshoring now."

Jan's pushback dissuaded Stephen at the time.

However, the buzz about offshoring had been increasing over the years and now, in 2003, the new VC was pushing for profits, and Stephen again wanted to pursue offshoring as a way to staff the development team more economically.

There was a three day offshoring conference to be held at the Chaminade Resort in Santa Cruz. Stephen thought it would be a good event for Jan to attend to learn more about the current offshoring craze. Stephen hoped Jan would return enthusiastic about the idea. Jan went open-minded. They could use more developers, and she definitely liked the cost savings potential.

It was a very informative conference. The meetings were very open, discussing the good, the bad, and the ugly sides of offshoring.

Jan sat by one manager who was bubbling over with excitement about his company's success in offshoring. He was one of the presenters, and described how they had their entire product development team in Russia. He had charts and graphs about their cost savings, and about how efficient and technically savvy the Russian developers were.

Jan had a chance to query him a bit more when he returned to his seat.

"How did you recruit the engineers in Russia?" she asked.

"We leave that up to our development manager there," he explained.

"How do you train them and bring them up-to-speed on your product?" she asked.

"Actually, they were the company that developed the product initially," he said. "We bought that company, including the development manager, several years ago, and there was no reason to move any of the development to the U.S., since the product technology expertise was all there."

"Ah," sighed Jan. That wasn't the answer she'd hoped for. Intelic was not in the same position at all, and his experience had no bearing for her.

Another speaker gave a thorough and motivating presentation on how to create a successful offshore team. He believed the best success came from planning, from the start, to eventually make the offshore employees, direct employees. He began his successful offshoring initiative by partnering with a service provider in India, to help with the initial hiring. The speaker traveled to India to lease a building with the intention of buying it later, once they converted the team to employees.

One main advantage to his approach, especially for a small software company, was employee retention. Employee retention was a big offshoring concern, especially in India. Regular job hopping was common to obtain higher salaries. Larger, more established software development companies were able to give their Indian engineers higher salaries and more prestige. It was hard for India-owned contracting companies to retain engineers. However, if a smaller U.S. company made the engineers permanent employees, with stock and other benefits, retention was much higher.

Going through the steps to buy a building in India wasn't easy. The speaker had lived almost a year in India, learning the ropes. First he had to decide on which city, and identify the best locations in that city. Closing the deal on a lease-to-buy building was extremely tough, and required many dinners with local officials, and a few bribes. It was also impossible, he said, for a woman to do it. Culturally, the Indian officials would only deal with men.

Once staffing began, the speaker believed it was imperative to spend sufficient time face-to-face with the new development team. He recommended that the lead product managers and development managers spend one or two months in India each year to train.

Technical schools in India were training engineers in the Waterfall development process. Indian developers expected to receive complete specifications before providing their cost estimates, or beginning work. The concept of iterative development, or the new Agile Methodologies, were foreign in India. Even when Agile was being used, Indian developers required extensive documentation to facilitate communications.

This was beginning to sound more ominous to Jan than her initial concerns.

Several speakers talked about what went wrong with their attempts at offshoring, including high turnover, rapidly increasing salaries, and lack of key technical resources. Many proposed the best use of an offshore team be solely for customer support (due to the global time) or QA (to avoid the issues with up-front complete design specifications). Although, even when a QA team was all that was offshored, the team still required extensive documentation to test to.

All speakers concurred with the need for extensive in-person face-to-face time, with the U.S. knowledge sources going to India and/or Indian engineers traveling to the U.S.

It seemed to Jan that unless the company invested in having a long-term establishment (building and employees) and significant travel, the risk was too high. Even then, at Intelic's small size, in order to compete with the gorillas that were adding offshoring sites rapidly, Intelic would need to either pay higher salaries (negating much of the advantage) or locate in a more remote city away from the main airports, top universities, and gorilla locations. However, that would mean more hours of travel for the managers traveling to and from the offshore site and more difficulty finding top notch engineers.

There were other options to consider. "Offshoring" didn't necessarily need to mean India, Russia, or China. Jan had experience with improved service at a lower cost in various onshore locations.

When she was a manager at ASK Computers, she managed Customer Service located on the East Coast (near Boston). This helped support East Coast customers in the same time zone. ASK also had a European Division outside of London, with less expensive customer support resources to reduce costs, as well to support global customers.

The advantage of ASK's approach was that ASK customers had a similar around-the-clock Call Center as they would have gotten if ASK had set up a call center in India, Russia, or China - without the language barriers. It is also much faster and easier to travel from California to Boston or even to London non-stop rather than the numerous days required to get to a city in India. The disadvantage was that the cost savings, while available, was not nearly as great as

India, Russia, and China.

Some discussion was held about the advantages of setting up Call Centers in less expensive locales than California, but still in the U.S. Jan would have liked expanding Intelic's Call Center support to Utah. Not only because it was her home state, but because the salaries were much lower in Utah than in Boston or California, the population highly educated, and because of the LDS missionary program, it was easy to hire people that were fluent in nearly every language. But Intelic wasn't large enough yet to consider customer support options in any other location - onshore or offshore. Her assignment was to evaluate offshoring development.

Jan returned and pondered the possibilities for acquiring offshore developers. She prepared a briefing for Stephen with the cost trade-offs.

Although many at the conference advocated moving only QA offshore, at least initially, the Practical Software process was too iterative to move only testing offshore. Plus, their bug count was so low and quality so high they didn't need many testers – it wouldn't be worth the effort and wouldn't significantly impact their budget.

If they were going to do it, they would need to include developers.

From the conference, she believed she would have more success in India than other options, such as Russia or China. While from a salary perspective, an India software center was more attractive than adding more resources in California, the number of staff needed for managing and tracking the process detracted from the bottom line. Adding to that the facility costs, travel costs, and additional management to coordinate efforts in both places, cost savings was significantly lowered. Then considering the degradation of quality reported in the conference due to global time, communication difficulty, and cultural differences, once all the information was analyzed - at least for a company as small as Intelic - there wasn't a sufficient cost savings to counteract the negatives.

The other concern was that a high percentage of engineers

graduating from the top-tier India universities came to the U.S. for employment. The top candidates that remained in India typically went on to get master's degrees, and then took management positions. High caliber hands-on developers that were satisfied with the lower rung wages were scarce in India. Added to that, a culture where the goal of developers with a few years experience is to move into management, leaves only junior and less skilled developers doing the actual coding.

Stephen reviewed the information, challenged it, but in the end he was forced to concur. For Intelic, offshoring was not the panacea it had appeared to be.

Years later, Jan consulted as a product manager for a company using an offshoring team that had been optimized for success. The company had done everything right, according to books and seminars. The company owned their own facility in India, the engineering team were employees with stock options, and the team included product managers located in India with the developers and QA. The perfect model.

Style guides, developer handbooks, and extensive product training were prepared to bring the new Indian engineers up-to-speed as quickly and completely as possible. Extensive up-front training had been done by experienced engineering and product managers. Agile training was given to improve interactivity. Ongoing travel was regularly undertaken by the company's managers and trainers to keep the Indian employees up-to-speed. Eventually, all development was done offshore with no U.S.-based developers.

For Jan, performing as one of their U.S.-based product managers was extremely difficult and challenging, even though there were product managers located in India to interface with.

Between time zone differences and communications issues (due to both language and the poor networking infrastructure in India), meetings and discussions were tiring and long. The meetings were "brutal," as one U.S. participant stated. Managers who worked with the offshore team needed to be on long phone calls nightly after a full day's work.

Even though the offshore team was trained in Agile, the Indian developers requested extensive documentation before any development began in order to minimize communications gaps. The up-front documentation before development began, and cultural resistance to changes once development occurred, resulted in a lack of innovation. Development estimates were inflated compared to Jan's experience with U.S. developers, and final code was not up to the same standards.

Jan spent some time evaluating the productivity of the Indian developers, both new-hires ramping up and those with several years product experience. Even though there were hard-working and dedicated engineers, because of communications issues, the need for firm detailed requirements, and lack of innovation, their performance statistics did not match the performance she'd measured with her local developers performing similar work.

Many companies who encountered similar lackluster benefits from offshoring are now moving towards more "onshoring" for technology-related endeavors (i.e., bringing the technical development back to the U.S.)

Jan decided her early inclinations were valid and was glad Intelic had not gone down the offshoring path. Even when done right, the issues related to offshoring far outweigh the overall benefits to the company.

BIGGER AND BETTER

"The journey is what brings us happiness not the destination." - *Dan Millman,*
Way of the Peaceful Warrior

The lease on the San Jose building was ending, and Intelic needed to look for a new location.

A brand new building complex in Milpitas had been suffering from low occupancy due to the economic downturn, and Stephen was able to negotiate a lease for an entire building at a good cost. The building was much larger than their current staff size required, but was advantageous in that visitors to the building assumed Intelic was a much larger company. Another big advantage was that the building backed right onto Highway 880 and would display a large, visible sign with their logo on a major Silicon Valley highway; as good as an expensive highway sign. Stephen was always focused on the marketing advantages.

Since Intelic was now a more mature company with some very major semiconductor manufacturers as customers, Gary and the IT engineer spent time thoroughly planning the move, including setting up computers in the new location many days prior to the move. This gave the internet's Domain Name Servers (DNS) the needed time to update the server directories worldwide. Stephen didn't want to lose any days with Intelic not being searchable. He felt it was very important to operate as professionally as possible which meant no downtime off the internet.

The move went without a hitch. Intelic's customers didn't even know the move had occurred.

Release 6.0 was being kicked off to include Multicurrency, Forecasting, and other new features. Frank took ownership of the Multicurrency features. Frank was the perfect one to own Multicurrency because of his European background, giving him knowledge of the complexities of doing business in different currencies. He was familiar with global currency nomenclature and business rules. He methodically mapped out the fields and calculations needed. Jan identified what fields needed to be added to the database to track the current exchange rate and currency type.

Another fairly new member to the product marketing team was Steven, who reported to Frank. Steven had a law degree, and was thorough and intelligent. Steven took responsibility for adding multicurrency to the Point of Sale (POS) module. That was a very tricky endeavor.

The POS module tracked the manufacturer's parts that were located at their distributors' warehouses and later shipped to end customers. The manufacturers received payment for the parts only when sold and shipped from the distributors to the end customer. Distributors were required to send the manufacturer POS reports monthly, stating the location and sale of all parts shipped from their warehouses.

Most transactions - such as opportunities, quotes, orders, and debits - were tracked in one currency. The user could chose the currency based on certain rules and parameters relating to the customers and what currency they used. There were various rules and complexities.

With POS, the process was even more complex. First, there was the currency the distributor used to do business with the manufacturer, which they would use to purchase the parts for their warehouse. Next there was the currency of the debit authorization. A debit authorization authorized the distributor to ship parts out of their warehouse at a lower cost to the distributor, due to economic or other justification, than they had agreed to buy the parts from the manufacturer originally. The debit could be in the currency the distributor bought the parts in, or could be in the currency the distributor planned to use when selling the part to a customer, or in the currency and exchange rate of a hedged contract. However, it didn't stop there. When the distributor reported the sale of the part back to the manufacturer, the customer may have paid in another currency. That means separate currency types for the original book cost, the new negotiated cost, and the resale price to the end customer.

Thus, there were three currency types, exchange rates, and values - with numerous business rules for how to manage them all.

Jan took ownership of the Forecasting module. A few years before, PMC had been interested in both Commissions and Forecasting. PMC had given Intelic briefings about their business processes and had walked Jan and others through, screen by screen, what they were looking for in the new modules.

Commissions had been prioritized over Forecasting at that time. Commissions was delivered as part of Release 4.0.

Jan brushed off the PMC Forecasting briefings, plus began to interview business people, including John and Stephen, about what should be included in the first release of Sales Forecasting.

All three (Frank, Steven, and Jan) worked with the developers as they implemented Release 6.0. For Halloween that year, Steven showed up in a "Multicurrency and POS" costume. He was like a superman with a cape labeled "Captain POS" and held an ice cube tray where each pseudo ice cube was marked with a different currency symbol. Geeky but fun.

During the same timeframe, sales deals were being closed including a large company that had been spun out of Motorola. Stephen was continually changing the sales methodology in order to refine and improve both the time to close deals and the revenue obtained. He reviewed the marketing approach yearly, grouped modules into different selling bundles, and changed selling options.

Sometimes every feature was extra cost, even features that engineering could not "turn off," which then caused the team to quickly work out updates to their licensing key or, if there was not enough time for that, add hidden properties to turn things on and off based on what the customer purchased. Stephen would then evaluate what selling strategies were best from both the customer and Intelic's perspective.

Intelic had been selling the software as perpetual, named user licenses based on the number of users that would use the system. Oracle then changed their selling model from selling "named user" licenses to selling "concurrent user" licenses, and many other software companies were following suit. Stephen was getting pressure from customers during sales engagements to offer ProChannel concurrent user licensing, because many of their users, such as distributer users, didn't log on very often. The price Oracle charged for concurrent user licenses was much higher than named user licenses, but customers felt they were overall paying only for what they used.

Stephen had been offering discounts on distributor user licenses, since the distributor users are not on the system as much as sales reps, but in response to the customer requests, he calculated a way to make more revenue with concurrent user licenses by charging the same price for all licenses regardless of if the user was a distributor or internal user. The customers were happy, Stephen was happy. Win-win.

Stephen had also been trying to engage a customer into purchasing the software as a term license instead of perpetual. Almost every software vendor was selling perpetual licenses - i.e., licenses that, once purchased, the customer owned forever. The customer would need to pay for yearly maintenance, but not need to pay anything again for software modules they purchased, including software upgrades. With their latest deal, Stephen successfully negotiated a five-year term license. A term license is only valid for a specific time, after which the customer needs to re-buy the software to continue to use it.

This would be Intelic's largest customer to-date, plus it was their biggest sale - even though it was less up-front than a perpetual license would have been. In addition, in five years the term license would expire, and the semiconductor manufacturer would need to re-buy the software. The customer was gambling that, because everything in the software world changes so quickly, in five years they would likely be ready to change vendors. Less money up-front seemed like a good deal to the customer. Since it was Intelic's largest deal to-date, Intelic was ecstatic to have closed the deal. Plus they were so confident in their software, they believed there would be another big sale to be made in five years. (In five years, that customer paid again to re-purchase the software.)

Their new customer hired a third party consultant to perform the implementation. That was a common practice in the software industry when implementing major software suites such as Oracle ERP or SAP ERP software, but to-date, the Intelic team had always done the implementations with no other company's help (besides the semiconductor company's IT team). Intelic had pursued relationships with various large consulting firms, but none had been interested in having a relationship with Intelic because the services revenues were so low. ProChannel was too easy to install.

However, the new customer already had a relationships with this consulting firm, and would use them solely, not anyone from Intelic's professional services.

This posed some challenges, since the customer's implementation would be following their big consulting firm's implementation process, and not Intelic's. The firm's consultants also did not have any prior experience installing ProChannel.

The consulting firm had brought in a large team, and was moving quickly through their implementation process when the customer complained about performance issues on their test systems.

Intelic engineering had, in parallel, been analyzing performance and running internal benchmarks in preparation for their largest customer implementation. Micah was working on a test database he coined Kablooie, named after the Calvin and Hobbs character, but also named because Micah wanted a database so big it was like the data blew up and went Kablooie! He had taken the sales demo database which only had a few hundred manufacturer parts in the system and one hundred customers, and used algorithms to multiply the data many fold until he had one million parts and one hundred thousand customers to match the big semiconductor company's data needs. To date, his performance tests had identified no performance issues.

Intelic's customer services team quickly reviewed the customer's situation. The problem was in the catalog module. Intelic identified that the consulting firm had loaded four million parts in the database. This was more than the Intelic engineers had anticipated, but when Micah quadrupled the parts in their Kablooie database, there was still no discernable performance issue.

Intelic asked the customer if he would send them a copy of their actual database for testing. When downloading the zipped customer database from their FTP server, it was taking a very long time to download, and a very long time to import into their local test server.

Lei, one of Intelic's service team members who worked on customer databases, came into Arun's office and said, "That database has 80 million customer part numbers loaded!"

From a business standpoint, that didn't make any sense to Intelic. They soon found out what had happened.

The Intelic professional services team's process was to start with data review and cleanup. They would only load the last six months of customer data to avoid loading ProChannel with tons of outdated and unused information. They would load more customers if they were linked to historical transactions being loaded, yet still the list was a fraction of all of the customers in a company's back office ERP system, where customer data cleanup is never done.

In addition, in an ERP system, each billing customer has multiple ship to addresses linked to it. Many of these are duplicates or slight variations based on someone manually entering a new ship to with each shipment, rather than going to the effort to look to see if that address already exists. ERP systems weren't always the most user-friendly.

The new customer's consulting team had not done any data cleanup and had loaded every ship to address in the ERP as a separate ProChannel customer. However, even that larger number of customers in the database would not have caused ProChannel any issues.

Most manufacturers only tracked customer-specific part numbers for a handful of their large, key OEM customers like IBM and Hewlett-Packard, who expected manufacturers to do quotes using the customer's own alternate part number scheme. All of the manufacturer's other customers order parts using the manufacturer's part number nomenclature. However, the consultants decided that for each customer, they would load a new customer part linked to the manufacturer's part number. There was no known business reason to do this since these "customer part numbers" were the same as the manufacturer part number. It was just the way this consulting firm implemented ERP systems. This explosion of data resulted in eighty million pseudo customer part numbers, mostly redundant. Kablooie!

The semiconductor customer had spent a great deal of consulting dollars getting all of the data loaded, and were adamant that they would not go back to the beginning and do any kind of data cleanup. The onus was on the Intelic engineers to make any changes necessary to handle eighty million customer part numbers.

The problem wasn't in the database performance itself. The Oracle database software can handle many millions of records. However, there was a ProChannel HTML component, a pull-down selector, on the Customer Part Search screen, that assumed a limited number of customers with part numbers. The huge number of customer objects linked to customer-specific parts in the system was overloading the pull-down selector, and caused the performance issue.

To solve the problem, the engineers added a business property so that, by property, the standard customer pull-down selector on that screen would be replaced by a pop-up search-type HTML component for large datasets. Jan designed it as a new business property, because all of their existing customers would want to retain the current pull-down selector which was easier to use and required less clicks. In addition, a new property and option was "acceptable" to add in a maintenance release. A change that would affect all customers would have had to wait for an enhancement release, and that would have delayed their new customer's implementation. The customer's plan was to go live on Release 5.0.

Unlike some companies, Intelic did not customize software for each vendor. Providing a common software code base for all customers made maintenance and upgrades very cost effective.

The engineering team quickly made the change, tested it, and sent a maintenance release including the change to their new customer. That solved the problem. The performance was then outstanding, and the project continued on-track.

Jan breathed a sigh of relief knowing that the issue was as simple as it was and overall, the product was as robust as she'd thought it was and scalable enough even for their new, largest customer.

One day Jan submitted a new SDR to report an enhancement request she'd thought of, but it seemed something was missing. She couldn't quite put her finger on it, though, so she entered a test SDR and looked at each screen more carefully. When she submitted the new SDR, she came to the "Thank you. SDR #5354 has been saved" page, but no quotable quote appeared.

She closed the test SDR, and submitted a new SDR against SD Tracker as a bug: "Quotable quotes aren't working in SD Tracker."

A few minutes later, Gary showed up in her office door.

"I'm sorry," said Gary, "I thought you were part of the discussion. We were thinking that since we're a more mature company, we should act more professionally now. We turned off the quotable quotes."

"Was that something Stephen asked for?" she questioned.

"No, I just thought it was something we should do and something Stephen would be asking for," he admitted.

"Can the customers see the quotable quotes when they enter issues online using Call Tracker?" Jan asked.

Call Tracker was the separate module in SD Tracker that allowed their customer contacts to directly add issues and enhancement requests.

"No," said Gary. "Quotable quotes are internal only."

"Did anyone complain about any of the quotes?" she asked.

"No," said Gary.

"Well then, let's turn them back on! I want to keep this company's fun, team-building atmosphere. Let's not get stodgy."

Gary smiled. He liked the quotable quotes too.

To maintain good relationships with their current customers, Intelic held an Executive Briefing day, and invited the executives from each of their customers to attend and receive briefings from various experts about business processes, market trends, and an update on ProChannel.

This year, as part of his presentation, Stephen wanted to include in his briefing a section about "Clean Data." Clean Data was a hot topic of discussion in the industry at that time, particularly because the ERPs had such huge, out-of-control customer databases, and IT organizations struggled to prepare consistent reports with such masses of inconsistent core data.

Jan happily helped Stephen prepare slides. They didn't name names, but their newest semiconductor manufacturer's customer data was what Jan used as the example of "Bad Data." In particular, she had one slide that showed sixteen "customers" in their database, all like "Flextronics – Milpitas 12345." The numbers at the end, which the manufacturer called their Account 5-Code, was the only real differentiation between these "customers." Drilling down to the details, each customer record had nearly the same address, except one would have an additional address line "Warehouse 24" or "Attention Robert Jones." All sixteen were the same billing company, but were just variations on the ship to addresses entered in the ERP.

When Jan had first seen the duplicates in their database and talked to the customer about it, the customer waved it off as a non-issue. "All of our sales reps know their customers by their 5-Code. There's no confusion," he replied.

Jan thought it was messy, and all those duplicates would slow down searching, causing the user to do more clicks to find what he or she was looking for. Plus, although they were starting out using ProChannel for direct business only, if they later expanded to the channel and had distributor users involved, the distributor users would not know the company's internal 5-Code naming convention. It would get messy.

ProChannel offered a "Customer Aliasing" tool. Perhaps a better name would have been "Customer Aliasing and Merging," because it did both.

The tool had two features. First, users could add in popular aliases for a customer name, such as "HP" to denote "Hewlett-Packard." When a sales rep typed HP, any customer named HP plus those named Hewlett-Packard would be returned. Aliasing could also be used to enter the name in alternate language, such as Japanese characters. A user in Asia could type the customer name in Kanji, and ProChannel would find the correct customer name.

In addition to adding aliases, the tool could merge two customer records together. This was a feature that, at the time, the big ERP software didn't do. If one sales rep created a customer "HP" and generated transactions for that customer, and another sales rep created a customer "Hewlett-Packard" and generated transactions for that customer, ProChannel's Customer Alias tool could merge the two customers into one. At the same time, it also moved all transactions from the merged customer to the final customer name. In addition, the merge part of the function took care of all other related data – users, contacts, customer program and assembly names, customer part numbers, etc. – and would link them to the final customer name or, if that would create duplicates, remove one and point all references to the non-duplicate.

Not all customers took advantage of the power of the aliasing tool. Stephen's pitch to the executives discussed all of the business value from having clean data, including improved tracking, reporting, and business insight. In addition, clean data meant better system performance. At that time, the aliasing tool was a separate price. Most customers had purchased it, but some had not. His pitch was to help those who owned it take the most advantage of the tool, but also to upsell the tool to those who did not yet own it.

The customer executives enjoyed the day, and enjoyed getting together to network. The semiconductor manufacturer companies were a small, tight-knit group. Some of the newer companies had been spun out of older, larger companies. Other executives would leave one semiconductor company to join another. Most of the executives knew one another; many had previously worked together.

To-date, Intelic enjoyed having a one hundred percent reference-able customer base. It had been important to Intelic's growth, because of how tight-knit the community was.

Every member of Intelic took pride in their product, customer support, and their company.

NEW AREAS OF OPPORTUNITY

"When you're finished changing, you're finished." - Ben Franklin ,

Stephen was like a whirlwind during this timeframe. He wanted to branch out into new verticals to expand their potential list of customers. A consultant was hired to review similar verticals to semiconductor companies, who could also benefit from the ProChannel product.

Attributes of semiconductor companies that made ProChannel a perfect fit were the semiconductor industry's very discrete products (chips, crystals, diodes, transistors), price volatility, short design cycles, and complex distribution network.

The consultant identified several verticals that had similar attributes. The most optimistic fit was building products (nails, lumber, etc.)

Besides expanding into other verticals, Stephen wanted to expand into other geographical regions. As of now, although the users of ProChannel were worldwide, the manufacturers Intelic sold to were limited to firms based in the U.S. Stephen hired a group in Europe - five sales reps, with offices in U.K., France, and Germany - to become an extended sales organization.

Even with all of the activity, they also took time to have special team-building events. John had moved to Morgan Hill, about twenty miles south of the office. There, he had a beautiful house with a lovely pool in the back and both a three-car garage and a separate carriage house with a guest house on top. Almost enough garage space for an avid car collector like John.

In addition, the property had a huge warehouse which he and Ed had set up for building race cars. John and his sons owned a racing team.

John offered to host a party at his house one Saturday. Nearly every employee attended, plus two board members.

There was fun and frivolity. Chaiya, an avid rock climber, even attempted to scale the rock wall of the garage and, after scraping himself on the fall down, required bandages and antiseptic. The company had previously had several outings to Planet Granite for rock climbing. Jan was now especially glad that those outings had been relatively injury-free, except for one outing where Stephen smashed two fingers while climbing and needed them taped up, yet continued to climb. At John's house, Chaiya was bandaged up and the party continued.

Everyone loved the pool. At one point, when Stephen was standing near the edge of the pool talking to John and a board member, Freeman thought about pushing Stephen in the pool but Stephen had his cell phone in his hand. Freeman solicited one of his friends, and both walked up to Stephen and John casually. Freeman asked if he could borrow Stephen's cell phone. Once Stephen handed it over, Freeman quickly tossed it to his friend and pushed Stephen into the pool. Stephen was not pleased, especially since it was done right in front of the board member, and Stephen was still in his clothes. Jan actually wondered if one time Freeman would go too far.

Freeman had said once that one of his goals, yet to be realized, was to be fired from some company.

"Well," said Jan. "Let's not get you fired from this company. We need you here."

Later, after the board members had left, Madhu walked up to the group of developers sitting in the shade, rolled her eyes and said, "Why is our CEO hiding in the bushes?" Just then Freeman walked by and Stephen jumped out of the bushes with a hose and drenched Freeman, getting his revenge.

The large warehouse was used to house a barbeque truck and tables for dinner. In addition, everyone, including the employees' children, got their pictures taken in one of the race cars being built. One of the race cars was white. Jan's husband, Mike, had his picture taken. While in the car, he'd noticed the clutch was floppy.

"John," Mike said as he got out of the car. I think there's something wrong with that car."

John laughed. "It's a 'pusher,' " he answered.

"A 'pusher?' What's that?"

John signaled him to come around the front of the car and opened the engine compartment. Ed had joined them. The engine compartment was completely empty.

"See," John was enjoying the exchange. 'If you want this baby to move, you need to push it!" He and Ed laughed at their race car humor.

The other car was the "Intelic" race car – a blue race car John had hired painted with the Intelic logo on the side. Typically John's racing team would be paid $30-40K for a full-side advertising space on one of his race cars. Instead, the Intelic advertising was his personal donation to the company.

It was a fun event.

Stephen was also committed to being charitable. Besides supporting the Salvation Army toy and food "Giving Barrels" during the holiday season, Stephen had, from the start of Intelic, invested each year in the spring Silicon Valley Charity Ball.

From a practical standpoint, he considered the Charity Ball a good marketing venue. But he also liked that the company was, as he said, "Giving back to the community." Stephen wanted to be a good corporate citizen. Although the Charity Ball had been cancelled in 2002, it returned in 2003. In 2004, Stephen was honored as one of their "Ten Outstanding Volunteers" at the event.

Stephen also found time to volunteer on the board of Big

Brothers and Big Sisters.

As the business grew and evolved, personnel changes were inevitable. Greg, their VP of Professional Services, due to health reasons took an early retirement. Stephen was able to find a replacement to lead their busy services organization who went by "JP." JP had significant software sales and consulting experience.

JP presented to Jan and Anita his concepts for improving the implementation process, based on lessons learned from the consulting firm he recently worked for. JP's suggestions included increased partnering between services and product development to more effectively feed customer needs into new product plans.

Jan and Anita both embraced his new ideas, and thought he was a great addition to the team.

The professional services team was very busy and performed many successful customer releases. The "organizational silos" were a thing of the past. Customer implementations were being completed successfully and most customers were happy.

However, one large customer implementation was not as successful. The customer's representative leading the implementation from their side was extremely opinionated regarding new features and functionality he demanded be added to the product. He claimed the features were simply "best practices," and no reasonable system would not support them (even though all of Intelic's other customers deemed them of low importance).

JP and his new services manager, Ken, worked closely with product development to expand the product to meet that customer's requests. Because the customer's representative had so many enhancement requests, the implementation had to be timed to coincide with a new enhancement release. But the release had many features besides this customer's requests. The customer would begin implementation with a pre-release of 7.0 and complete their implementation using the production release of 7.0.

The customer remained difficult and unhappy, and the professional services team became tired and depressed. Finally, services (and Stephen) considered the implementation complete, but the customer would not sign off on the final delivery, for reasons that were not clear to Intelic. There was nothing more to be done at the customer's site, so the services team returned to Intelic.

After the Intelic team left the customer's site, automated reports received by customer support via email made it appear that the production version of ProChannel had been turned on and was in use. The customer claimed the software was only being tested, and wasn't actually in use. Although the customer paid for the implementation costs, ultimately, the customer refused to pay for the software, claiming it had not been satisfactorily delivered and installed, and never paid any maintenance.

It was their first unhappy customer and unsuccessful install.

The quarterly board meeting was coming up. While the first unsuccessful install was disappointing, it was not a significant hit to Intelic's business or an indicator of an issue that management felt needed to be addressed. There were other new customer implementations and modules being upsold to existing customers. All of the other customers were happy and renewed their maintenance contracts again for another year. As usual, Stephen spent time before the meeting evaluating the state of the business, plans for the next quarter, and analyzing if any change was needed in their current direction and activities. As usual, he solicited slides from Jan and John to represent the product and sales progress to incorporate into his professional-looking board packet.

Sitting with Jan outside for lunch the day before the board meeting, Stephen took a sip of his drink and threw it down and yelled.

There had been a bee in the can that stung his lip. Jan ran to get some ice cubes.

The next morning was the board meeting. Stephen was in his office at his desk first thing in the morning, facing away from the door working on his computer, when Jan entered to see if he needed any help preparing the board packets prior to the meeting. As she entered she asked, "How's that bee sting?"

He turned his chair to the side and said, in a grumpy, muffled voice, "What do you think?"

His top lip was at least three times its normal size. She was so taken aback she had to try not to burst out laughing. She could see he was totally upset and in pain, so she controlled herself.

Poor Stephen.

At the board meeting, he tried valiantly to do his typically outstanding Chairman report, but his words came out so muffled, "Whe dhid vhery well thish quartersh," that the board members could barely maintain their composure. They tried to stifle their urge to snicker, without complete success.

The good news was that Stephen was able to report to the board that business seemed to be improving. Although they were not yet back on-track based on their year 2000 projection of doubling every year, they had made progress along many fronts. They were improving the forecast and increasing revenues by pursuing different verticals, different geographies, and providing a new product offering they were calling "ProStart."

THE ADVENT OF THE CLOUD (2004)

"They don't call it the Internet anymore, they call it cloud computing. I'm no longer resisting the name. Call it what you want." - Larry Ellison

Salesforce.com had just gone public, and was a concern to Intelic due to Salesforce's growing success as a software vendor in the Customer Resource Management (CRM) space. The market position "CRM" included, as a subset, sales force automation - the sales transaction tracking modules ProChannel provided.

While there had always been many vendors selling CRM software, previously Siebel was the only vendor Intelic would come up against during customers' vendor evaluation exercises. Most of the other CRM vendors focused on the Call Center and customer contact management side of CRM, not sales transaction tracking. Salesforce offered a simple opportunity tracking form, but not quoting or other transaction modules. Only Seibel offered all of the transaction-based modules the sales force wanted, including quoting. Prior to Intelic, sales force automation had been dominated by Siebel.

Then Intelic came along, and became the CRM vendor of choice for semiconductor manufacturers. Even when Siebel was previously implemented at semiconductor customer sites, the customers were now buying ProChannel and unplugging Siebel. Intelic had also successfully replaced Salesforce more than once for opportunity tracking. Now Intelic was the market leader in CRM for semiconductors.

However, now interest in Salesforce was growing. Salesforce was one of the first vendors of cloud software, also referred to as "Software as a Service" (SaaS).

Much ado was being made about SaaS and the cloud, software available to use via the internet without the customer's internal IT team's involvement, versus on-premise software, software that a company would purchase and install on their own computers and have their internal IT team operate. ProChannel was an on-premise solution. So was Siebel.

Cloud solutions offered the advantage of quicker implementation and lower operating costs, since the software ran in an external, hosted service center and required little, if any, of a company's internal IT team to support. However, for many of ProChannel's functions, customers wanted to maintain an on-premise solution because of the higher security and better control they felt their own IT teams could provide. Functions such as the company's price list were highly proprietary, and the large semi-conductor companies were more comfortable keeping that data inside their own computer center.

Even though ProChannel was housed internally, ProChannel was web-based. External users such as sales rep firms and distributor users, would access it from outside the company's four walls via the internet. Because it was web-based, there was often a sales challenge to obtain the sign-off from the customer's IT security team that was needed to close a deal.

Jan had provided technical briefings for sales to address the objections she knew the customers' security teams would raise during the sales cycle. ProChannel was architected from day one to provide top security and multi-level user access protection, which ultimately addressed the concerns of even the most stringent security experts.

However, with the expansion of the Internet and more and more applications starting to be offered as SaaS solutions, even semiconductor companies were becoming open to running more and more functions in the cloud. In general, using a SaaS solution avoided the lengthy and expensive implementation project typical with on-premise software. The cloud vendor or partner service provider hosted the computer servers that ran the software.

The cloud was particularly attractive to start-ups as a cost avoidance measure.

Stephen wanted to be able to sell ProChannel to the numerous small start-ups that were starting to flock to Salesforce. Semiconductor start-ups didn't have as complex a sales channel, or as much of a need for many of the advanced functions ProChannel provided, and could "make due" using the more limited Salesforce functionality. However, Stephen reasoned, as a small semiconductor company grew and matured, if the company started out using ProChannel, maintaining the company as a customer by upselling to them when they needed more advanced functionality would be much easier than going into an existing Salesforce customer and starting a new sales process.

Salesforce was architected as a "multi-tenant" solution, meaning that multiple customers use the same computer application and multiple customers' data is stored in one database. The multi-tenant application keeps each customer's data separate and secure, even though they share a single database instance.

ProChannel, on the other hand, was architected to be hosted on-site (on-premise) for one company (single-tenant). Each company had its own local database.

One advantage to multi-tenant solutions was that demos were easy to access, since the software was always running. Only a new tenant and users needed to be added to the existing database. Customers could start accessing the software without installing copies of the software, the database, or any hardware. After giving the software a test run, it was a click of a button to convert it to a production system.

Converting ProChannel to a multi-tenant architecture would be a large task. ProChannel's architecture utilized local shared data caching for high performance, and the database and application did not have the concept of tracking which data belonged to which tenant.

How could Intelic compete with Salesforce without having a

multi-tenant solution?

One problem cloud computing vendors had to solve was how to improve the ease with which new versions of the software could be implemented. To be successful, cloud computing software companies had to evolve away from the huge, monolithic, hard to install and hard to upgrade applications of the past. When all customers are on a shared, multi-tenant software application, upgrades to the software for new releases needed to be quick and painless, since all customers are affected. Software that runs in the cloud can't take years to implement and years to upgrade. Cloud software needed to be able to be continually released and upgraded transparently.

Intelic had a big advantage over other on-premise software vendors, since ProChannel already had the tools and framework for quick installations and easy upgrades. Secretly, Jan was pleased with the software industry's new cloud focus. She thought it would be a wake-up call for monolithic, gorilla software vendors who were making billions in installation and services costs. Cloud software vendors would have to revolutionize the way software was done to meet the need for easy, seamless upgrades. Gorilla software companies would need to learn how to build practical software.

Another advantage Intelic had over other on-premise applications was that ProChannel - due to its clean, simple architecture - was very lightweight. It could handle the largest semiconductor company with millions of reference parts in its catalog, global worldwide customers, and a large number of daily transactions; but was not a huge, behemoth, gorilla application. The main storage impact was the amount of data in the database, not the footprint of the ProChannel software. For smaller semiconductor companies with a small product catalog, short customer list, and a handful of sales reps, ProChannel required very little space on a computer.

The team calculated that ten smaller-sized companies could run ProChannel in parallel partitions on a single, fairly small server that Intelic would host and maintain. That would make it as inexpensive for start-ups to use ProChannel in the cloud as it would be for them to use Salesforce.

Stephen didn't want to offer the complete version of ProChannel's features and functions to start-ups, because he wanted to start with a version that was very reasonably priced. Later he wanted to be able to go back and upsell the more robust ProChannel functionality when the small customer grew and was more able to afford it.

Stephen named the small-company cloud version of ProChannel, "ProStart."

The Intelic team would be able to market a perceived security advantage for ProStart over Salesforce because each customer's data would be in a partitioned database, physically separated from other customers' data. In multi-tenant solutions, the application itself must keep proprietary data from one customer separate from the other, but they physically share the same database. IT security experts in the early years of multi-tenant applications did not trust the multi-tenant security model.

Jan worked on designing a subset of ProChannel modules and features to bundle and install as ProStart.

Salesforce was extremely easy for a user to request their own sandbox system to try out, and then very easy to set up a production version.

Jan and Julie created an easy-to-use "ProStart Quick Start Guide" to step a new customer through how to set up their small ProChannel system.

Intelic hired Jean, who had been their contact at QuickLogic and was now an independent consultant, to walk through setting up a ProStart system by following their new "ProStart Quick Start Guide." Within a couple of hours, Jean had completed the exercise and had set up her test customer's ProStart system.

"Wow," said Jean. "I'm not that technical and that was easy to do!"

At first, Intelic tried to use their existing sales reps to sell

ProStart. But because the reps were commissions-based and the commissions on ProStart were so low, the reps would end up trying to upsell the customer on the ProChannel solution instead of ProStart.

Stephen started thinking about how to approach ProStart sales differently.

Frank had spent a lot of time investigating Salesforce and recognized that one thing Salesforce could offer that ProStart could not was easy configurability and customization. Jan challenged the development team to come up with a technology that would allow companies to change the look and feel of the pages, plus extend the forms with additional data.

With Release 1.0, Jan had designed a configurability option using metadata. She liked it, but the developers argued it caused performance issues, and had talked her into moving away from that approach and using external pages configurable by property instead. Over the years they had worked to improve configurability on some pages in a limited way, but now they needed a very robust approach.

Arun and Ketan took up the baton.

Ketan was back at Intelic. After having left Intelic's original contracting company and returning to India, he had later returned to the U.S. with a different contracting company that allowed and encouraged contractors to convert to direct employees. Intelic had recently hired Ketan as a direct employee.

Arun and Ketan worked together to design a "configurator." Ketan took the initiative to write a design document, and reviewed it with Frank and Jan. The configurator would let users, using GUI forms, graphically redesign screens and even add custom fields of any type (date, numeric, string, Boolean, etc.) The output of the configurator were XML (eXternal Markup Language) pages that ProChannel would read to configure each screen. The configurator handled error checking and consistency, making it easy for the user to make extensive customizations to ProChannel without knowing how to program. The approach was quite brilliant.

Frank named the new configurator module the "Advanced Developer Kit," released as part of Release 7.0. Frank nicknamed the release the 007 Release.

A new Director of Marketing had been recently hired. Stephen had chartered her with creating new marketing items that could be given to customers upgrading to Release 7.0.

A company celebration was planned to commemorate the 007 Release, including Champaign and a James Bond theme. As the employees were starting to head to the Conference Room, Jan entered before the others. Only Stephen and the new Director of Marketing were in the Conference Room. Stephen had just unfurled one of the new marketing items, a beach towel with the words, "Intelic's ProChannel 007," displaying a James Bond revolver. However, instead of saying "Intelic," it read "Intelc" without the "i." Stephen held the towel opened up and just stood there.

"Notice anything?" he said to the Director of Marketing.

She looked at it a minute, perplexed, and then started to laugh. "Ha ha – I spelled Intelic wrong."

Stephen was a complete perfectionist when it came to marketing, and didn't appreciate her cavalier lack of concern for the sloppy job and wasted money. Needless to say she wasn't the Director of Marketing for very long.

Frank became head of both marketing (working with the analysts and focusing on outbound marketing campaigns) and product marketing (working internally with the product development team on the next generation product releases).

DISCOVERED BY THE SOFTWARE GORILLAS (2005)

"Don't worry about people stealing your design work. Worry about the day they stop." - Jeffrey Zeldman

One day Jan received a call from an Oracle representative. Because Intelic used Oracle as their database, Intelic was listed as an Oracle customer.

"Hello," he said. "We are having an Oracle User Group Meeting next month, and wanted to invite you to attend."

Oracle produced both database software and the ERP software many of Intelic's customers used to run their back office manufacturing systems. ProChannel interfaced to Oracle, SAP, and other ERP software to send order requests and financial information to the back office, and to receive new customer and shipment data from the ERP. Oracle was also selling modules that directly competed with ProChannel.

Jan wasn't interested in going to a database meeting, but she would love to get more insight into their ERP and CRM modules. Oracle was showing up more as a competitor in Intelic's sales cycles when evaluating quoting, pricing, and channel management software. ProChannel provided much better quoting, pricing, and channel management software for the semiconductor companies. Since ProChannel interfaced easily and seamlessly with Oracle's Order Management and Financial tracking software, adding ProChannel as the quoting, pricing, and channel tool had been proven to be a better

236

choice for semiconductor companies than buying competing Oracle modules. However, prospective customers' IT organizations were knowledgeable and comfortable supporting Oracle ERP. The IT managers often pushed their company to use more Oracle modules, instead of adding a new vendor to the mix.

"What products are you going to be covering at the User Group Meeting?" Jan asked politely.

"All of them – database and ERP products. We will also be hosting special sessions showing our new Customer Hub and our new Configurator product," he stated.

This would be a great opportunity for Jan to find out more about one of their big competitors from the inside!

"That sounds very interesting," Jan replied, trying to sound nonchalant. "Can I bring another member of our company as well? Our Product Manager?"

"Of course," the caller said, "that would be great."

She asked the Oracle rep to send her the registration email, and quickly went to Frank's office.

"Frank," she said. "How would you like to go with me to the Oracle User Group Meeting next month? They just called and invited us and are showing all of their competing products!"

"Really?" said a surprised Frank. "That would be great. Don't they know who we are?"

"Apparently not," grinned Jan.

The day of the Oracle User Group Meeting arrived, and Jan and Frank drove to Oracle's offices in Redwood Shores. They were greeted amicably at the sign-in desk, and received pre-printed badges with their names and their company name, Intelic.

Jan and Frank were aware that Oracle had also been building a product to compete with the Intelic Point of Sale module.

Jan and Frank went into the demo room and saw a workstation with a sign overhead "Oracle Channel Management."

"That's it, their POS-equivalent solution," said Frank.

But there was no one giving a demo. Frank asked when the

demo would be given and was told to come back at 2 o'clock.

They left the room to see what other topics were being presented now.

Jan attended the Configurator meeting. There she discovered that the Oracle "Configurator" was nothing more than the ability to write custom Java code that would then actually replace the Oracle code used to display the screens. That meant Oracle's IT administrators needed to be Java developers and do actual software development in order to configure their ERP system. That would be difficult and error-prone.

ProChannel's Configurator was GUI based, and automatically saved XML files with complete error checking and guaranteed compatibility. The XML files were then read by ProChannel to display. There was no need for manual software development, since it was all GUI based. Any IT administrator or business analyst could modify the screens and add database fields.

The ability for the customer to add more complex Java algorithms for the Configurator to use was an available feature, but not required for most business needs.

In addition, with Intelic's configuration approach, upgrades to the next release were automatically handled by the Installer. For Oracle's custom Java files, the IT organization would need to make changes to the code, recompile, and test with each upgrade - adding to Oracle's already time consuming and expensive upgrade process.

This was a fact that wasn't lost on the attendees. Many people started raising their hands and complaining about the complexity of the approach, the lack of real tools, and the fact that it was just giving them the ability to change Oracle's Java code. The meeting became quite boisterous.

"This is interesting," thought Jan. It was clear how Intelic's sales team could leverage the differences between ProChannel and Oracle when competing against Oracle.

At the stated POS demo time, Jan and Frank returned to the

demo room. There was a woman sitting at the Channel Management workstation getting ready to give the demo. Her badge said she was Tisha.

As Jan and Frank walked up, Tisha glanced at their badges and was aghast.

"What are you doing here?" Tisha exclaimed.

"We were invited by an Oracle rep," Jan said, smiling nicely.

Tisha leaned forward and covered the screen with her arms.

"Out," she yelled. "This is the 'Intelic Killer' application and I'm certainly not going to show it to you two!"

Tisha shut down the computer and waved at two other Oracle employees who apologized, but escorted Jan and Frank out of the demo room.

They were disappointed, but also thought it quite interesting that Oracle was concerned enough about their little company to put resources into an "Intelic Killer" app. When Jan worked at Ingres, the sales people were always hopping between the big three database companies: Ingres, Oracle, and Sybase. Ingres had a "Sybase Killer" project, where an ex-Sybase sales rep was giving Ingres management the "scoop" on how to combat Sybase's sales pitch. It seemed the ERP software companies were no different.

The incident proved that Intelic was not under-the-radar of the big software gorillas any longer.

Jan and Frank had not been asked to leave the Oracle building, so remained to see if there were any other sessions of interest.

They spoke to Oracle's project manager for the new Customer Hub feature, who didn't seem to be aware of Intelic as a competitor. They learned that Oracle was significantly behind Intelic's management tools for maintaining clean customer data. That was good news.

Afterwards, they entered a break-out room, which had stand-up tables for the attendees to use while sipping coffee during the break. There was nothing else they needed to check out, so they both got a cup of coffee and joined a table with three people standing at it – two men and a woman. Only after they had approached did the men turn so that Frank could see they had Oracle badges on. The woman was obviously a prospective customer, since the two Oracle men were giving her a sales spiel about their great Forecasting product. She looked at Jan and Frank, saw their badges, and said, "Intelic? That's the other software we're looking at for our Forecasting solution!"

The two Oracle salesmen glared at Frank and Jan, who decided now may be the time to head out. Before they did, Frank slipped the prospective customer his business card.

Later that year, Oracle acquired Siebel, one of Intelic's main competitors, which increased Oracle's desire to squash the smaller company.

SAP had entered the CRM arena a few years earlier. Semiconductor companies that used SAP as their ERP system, evaluated SAP's CRM when considering a new CRM tool. Even though SAP CRM was nicely integrated with SAP's other modules, Intelic remained the CRM of choice for semiconductor companies. SAP tried for years to win the semiconductor channel management business with a product similar to Intelic's POS module and Oracle's new "Intelic Killer" module, but had not had success.

Both Oracle and SAP continued to pursue semiconductor companies both in channel management and CRM, but without success.

The gorillas had woken up and taken notice of the small company, growing rapidly - a threat to no longer be ignored.

The gorillas were not happy with a small software company providing significant functionality to such a large customer segment as semiconductor companies, while they themselves had not been able to make any inroads into the same companies to automate their quoting and pricing or CRM initiatives.

The gorillas knew how to spread rumors and innuendo, and just enough flack to worry some large, conservative manufacturers into not taking a chance on a small company. While the gorillas had not been able to steal any existing customers or divert any new sales, they started to become successful at slowing down sales while the manufacturers took a "wait and see" attitude. Semiconductor manufacturers were notoriously conservative and risk adverse. In addition, the semiconductor manufacturers hadn't yet recovered from the recession. Intelic sales had come to a standstill.

What would become of the start-up, which had grown to become a small but successful software company? Intelic had claimed ownership of the semiconductor market space.

Customers lauded Intelic's software as providing a return on their investment in just a few months. One semiconductor company that previously had no control of their quoting practices reported a savings of $9 million in improved revenues in three months' time after installing ProChannel. Another claimed ProChannel saved their channel business. Another said with ProChannel, they finally were able to get their sales revenues in line.

All of Intelic's customers were saying that the little software company was different, that Intelic understood their business needs, delivered quality software, and met their most pressing requirements.

But was it enough?

MORE UPS AND DOWNS

"It is not the strongest of the species that survive, nor the most intelligent, but the one most responsive to change." - Charles Darwin

The whirlwind of activities continued.

Their new SaaS offering, ProStart, was ready for customers. Stephen had decided that selling cloud-type software is completely different than selling on-premise solutions, and that the same sales rep should not be tasked with selling both versions. Julie took the assignment to manage the new ProStart Sales initiative, and hired a ProStart-dedicated sales rep. Soon they had five companies signed up for Beta tests of ProStart.

Following the "ProStart Quick Start Guide," Rich was able to create an instance of ProChannel for each new ProStart customer quickly, ready the day after a customer requested their Beta version.

It looked like the endeavor was going to be a real success.

The expansion into the new building products vertical was going more slowly. Julie had created a building products version of their sales demo and Frank had worked on new marketing and literature geared to building products companies.

However, Intelic had always recognized that one of the reasons for their success was that so many of the Intelic employees came from the semiconductor space; hence the product, marketing, training, and implementation process all reflected keen knowledge about the semiconductor company's business. Selling into a new vertical was going to take some time for the previously single-vertical company.

Stephen began recruiting for a sales person from the building products industry to help facilitate their introduction to building products companies.

Plus they were making some progress with semiconductor companies. Several new semiconductor company sales deals had closed and software implementation projects were underway. Global expansion was also forging ahead. Intelic signed two semiconductor customers headquartered in Europe and began installing ProChannel overseas.

In addition, Stephen was actively pursuing companies that Intelic could acquire in order to grow the business more rapidly. Jan traveled to Boston to evaluate a promising company, Stephen and Jan performed due diligence on a company in San Francisco, plus there were a dozen or so small companies that Stephen had identified as potential acquisitions.

Although there was a lot of activity occurring on various fronts, the economic downturn was still very evident. Intelic's sales funnel had improved, but most of their sales prospects were not taking action.

Although prospective customers had often compared big gorilla software against ProChannel as part of their sales process, now Intelic was getting pushback from their customers and questions Intelic soon learned were coming from the big gorilla sales team.

The gorilla marketing teams had taken aim at Intelic, and were giving their sales reps ammunition to use against Intelic during the sales process. The gorillas were pitching that little Intelic was not large enough to take care of the customer's large, important needs; that ProChannel was not a robust enough application to manage the high volume, large-scale transactions which were mission-critical to a large semiconductor manufacturer's business. Intelic's sales cycles were getting slowed down significantly due to flack being generated, and the increased competition from the big software gorillas.

Although the gorillas hadn't been able to take any deals away from Intelic, sales cycles were requiring more effort. It was not enough to have the references and praises of existing customers. Potential customers were requesting new benchmark reports, sizing data, and other information to prove to their IT organizations that ProChannel was indeed a robust, enterprise-worthy application.

One of their large customers was discussing purchasing additional modules. However, their IT manager was pushing back, questioning ProChannel's ability to continue to support their business. The IT manager had just returned from an SAP conference where new modules that competed with Intelic's were being showcased.

Jan knew there was a huge difference between Intelic's architecture, focused on simplicity of design, versus complex bulky gorilla software. A simple, uniform design reduces development time, improves maintainability, and makes modifications quicker and easier. Over-designed, bulky software is costly to develop and maintain.

Jan had guided the ProChannel architecture using five principals:
1. Is it the simplest approach?
2. Is it customer-focused?
3. Is it designed for the expected user base?
4. Was performance considered?
5. Is it reliable, maintainable, supportable?

ProChannel's architecture was simple, but the functions it automated were complex, scalable, and robust.

The engineers set up a performance system and Mike, their IT administrator, ran numerous tests, gathering benchmark data that proved the scalability of ProChannel. Jan also updated the architecture briefing to address IT concerns. Intelic was able to persuade the IT manager that it was both safe and smart to buy the new modules from Intelic.

Sales used the performance benchmarks to address prospective customers objections. Most deals were, however, still on-hold.

Stephen was noticing that more and more of their competitors' products featured a nice graphical dashboard on their home pages to enable managers to quickly view the status of their business when they logged in each day. Frank noted that Salesforce had nice charts and graphs. This wasn't the first time Stephen had thought about adding colorful charts and graphs to the product. Colorful graphics appealed to his marketing side.

Five years earlier, Stephen had formed a partnership with a small company in Florida that was interested in working jointly with Intelic to integrate the Florida company's graphical analytics tool with ProChannel. Their analytics experts came to California to meet with Intelic team members. Together, they identified twelve Key Performance Indicators (KPIs) that were the most important business indicators for semiconductor companies. The KPIs included indicators like billings, bookings, design productivity, quote activity, etc. Once the twelve were selected, the analytics experts then led the Intelic team through the exercise of identifying the objective of each indicator. For example, the objective of reviewing billings data was to analyze growth and productivity. Other objectives included customer satisfaction and cost. Next the joint team worked through the details of what data in ProChannel should be used to calculate each KPI. For billings, data included revenue dollars (what the manufacturer made selling to distributors or end customers), consumption dollars (what the market paid whether purchased from a distributor or directly from the manufacturer), quantity shipped, and so on.

Last they decided what views of the data the customer needed to see: monthly, quarterly, daily, same quarter as last year, average dollars, etc.

The analytics experts then defined the screens and drill-down options that the user would be provided. The Intelic team built the data exports and utilities. The analytics tool allowed users to filter by geography, timeframe, etc.

The resulting product was named ProVision, became Release 4.5, and was offered as a Beta Release to one of Intelic's customers. Frank created an outstanding demo disk showing the dashboard with easy to read KPI summaries and impressive drill down and search capabilities, comparison charts, and graphs. Chaiya provided the demo "voice."

Although ProVision was a beautiful product, once it was installed at the customer site and Beta testing began, it was discovered that, unlike the analytics company claimed, the analytics tool simply couldn't handle the amount of real data that a mid-sized semiconductor company needed to evaluate. The analytics company worked closely with Intelic to resolve the problems, but the performance issues continued, frustrating Intelic and the customer.

Then Intelic found out that the analytics company had recently been acquired by a very large analytics firm, and that many of the key analytics experts from the little company had resigned. The parent company was not very interested in the small deal with Intelic, and now did not have the expertise to work to improve performance.

Ultimately ProVision was removed from the Intelic's offerings. It was the first time in Intelic's history that a module was unable to be completed and was removed.

Since then, ProChannel had no drill-down charting or analytics capability. Now, in 2005, Stephen believed they were losing a competitive edge during the sales cycle without graphics.

Stephen tasked Frank with quickly designing a dashboard module. Release 7.0 was out, and Stephen wanted to release the "Dashboard" as a new Release 7.2, in a few months. Anita ran the ongoing engineering development efforts while Jan worked on the Dashboard technical requirements and Arun and Ketan researched potential graphical charting components to add to the product.

The decision was to incorporate an open source set of graphical components into their toolbox to use to build snazzy graphs and charts.

The challenge in building an analytics tool is to take the extensive amount of business data and store it in a way that users could use to see a graphical representation of the data very rapidly. The data also needed to be stored to support quick drill-down and filtering of the data.

Frank and Jan dusted off the ProVision specs as a basis for the KPIs that would be most meaningful. Frank worked to identify the graphical views and business components to provide for analysis. Jan designed a database star schema for the analytics module to use and a high-speed process to perform nightly exports from their business database tables into the star schema tables. Jan worked with Arun on the best way to run the processes to minimize any downtime for the user when the data was refreshed. The use of a star schema and nightly updates was how all analytics systems worked. Drill-down, slice and dice data analysis could not be done using standard transactional business tables.

ProChannel would start exports into the start schema tables at 2 a.m. nightly (or whenever the customer decided was their company's lowest use of ProChannel's resources), and populate a copy of the Key Performance Indicator (KPI) tables. During this time, users could still access data and view charts and graphs based on the prior day's data. Once all of the KPI tables were populated, ProChannel issued a command for Oracle to do high-speed table mirroring to switch the graphics to point to the new KPI tables. This process took less than a minute, even for the largest company's database, so there was only a short window of time where the dashboard would not be available to users.

It was a complex module, and the engineering team enjoyed the technical challenges. Release 7.2, with the Dashboard, was available in May 2005, six months after Stephen's request.

With Release 7.2, sales was able to compete more aggressively with their competitors.

The good news was that with the Dashboard, the semiconductor manufacturers were not finding SalesForce to be a better fit for their needs. In addition, they were not buying the big ERP gorilla software to meet their sales force automation needs. The big gorillas were still not making any inroads into Intelic's vertical space.

The bad news, however, was that the semiconductor manufacturers were still buying no software. The continuing economic downturn had stalled Intelic's sales activity again. The prospects were in a wait and see mode. Thus, revenues were not keeping up with projections or headcount.

Stephen was becoming very concerned that they were not going to have enough funds to last until all of the customers' yearly maintenance contracts were renewed in July. He was also concerned that, because of the continued economic depression, many of their customers on stable releases may decide they didn't need to continue to pay maintenance.

Intelic needed more money to guarantee survivability, and needed it quickly.

Stephen met with the board for advice and they recommended going for another round of funding to make sure the company had enough leeway until mid-2005.

But their VC was not willing to infuse any more capital into the venture and, as the Series C investor, had the majority vote.

That was a hard blow, a show of no confidence.

Stephen was sure that Intelic's problem was the slow recovery of semiconductor companies and not any basic issue with the underlying company plan. The various activities to expand the sales channel to other verticals and to provide the hosted ProStart version were in hopes of buying time until the big semiconductor companies started to purchase IT software again. Stephen argued that the sales opportunities were still there. Try as they may, the big gorillas had not stolen one customer away from Intelic. Intelic wasn't losing deals. However, Intelic's potential customers were in a "wait-and-see" mode until the economy improved.

Stephen gave up on the VC and went to solicit additional funding from other sources. He found another VC who was excited about the company and willing to provide bridge money for a year.

He presented the option for the bridge loan to the board at the next board meeting. In fact, he had two parties, other VCs, willing to step up to the plate.

"That won't happen," said their one current VC board member.

"Why not," said Stephen in surprise.

"We have rights of first refusal to any new rounds or any new investors, and we are refusing."

"But you aren't willing to invest more. You also won't let us get a bridge loan?"

The two of them left the board meeting for a private consultation. It ended up that the VC had already written Intelic off, and was in a non-supportive, wait-until-the-end mode. He was pushing Stephen to give up and close down the business.

Stephen wasn't about to give up yet, and began to think about other potential options. First, the three founders took significant pay cuts to bridge the gap. Next, he found a private party willing to give him a short-term one-year loan, with guaranteed payback. Third, he began negotiating with the building manager to lower the lease on the building they were renting.

The option he discussed with the building manager made business sense to Stephen. The building manager's choice was to either have Intelic move out, which would increase the building complex's already high vacancy rate, or keep a good tenant (Intelic) in place, albeit at lower rent income. At least with the second option, the owner would still have some income coming in.

Stephen's playing hard-ball with the landlord is what resulted in the eviction notice on the front door that a couple of employees saw returning from lunch before Stephen, John, and Jan got there. That eviction notice resulted in Stephen, John, Jan, and Gery quickly and quietly moving excess equipment to Jan's SUV. Jan also made sure she had a copy of the latest backup tapes.

Hence, the next morning, Jan was driving into work in a drizzling rain with the spare computer equipment in her SUV, fearing what she would find there; fearing she would arrive at work to find employees milling around the parking lot (or sitting in their cars to avoid the drizzle), and a Sheriff's padlock on the front door.

Thankfully, when she arrived, there was no sign of concern. The building was open, and employees were doing business as usual. However, Stephen was in his office with the door closed much of the day, negotiating options with the landlord.

The final agreement with the building manager was for Intelic to move to one floor in another building in the same complex. In reality, with their current headcount, they were now using less than one-third of the office space they were renting. Stephen had been able to originally negotiate a great price for their current location. The large building had also been impressive to customers when they arrived for a visit, to have Intelic have a wide two-story building solely for their use. The fact that there were no employees housed upstairs and that one wing wasn't occupied, was restricted from any visitor's view.

The new space in the next building would just be the top floor in half of a building - much smaller than their current accommodations and no highway signage.

Stephen, John, and Jan did a walk-through of the new office space they would be moving into.

"Argh," Jan was unable to avoid uttering when she saw the small break room with horrible orange and beige checkered linoleum flooring tiles. Right next to the orange and beige flooring was a clashing deep gold accent wall. "Can we remodel?"

"Sorry," said Stephen. "One of the landlord's requirements is to move in as is. I already tried."

The office definitely hadn't had a good interior decorator.

While none of them liked the décor, the three of them agreed that the move was necessary.

They had two months before the landlord would require them to move to the new office space. Stephen negotiated with the landlord to let them pay at the lower office space rate in the interim, while they planned and coordinated their move. Because the landlord's choice was to give them sufficient planning time or lose Intelic as a longer-term occupant, he finally relented. Stephen was a hard negotiator.

The facility cost reduction would help them bridge their current cash crisis. Stephen didn't want to assume the business would fully recover during the next year, but wasn't ready to wave the white flag and declare defeat yet. He was hopeful and would pursue more business options. But in parallel, he believed they needed to take the cautious approach.

Stephen suggested that the three co-founders suspend their salaries until the maintenance dollars started to come in.

"Once we know the majority of the customers will renew maintenance, Intelic can pay our back-salaries. Until then though, we should suspend our paychecks."

All three were in quick agreement.

Stephen also recommended downsizing once more, before the move date. Even with the reduced facility cost, cofounders' cut in pay, and the bridge loan, if the economy remained sluggish, they could run out of money before the July 2006 maintenance renewals.

Besides, Stephen reasoned, one other option still open to them, was that, instead of acquiring a company as they had previously sought to do, Intelic would become the acquired party.

If they ended up going down that path, Intelic would be much more attractive to be acquired if the employee size and total salary costs were smaller, matching Intelic's ongoing worst-case operating expenses.

That meant they needed to go through another layoff.

For the three co-founders, this was the most painful step yet. Outstanding managers and developers, along with excellent workers in every organization, would need to be let go. The layoff even involved most of the senior managers. Jan was distraught at cutting engineering back so far. Losing Anita, Jan's close friend, was heartbreaking.

At least they didn't need to let everyone go right away. Some of the managers agreed to stay to help during the transition until they moved to the smaller facility.

As part of the cutback, instead of having a full-time IT manager, Jan found an IT consulting company who would manage their internal systems with a half-time, less expensive employee. Gary would continue to manage IT and the consultant until the move. Then Jan would take on engineering and IT.

The IT consulting company brought Dave over and introduced him to Gary, who would train Dave on the systems. Jan was less than excited about the IT company's choice of Dave as Intelic's IT person. During their meeting, Dave seemed low on energy and not very engaged. Afterwards, in private, Jan discussed Dave more with the IT company manager. The manager was an advocate for Dave, and assured Jan that Dave had extremely strong system administration skills.

"Besides," the manager said, "Dave is the only person we currently have available who could work on a part-time basis."

Dave it was.

Over the next month, Intelic started experiencing system difficulties. Users' laptops were freezing up. Dave would go to each user with problems, do some cleanup on their computer, and things would work all right again. For a while. One of the servers crashed. Gary had complained to Dave's manager at the IT company, who said she had talked to Dave and he'd said he was doing the best he could, but the problem was just that some of Intelic's systems were older.

A week later everyone was complaining, and it was getting so bad that Jan escalated the issue to the IT company's President. Jan and Gary were sure they weren't suddenly having all of the problems because the systems were suddenly older, and thought Dave must not be doing what he should.

The IT company's President decided to bring in a different IT expert to evaluate the Intelic situation.

The IT expert, Steve, owned his own IT computer and data security firm. Steve was called in often by the IT company to trouble-shoot difficult issues.

Jan was in her car driving back from a customer visit when she received a phone call. Steve was on the phone.

"Hi," Jan answered.

"Hello. This is Steve. I'm helping your IT company on your situation."

"Great. Do you have any information about what the problem is?" Jan asked.

"Yes," he said. "Dave said that he was told to not update any of the laptop, desktop, or server virus protection software. Your version of virus protection software no longer works with the older Windows XP, which many of your computers are still running. Because of that, your systems are writhe with viruses."

"What!" Jan exclaimed. "What do you mean? We've always kept our virus software up-to-date. We ship software to huge manufacturing companies. We have always been diligent about making sure we protect our customers' systems by keeping our computers virus free!"

"Humm," pondered Steve. "Dave said he was directed that funds were tight and Intelic wouldn't pay for any virus software upgrades."

"That's crazy," said Jan. "I'm sure Gary would never have said that. Dave must have totally misunderstood. Regardless, what do we do now?"

"Well," said Steve, considering the tone of her reply. "Fortunately for you, I'm an authorized Microsoft distributor. I can update all of your company's virus software within the next hour. But it will cost you almost $20,000 in software upgrade fees that I will owe Microsoft for the upgrade." Steve provided her the basis for that estimate including his discount percent and said, "You sound like a trustworthy person. If you authorize me to start right now, over the phone, I'll start the upgrade and we can sign the paperwork when you get to the office."

Jan knew it was a lot of money, but had priced security software in the past so knew the amount was reasonable.

"Yes, definitely," said Jan. "Proceed."

Jan knew it didn't matter how tight their finances were, they would be out of business in a day if any customer thought there was a chance of them shipping infected software. She was one hundred percent confident Stephen would agree. Plus, one of the advantages of being a co-founder is each co-founder has equal say.

She called Stephen and explained what Steve had uncovered. Of course, Stephen was in total agreement with the need to update their virus software, regardless of their tight funds.

Back in the office, Jan talked to Gary, who was shocked.

"I never talked to Dave about virus software," Gary replied. "I did tell him in general we wanted to minimize expenses, but he never came to me about needing a virus software update."

Steve quickly ascertained that the server they used to ship software to their customers, which was new, was free of viruses and there had been no impact to their customers.

Whew.

Next, the infected computers needed to be cleaned up. The central Gates computer had crashed. When the computers were first installed in 1998, Martin had named the servers after famous entrepreneurs, wanting Intelic to follow in their footsteps. Gates was named after Bill Gates, and was one of the oldest servers.

Gates ran their internal internet plus hosted SD Tracker. Gary and Jan went into the computer room, but Gates' computer chassis was open, the motherboard removed, and parts were everywhere. Dave had been trying to fix it, but had left for the day.

Jan was furious and called the IT company. Because Dave had caused the problems, Jan told Dave's manager at the IT company that Dave would need to work at Intelic until the Gates server was back online, no matter how long it took, at no extra charge to Intelic. Although Dave had already put in his half day, he returned to join Steve (the new consultant) and Gary, to work to fix the problems until Gates was back on-line. Gary finished everything he could do. While he knew a lot about systems and IT, it wasn't his forte. It was up to Steve and Dave to complete the cleanup effort.

Kevin, Intelic's QA tester, came to Jan and volunteered to stay after work as long as it took to escort the consultants out, and to lock up when the systems were restored. It ended up that Kevin, who, as QA, was also in the computer room a lot, also had a less-than-stellar impression of Dave. Kevin didn't like the idea of Dave being left alone in the computer room without an employee in attendance, and didn't think Jan or Gary should have to baby sit all night. Jan appreciated Kevin's willingness to fill in. It took all night, but by morning, the systems were back online.

After that fiasco, Jan fired the IT consulting company, and hired Steve as their IT consultant. Steve was able to do more for a fraction of what they had paid before, and all systems were soon humming like new.

In addition to the layoffs, John had to cut back his time due to health issues. Deb and Jay had both moved on a few years earlier. Sales people typically don't stay at one company a long time. Although Deb and Jay had been replaced, Intelic was now losing those new sales people due to the downturn in business. The sales people were all on commissions. No sales, no income.

It was a blow to the sales effort at a time when revenues were key. Stephen quickly sought more sales expertise.

Moving day came and - because they had more equipment, cubicle walls, and larger pieces of furniture - they hired a professional moving company to move them from one office building to the other.

Jan was walking from the parking lot into the new building as the main computers were being unloaded, several on a single pallet. The mover turned around and Jan gasped as she saw an entire pallet-full of their primary servers topple over onto the cement. Steve, their new IT person, was right behind her. He whisked out his cell phone and took numerous pictures. He confided later that his prior job had been as a private eye, hence his immediate thought was to take pictures as evidence.

Fortunately, because the computers were bubble-wrapped, there was no damage, and all systems came up cleanly.

CONTINUING TO RUN THE BUSINESS

"Life is like riding a bicycle. To keep your balance, you must keep moving." -
Albert Einstein

The new office facilities were small, only one-fourth of the space of the prior building, but Intelic had never even filled half of their prior building, even before the layoff. Now the close quarters gave them a tight-knit start-up feel again. They were back to the employee size of their earlier years.

One Monday, Lei, who worked for Rich in customer support, was working on a data issue and asked Jan for some advice. At about 5 p.m., Jan and Lei were sitting in Lei's cubical when Rich found Jan and said, "We have a customer High/Critical!"

Customer calls and SDRs were given a priority and a severity to rank them. Priorities were 1-High, 2-Medium and 3-Low. Priority denoted how soon the customer needed a bug fix or an issue resolved. Severities were 1-Critical, 2-Serious, 3-NonCritical, and indicated how important the problem was to fix.

The only way an issue could be a High/Critical was if a customer's production system was hard down and/or significant production data corruption was occurring which would also cause the customer to shut down their production servers.

Jan could count on one hand the number of production High/Critical issues she had had to deal with over the years. Hearing a customer production system had a High/Critical issue caused the company to act as if flashing red lights and sirens were going off.

Immediately Lei and Jan stopped what they were doing to find out what the situation was. Arun had seen the SD Tracker High/Critical SDR email and came out of his office next door to ask Rich what engineering resources may be needed.

One of their favorite customers had upgraded from Release 6.9 to 7.1.5, the latest maintenance release. The customer was one that was slow to upgrade, and skipped Release 7.0 and waited until Release 7.1 was stable.

The customer had done the right steps, including first testing the upgrade on a non-production separate test server. The customer's team had then run extensive acceptance tests, and everything appeared to be functioning correctly. The customer then completed the production upgrade the day before, on Sunday. The upgrade was successful. But then, during the day Monday, they started seeing duplicate shipments occurring in their Order Management module.

Rich asked the customer to read off their property settings for importing orders. Sure enough, one property was set wrong.

"How could that be?" the customer asked.

During the years, Intelic had always been extremely careful about not making changes that could cause unanticipated impacts to their customers' production business processes when they upgraded. However, Release 7.0, being a ".0" major release with significant architecture and other infrastructure changes, required more attention to upgrade to than other releases. It was also deemed a good release to change some properties which controlled business processes that had evolved over the years. Intelic and their services team wanted the property defaults to reflect Intelic's recommended "best practices."

The property changes were carefully documented in their Release 7.0 conversion document and notices had gone out to all customers about the change. However, this customer did not upgrade to 7.0 when it was first released. Instead they moved from Release 6.9 to 7.1.5. Release 7.0 was released over a year earlier, and the property change warnings hadn't been repeated in the 7.1 conversion documents.

Intelic took part of the responsibility for the issue because it was rare for them to make any property changes, and the 7.0 release changes were obviously missed by the customer.

The customer didn't point any fingers, but just asked for prompt help to get the data cleaned up, and get them back online.

The customer had shut down their production system so no more data corruption could occur. It was the first time an Intelic customer would take their production system off-line for any significant time period.

Arun quickly started brainstorming with Jan how they could back out the duplicate information, which had been incorporated into the total numbers for the main orders and carried throughout the system to generate sales commissions records, sales forecasts, and other side effects.

They couldn't simply take the snapshot of the production data from before the release upgrade and re-run the shipment data, because during the day, sales and distributor users had been using the system, adding new quotes, design registrations, sample requests, and other transactional data that would be lost if they reverted to Sunday's data.

It was a gnarly problem to solve, and had many facets.

Jan updated Arun on the algorithms that ProChannel ran when the order shipment property was set to true, which she'd designed a few years earlier and which Chaiya had implemented. Chaiya had since left Intelic to pursue a medical degree.

Arun reverse-engineered the import function and wrote a program specifically to read the prior shipments and reverse the duplicate calculations. Jan and Lei obtained a copy of the customer's database and ERP order shipment files to start testing. Kevin helped set up the test scenarios.

After loading the customer's database and running their tests against the order shipment files several times, they were confident that they could successfully reverse the bad data.

They sent the customer the program and step-by-step instructions about what to do. Everyone working on the problem stayed in the office while the customer ran through the process. He eventually called them and said, "Yes! It looks perfect now. The shipments are as we would anticipate, and commissions and other data is in alignment. Thank you!"

It was 1 a.m. and the Intelic team, weary, left the building to drive home.

One day Marsha, the Marketing Manager, arrived at the office and sat down at her desk in her cubicle. She stared a few moments, confused, then went to Gery's office.

"My laptop is missing!" she exclaimed.

She was sure she had left her laptop on her desk when she left work the evening before, but now it wasn't there.

As people arrived for work, two other people reported their laptops missing from their offices.

Gery went to the computer room to review their security video tapes.

This wasn't the first time Intelic had had security issues. A couple of years earlier, when they were in the larger building in the same business complex, the police had been called on a Saturday afternoon due to the alarm going off. The police discovered that the conference room windows on one side of the building were shattered. Apparently someone had entered the conference room, but left quickly due to the alarms. Nothing was stolen.

The next year, in the same building, Gary went into the engineering conference room to prepare for an engineering design meeting. He noticed the laptop used with the projector during engineering meetings was not on the table where it was always left. He went to Stephen to report the loss.

Stephen asked Gary when he saw it last. Gary remembered using it for the SDRB meeting on Tuesday, earlier that week.

Stephen alerted Gery, who went into the computer room and started to review the security tapes. There was a three-day lapse during which the computer may have been stolen, so there were a lot of tapes to review. There was no security camera in the conference room, but there was one viewing the hall leading up to the conference room and the conference room door.

Gery reviewed engineers coming and going, and the janitorial service in the evenings. Then he paused and re-wound the tape to view that last part again.

The normal janitorial process was to roll a large garbage barrel up and down the halls. The female janitor would walk into each office or conference room to get the small office trash can, bring it to the hall to empty it into the barrel, and move on to the next office.

On Wednesday night, she followed this process. She went into the engineering conference room and returned to empty the small trash can into her garbage barrel. Then she did something odd. She pushed the large rolling garbage barrel into the conference room. That was a different process than Gery had seen on the tapes before.

Gery was convinced that the janitor had seen the laptop and decided to roll the barrel into the conference room to put the laptop in the barrel to secretly remove the computer from the premises.

Stephen and Gery showed the tapes to the janitorial service, but they did not believe the evidence to be convincing.

Intelic hired a new janitorial service.

Now this latest robbery had occurred. During all the years Intelic was located in San Jose on the route between the homeless encampment and needle exchange center, nothing had been stolen. Here, in a new, large building complex in Milpitas with security guards, it was their second robbery and third break-in.

Once again Gery was in the computer room reviewing surveillance tapes.

Gery called Stephen and Jan in to see what he had found.

There was a camera recording events on their office's back door which lead to a stairway down and out of the building's exit door. After 6 p.m., both their office back door and the door downstairs to outside the building automatically locked after someone exited.

The angle of the camera included the Marketing Manager's cubicle. They could see the Marketing Manager's laptop sitting on her desk.

Later in the evening they saw the male janitor go out the back door to the stairway carrying a large bag of garbage, apparently to take the garbage out the back door to the garbage bins outside of the building. The janitor didn't return.

Some time later, they could see a shape outside the frosted window of their office back door – someone was on the landing. He then knelt down or otherwise wasn't seen in the door's window. Then the back office door opened. A tall thin black man they didn't recognize wearing a hoodie and a backpack came in. He walked up the hall between cubicles and was lost from the camera, but was going the direction of the other two offices with missing laptops. The camera was still viewing the Marketing Manager's laptop. The hooded man returned, entered the Marketing Manager's cubicle, and when he left, the laptop was gone!

The tape seemed to display cut-and-dried evidence.

Inspecting the scene, Gery noticed some scratch marks outside their office back door he assumed were caused when the perpetrator hunched down in the video to jimmy the door lock. There were no marks on the main exit door to the outside, though. Stephen conjectured that perhaps the janitor was in cahoots with the thief, and had propped the outside door open.

The police were called and met with Stephen and Gery. One policeman looked at the tape and said, "Hey, that's Eddie!" The officer explained that someone named Eddie had been involved in various incidents around their building complex. "His beat-up old green Chevy was also reported to have been spotted in the complex that day," he added.

"Great!" exclaimed Stephen. "So you can pick him up?"

"I don't think so," replied the policeman. "That video tape is really grainy. I don't think it's sufficient evidence to indict him."

Stephen was incensed. When Stephen told Jan the outcome she was also incensed.

"You mean the policeman could recognize and name him, yet it was too grainy to indict him? That doesn't make any sense at all!" Jan complained.

Intelic's insurance covered the stolen laptops, and they changed cleaning services again. But the incident was still unsettling.

It was particularly unsettling for the engineers who were working late that night during the timeframe of the burglary. Ketan, Kevin, and other engineers were in the front of the office working at the same time that the burglary was taking place. Ketan, in particular, was shaken by the event, and was nervous to stay late unless a large group was in the building.

The small office area had limited hard offices. Stephen had the fairly nice corner office with a solid door, appropriate for the CEO. Most of the remaining hard offices were centrally located in the building. Each had a wall of glass and glass door. Jan had lobbied to put Arun, who was now the Director of Engineering, in one of the window offices instead of a cubicle. Stephen agreed, and Arun's office was on the same side as Jan's office. The developers were located in cubicles nearby.

Stephen then hired Anne, a senior sales rep from the building products arena. When Anne was hired as their Building Products VP of Sales, Stephen decided to give her a hard office and move some of the team around. Arun was out, and back into a cubicle.

Stephen was going to move Arun and the developers to the other side of the building so services and support could move over by JP and Rich and sales could be nearer to Anne. That put the developers on the opposite side of the building from Jan's office.

Jan decided if Arun couldn't have a hard office, she didn't need one either. Jan decided to take a cubicle in the corner next to where Arun and the developers would be located. Jan solicited Gery to help remove a couple of cubicle walls so she could claim a space large enough to hold small engineering meetings. As a side benefit, removing the walls gave her a direct view out of a window.

Jan liked the cubicle better than the central hard offices that were all glass and made her feel like she was in a fish bowl. Plus it felt more like they were back in their first start-up building because she could interact with the developers nearby.

THE END OF THE ROAD (2006)

"You've got to know when to hold 'em, know when to fold 'em." - Kenny Rogers

Even though Intelic continued to retain all of their customers, plus upsell modules to a few existing customers, it wasn't enough.

The semiconductor industry had not fully recovered from the economic downturn of the past few years. Although Intelic had lost no existing customers, and no new customers had purchased gorilla software to solve the business processes ProChannel automated, semiconductor customers remained in their "wait and see" mode, and were not investing in new IT software.

Intelic had been trying to solicit a strong sales manager from the semiconductor industry into taking a VP of Sales position. The candidate Stephen and Jan thought would be outstanding decided, at the last minute, against coming into Intelic because of the current revenue risks. Good candidates would be almost impossible to solicit during this downturn.

The writing was on the wall. It was time to sell.

Stephen had been going through due diligence with various companies interested in acquiring their business, and there was one company who showed the most interest in being the acquirer. Interestingly, it was a company that previously had been on Stephen's list for Intelic to acquire.

Over the next few months, several due diligence meetings took place with the New Company and Intelic.

Neither Jan nor John were excited about a potential sale, but it was prudent to cover all bases.

Only six months earlier – when it looked promising for Intelic to either expand their revenues from new sales, an acquisition, or both – the three co-founders had been out to lunch when Stephen posed a question.

"How much money do you personally hope to get out of this venture?" Stephen inquired of John and Jan.

All three of them were aware it was not going to be anywhere near the millions they'd dreamed of in the '90s, during the dot.com boom, when small start-ups were quickly realizing IPOs or multi-million dollar buy-outs.

John said, "I think the minimum should be at least $2 million each."

"I'd be more than happy with $1 million," Jan chimed in.

Now it was clear that even their more modest dreams were out the window.

It was March, nearing the time when the bridge loan from the private investor a year ago would need to be re-paid. Maintenance dollars were not due for two months. The projected income was not looking good.

At one of their executive staff meetings, JP suggested that they call every customer and ask them if there's any modules they don't own that they want to buy at half price. He also suggested giving the customers an incentive if they paid their maintenance early.

Stephen believed it would panic the customers if word got out that the small company was scrounging for money. He feared it would jeopardize maintenance renewals.

A formal offer to buy Intelic was made by the New Company, a small privately-held corporation.

The Intelic managers who had participated in the due diligence meetings were aware of the offer, and were also painfully aware of the lack of sales, yet still there was angst.

Rich and Arun came into Jan's office. "Don't sell!" Rich implored. "We have to be able to do something."

Arun suggested, "We can all take pay cuts. We can even work without pay, if needed, until the maintenance dollars are in."

Stephen and John were adamant that, although it was acceptable for the co-founders take cuts or no money at all, Intelic could not withhold pay from the employees. In addition, it was not guaranteed that even that step would cover the gap. Stephen reasoned that it wouldn't be fair to the employees for them to work for three months without pay and still lose the business.

The next day Stephen had the paperwork for the sale prepared and brought it in for Jan's signature. He had already signed, and left the paperwork on her desk for Jan to decide what to do.

Jan felt horrible. She had already talked to John who wouldn't sign. The company was his "baby" and he was loath to let it go. So Jan's was the necessary second signature to close the deal.

She desperately wanted Intelic to continue. She knew the employees all wanted to continue.

At the emergency board meeting, it had been clear that the board, although they said they would support management's decision, whatever it was, thought that the company had little choice but to sell. Besides, Bob said, the board felt that both the board and management were tired out and ready to sell.

Jan was willing to continue, but Stephen was recommending they sell. The partners had always planned that their exit strategy was likely to be through acquisition. However, in their plans, everyone would be getting money from their stocks for themselves, their employees, and the angel investors. With this deal, only the Series C VC would receive any payout.

Even if she could convince Stephen to continue on, that action would pose a real risk to their customers. If they were unsuccessful, and Intelic came to a screeching halt, their customers would suddenly be without software maintenance. ProChannel was a mission-critical system for their businesses. The customers would have no ability to quickly move to another vendor's solution. It could be disastrous for Intelic's customers' businesses.

The New Company had offered to take every employee, except three top-level employees who the New Company felt were redundant to their own executive team. At Intelic's small size, that left only 17 employees. For the employees who would be transferring, the New Company offered to match their current salaries plus provide fairly generous stock packages to replace the stock the employees would be losing in the deal. The New Company offered Stephen a 6-month transition contract with significant stock. The provision that Jan remain with the New Company for a minimum of one year was part of the deal.

Jan sat at her desk, weighed the alternatives, and couldn't see a way for Intelic to continue on.

She signed.

Stephen planned a final board dinner (for all except the VC), to show the board the three co-founder's appreciation for the board's years of support and effort.

Bob made a toast. He said although neither the board nor the founders received a cash buy-out from the deal, he still considered the venture a success.

"Look at what you accomplished," he said to the three co-founders. "You provided significant return on investment for your customers. You built a brand to be proud of, one that owns the semiconductor space. The big competitors were never able to get a foothold."

"With the merger, your customers are protected. The New Company will take care of maintenance and the ongoing evolution of the product. Your employees have good jobs and good stock packages."

"I consider this venture a success."

They all toasted.

COMPANY PHOTOS

"Don't cry because it's over, smile because it happened." - Dr. Seuss

"We Need a Boat Ride," 1999. Front Row: Stephen, his son, wife Mary, Frank, Ketan, Chaiya, Arun. Back Row: Freeman, Starr's son, Starr, Julie Anne (Jan's daughter), Jan, Julie, Starr's other son.

The last day. Front Row: Hang, Kevin, Arun, Susan, Ashish, Gery. Back Row: Linda, Ken, Stephen, Michael, Ketan, Dale, Jenn, Rich, John, Jan.

EPILOG

"The only way to make sense out of change is to plunge into it, move with it, and join the dance." - Alan Watts

In February 2001, Intelic changed its name due to pressure from Intel, the world's largest semiconductor company, whose lawyers claimed the name Intelic was copied from <u>Intel</u>'s <u>I</u>ntegrated <u>C</u>ircuit (IC) Division, instead of the co-founder's intended meaning, "<u>Intel</u>ligent <u>I</u>nternet <u>C</u>ommerce." Intelic didn't have the money to argue and chose the name Azerity.

Azerity was acquired early in 2006. Many of the prior Azerity employees have continued to work for the new company since then.

The Azerity team and ProChannel software are now referred to as High Tech or HT. The new company's HT product line has been able to retain a high percentage of the Azerity customers and has added many more customers.

The ProChannel (HT) software is in-use worldwide today.

The stories in the book are based on actual events, although some of the names have been changed.

REFERENCES

1. Agile Manifesto and history were from the website www.agilemanifesto.org.
2. "Nine women can't make a baby in a month" quote was first coined by Frederick P. Brooks, Jr. in his book, "The Mythical Man-Month," according to Wikipedia: en.wikipedia.org/wiki/Brooks'_law.
3. Quotes by Dan Millman were from "The Way of the Peaceful Warrior," by Dan Millman, published by HJ Kramer Inc., 1980, 1984.
4. Other quotes were from various quote websites:
   www.brainyquote.com
   www.goodreads.com
   www.keepinspiring.me
   www.searchquotes.com
5. For more information about Practical Software, go to www.duckpondsoftware.com.
6. For more information about Software 2020, go to www.duckpondsoftware.com/software-2020.
7. To view/make comments about this book online, go to: www.duckpondsoftware.com/my-books.

ACRONYMS

ATP   Available-to-promise: The inventory of parts that is available to be sold/shipped.

CM   Configuration Management: The discipline of managing versions of software code.

CVS   Concurrent Versions System: An open-source software code management tool.

DOORs   Dynamic Object Oriented Requirements System: A requirements management tool.

ERP   Enterprise Resource Planning: Software that automates back office functions such as orders and shipping, accounting, sales, and customer management.

HTML   HyperText Markup Language: Web page code.

IT   Information Technology: The organization responsible for running a company's internally used computers and software, such as Enterprise Resource Planning systems.

NIH   Not Invented Here: Software that is purchased from another vendor. The NIH Syndrome is the philosophical principle of not using third party solutions.

PM   Product Manager: The person responsible for software requirements and design.

QA   Quality Assurance: The organization in a software company that does the testing.

SAP   Systems, Applications & Products in data processing: A large ERP software vendor, based in the Germany.

SDR   SD Tracker Request: A task that a developer needs to work on, such as an enhancement request, bug fix, etc.

SDRB   SD Tracker/SDR Review Board: The Intelic cross-functional team that reviewed SDRs and decided when they should be fixed or implemented.

UNIX   Not an acronym. All caps is a trademark. A family of multitasking, multiuser computer operating systems.

VC   Venture Capitalist: An investor who provides capital to startup ventures.

ABOUT THE AUTHOR

After graduating from the University of Utah, Jan (with a BS/MS in Math) and her husband Mike (with a BS in Physics/MBA) were both offered positions at Ford Aerospace in Palo Alto, California. Ford Aerospace didn't realize they'd hired Ford Aerospace's first married couple.

Jan spent almost twenty years in various software engineering positions at Ford Aerospace, from hands-on developer to senior software manager. She designed and developed satellite management and tracking software, imagery systems, and database tools. She managed multi-level software security projects, artificial intelligence, computer-aided software engineering, and government defense software programs. She then decided to move from the satellite and defense world to the commercial software world.

Because of her love of database software, she accepted a Director position reporting to the President of the relational database company, Ingres, a division of ASK Computers, Inc. Her role was to assist the company in streamlining and improving their processes, from engineering to customer support. She later became Product Line Manager for ASK/MANMAN Enterprise Resource Planning (ERP) software, which was being sold to manufacturing companies worldwide and operated by IT organizations. Later as Director of Engineering for MANMAN/X, she helped architect ASK's next generation ERP solution. After ASK was sold, she took a short-term role at Varian in their IT organization to learn about ERP software from the IT perspective. She has also worked as a software Director or VP of Engineering at small software companies, where she enjoyed the start-up feel. Jan was excited when John Miller and Stephen Gold wanted her to join them as one of the three co-founders of Intelic.

Jan retired from software at the end of 2014. She and her husband live in Discovery Bay, California where they enjoy golfing, boating, traveling, and being grandparents.

Jan is currently President of Save the California Delta Alliance (STCDA), www.NoDeltaGates.com, a non-profit grassroots organization dedicated to keeping the California Delta a safe and healthy environment.

Her first book, a children's book titled "The Fable of the Farmer and the Fish," provides a simplified explanation of the California water wars and the need to be good stewards of our environment.